Further Praise for *West Wingers*

"*West Wingers* is exceptional because of the people in it: ordinary citizens who did extraordinary work and always put the American people first. We have so much to learn from their stories."
—Joe Biden

"There is no calling higher than public service. *West Wingers* brings us inspiring stories of women and men who unselfishly answered that call, remarkable citizens who worked for President Barack Obama to shape a better future for all Americans. These deeply moving stories offer more than a fascinating view into the window of history: they show us how hope becomes real, sustainable change."

—Valerie Jarrett, former senior advisor to President Obama

"These gifted thinkers will lead us to a better place. They will make a major contribution to our future—as a nation, as a people—with what they have learned working for President Obama. We all should be inspired by their involvement, their passion, and their work. Their contribution to our nation will inspire our young people to dream dreams, to be hopeful, and to never give up or give in."
—Congressman John Lewis

"These are essential American stories. Through diverse voices sharing their amazing experiences working to move our country forward, *West Wingers* creates an inspiring roadmap to a better future."

—Sheryl Sandberg, *New York Times* bestselling author of
Lean In and *Option B* (with Adam Grant)

"There are few things more enthralling than a backstage seat in the White House, and West Wingers brings together a powerful group of Obama administration insiders to shine a spotlight on what it really takes to fight for social change."

—Adam Grant, *New York Times* bestselling author of
Give and Take, *Originals*, and *Option B* (with Sheryl Sandberg)

PENGUIN BOOKS

WEST WINGERS

Gautam Raghavan served as President Barack Obama's liaison to the LGBTQ community as well as the Asian American and Pacific Islander community from 2011 to 2014. Earlier in the Obama administration, he served as deputy White House liaison for the U.S. Department of Defense and as outreach lead for the Pentagon's "Don't Ask, Don't Tell" working group. Prior to joining the Obama administration, he worked on the 2008 Obama campaign and at the Democratic National Committee. Raghavan is currently a consultant to progressive organizations focused on securing political power and social change. A first-generation immigrant, he was born in India, raised in Seattle, and graduated from Stanford University. He lives in Washington, DC, with his husband and their daughter, Maya.

WEST WINGERS

Stories from the Dream Chasers, Change Makers, and
Hope Creators Inside the Obama White House

EDITED BY GAUTAM RAGHAVAN

PENGUIN BOOKS

PENGUIN BOOKS
An imprint of Penguin Random House LLC
375 Hudson Street
New York, New York 10014
penguinrandomhouse.com

ISBN 9780143133292 (paperback)
ISBN 9780525505068 (ebook)

Printed in the United States of America
1   3   5   7   9   10   8   6   4   2

DESIGNED BY LUCIA BERNARD

Penguin is committed to publishing works of quality and integrity. In that spirit,
we are proud to offer this book to our readers; however, the story,
the experiences, and the words are the authors' alone.

Contents

* * *

Preface

On my last day at the White House, my dad called me up and told me I should write a book.

After three years working for President Obama, I knew my parents had a more-than-slightly inflated sense of my job and importance. I imagined them telling friends at dinner parties that *Barack* relied on my counsel for every major decision, that I had been a key player during some of the most historic moments of the Obama presidency: the hunt for Bin Laden, the Arab Spring, the tan suit crisis.

My reality was far less glamorous. I wasn't a member of the senior staff. The President didn't know me on a first-name basis. I wasn't one of those "day one" folks who started at the White House on January 20, 2009, let alone one of the storied band of brothers and sisters who traced their service back to the Iowa caucuses or—even more rare and special in Obamaland—the early days in Chicago. While none of this ever bothered me because I was living my dream working for President Obama, what could I possibly have to say in a book?

I smiled, thanked my dad for the suggestion, and put it out of my mind. Until the 2016 election.

Enough has been said and written about the ongoing impact of that election, but one of the more immediate effects was that over the coming weeks I started feeling awfully nostalgic about Barack Obama *and he wasn't even out of office yet.* I have it on good authority that I wasn't alone in this sentiment.

By that point, I had been out of the White House for two years and I missed it like crazy. The pace and the excitement. The thrill that comes from watching history unfold and actually helping shape it as it happens. The satisfaction that comes from knowing that, even if you can't see it, your work is making a positive impact in people's daily lives.

But more than anything, I missed the people.

I missed the idealists who followed Barack Obama's call to service all the way to the White House, often taking the path less traveled to get there. I missed the fiery activists and organizers eager for "change we can believe in," who knew they had to make each day count because their communities were counting on them. I missed meeting people every day who challenged me to think differently, know better, and dream bigger.

In so many ways, working in Barack Obama's White House was like watching Aaron Sorkin's *The West Wing* brought to life. It had all the necessary elements: the brilliant, articulate professor in chief with an unapologetically progressive vision of America; a narrative arc rooted in ongoing themes of idealism and public service; but most importantly, a cast of patriotic Americans who labored every day, as members of the President's staff, to serve the country they loved.

As I wallowed in my postelection malaise and began to understand just how much things were about to change, I also realized the importance of capturing the momentousness of the last eight years and contributing to the American public's understanding of what many believe will be remembered as a historic presidency. A question began to take shape in my mind: could I help tell the stories of the incredible people I worked with in the Obama White House?

Countless books and articles had already been written about

President Obama—his victories and his flaws, his biography and his accomplishments—and about key conflicts and moments of the eight years of his presidency. And I knew more were being penned by central figures in the administration eager to share reflections and lessons learned from working in his orbit.

But despite this growing body of work, it felt like one broader set of key voices was missing: those of the President's staff who worked tirelessly, and often behind the scenes, to help him fully realize his commitment to hope and change. The American public doesn't usually get to hear from most of these people, or see their often-unheralded contributions to shaping the presidency.

It occurred to me that some of my colleagues might share my reticence about writing an entire book, but might want to tell their stories within a smaller space. Together, we could create a collection of stories capturing moments, big and small, throughout his presidency. I imagined this collection as a kaleidoscope with Barack Obama in the center and all of us around the perimeter, each seeing and reflecting back our unique perspective, all of it adding up to something meaningful. Not a work of nostalgia or hagiography, but a new way of looking at both the Obama White House and the inside workings of the executive branch.

There was a saying in the Obama White House, "People are policy," meant to emphasize the direct relationship between policy makers and policy outcomes. In any White House, you can tell what's on the menu based on who's at the table. That's why this book focuses on stories in which the storyteller isn't just narrating an interesting anecdote or a historical moment, but plays a key part in the story itself. For these individuals, public service isn't just a day job; it gives purpose and meaning to their lives.

That's also why so many of these stories are by my former colleagues from the Office of Public Engagement (OPE). As the President's team of "liaisons" to communities across America, many of us had to balance the hopes and needs of the communities to which we belonged against the agenda of the President in whom we believed. That meant the bad days were incredibly hard, but the good days were extraordinary. But as I spoke with more colleagues, including former staff who came before or after my time at the White House, it became clear that our OPE team did not have a monopoly on deeply personal stories. From the National Security Council to the First Lady's Office, I found stories, heartbreaking and inspiring, that underscore the personal nature of our work in the White House—and illuminate the impact of that work on communities across America.

Now, a disclaimer: although some of the most important moments contained within this book happened in the West Wing, many of us—myself included—didn't actually work there every day. The West Wing is fairly cramped quarters, and necessity dictates that much of the staff spread out across the White House campus, including in the impressive Eisenhower Executive Office Building, immediately adjacent to the West Wing. And an additional disclaimer: while this book is ultimately about President Barack Obama, in many of these stories he's a supporting character. The unique perspectives here offer a fresh look at Barack Obama as a boss, a mentor, and a man, but our primary goal was not to report on the President. Rather, our goal was to give you our version of The West Wing, a glimpse behind the doors of 1600 Pennsylvania Avenue, a fuller view of the highest office in the land.

As the collection started coming together, I became increasingly hopeful that anyone who picks up this book will be able to see themselves in at least one story and one author. I can't speak for other White House staffs, but many of us who worked in the Obama White House came from well outside the circles of wealth, access, and privilege. That's especially true for people of color, immigrants, LGBTQ individuals, veterans, women, people with disabilities—all identities that were represented in significant numbers on President Obama's team, but whose stories have not yet been told. These stories are a testament to what happens when everyone gets a seat at the table.

At a time of rising cynicism about politics and growing distrust of government, stories of idealism, patriotism, and service are more important than ever. As we think about the future, it is essential that we remember a more optimistic and inclusive vision of government—and know that time will come again.

Our hope is that whether you're looking for insight into the political process, an insider's view of a fascinating period of American history, or perhaps even inspiration for your future, there's something in this book that will speak to you, reassure you that even the most improbable change is possible, and give you hope for what's to come.

Gautam Raghavan

WEST WINGERS

EVOLUTION

Gautam Raghavan

never thought that one of my career highlights would involve weeping uncontrollably on the second floor of the West Wing, but we don't always get to pick how these moments play out.

It was a moment decades in the making, a turning point not just in the arc of our nation's history, but in my own journey as a married gay man who found himself working for the President of the United States.

* * *

I came out in the summer of 2003. Twice.

As is true for many gay folks deciding whether to come out and when, I arrived at a point where loneliness overcame all my hesitations and reservations. By the end of my junior year at Stanford University, I knew that I had only two options: alone and miserable in the closet, or fulfilled and happy outside of it.

I chose happiness. I was going to spend the summer interning in Washington, DC, and as a newly out and proud gay man, the possibilities were endless and exciting: Would I go to a gay bar? March in a Pride parade? Maybe even meet someone?

But when I got to Washington, all my hope and optimism was tempered by powerful forces seeking to limit possibility and opportunity in my life.

As it happens, I came out in the middle of a raging national debate over gay marriage. We were in the early days of the 2004 presidential campaign, and George Bush and Karl Rove were determined to use LGBTQ rights—my rights—to divide the country and mobilize their base. At the time, the LGBTQ community had few political allies. Of the entire field of Democratic candidates, only former Vermont governor Howard Dean had adopted anything close to a pro-equality position, largely consisting of his support for civil unions.

This timing made my decision to come out feel as political as it was personal. It not only meant becoming part of a community that was under siege, but also owning an identity that I would need to fight for. In that climate, coming out as gay but staying in the political closet just wasn't an option.

I returned to Stanford for my senior year determined to get involved. I volunteered on Howard Dean's presidential campaign and started reading the political blogs. A few months later, hundreds of gay and lesbian couples flocked to San Francisco's city hall to get married by newly elected mayor Gavin Newsom and other city officials eager to thumb their noses at the Bush administration. As I looked at photographs and watched videos of these brave men and women, some having waited decades for such a moment, I felt inspired—and resolved—to become a part of my community's fight for equality.

*　*　*

After graduation, I went back home to the Seattle suburbs for the summer to work for a congressional candidate running in the 2004 election. One warm July evening, I was knocking on doors for the campaign when, through a window, on somebody's television screen, I saw Barack Obama for the first time.

Even from my limited vantage point from the sidewalk outside, something about his poise or expression immediately grabbed my attention. Later that night, I watched his speech at the Democratic National Convention in Boston in full. I didn't know that night that his words would inspire an entire generation of activists, organizers, and public servants. For me, a newly out gay man just beginning to develop his political consciousness, there was nothing more moving than his description of the "improbable love" of his parents, and the line, "We coach little league in the blue states and, yes, we've got some gay friends in the red states."

I was hooked. I told my parents—but only half seriously—that one day I would work for Barack Obama. I didn't dare dream for a moment I'd ever *have* that opportunity. I did, however, hope that I would have the chance to work for someone *like* him—someone who sees America and loves America the way I do.

So I moved to Washington, DC, to get in the fight. What I didn't count on was falling in love.

* * *

In February 2005, just six months later, I met Andy. We were both graduate students: young, eager, mostly idealistic. We met almost by accident on Friendster, one of the many social network predecessors to Facebook that was (for a hot moment) all the rage. After exchanging messages for over a week, we finally met for a drink—and it was clear there was something there.

On our second date, Andy's dad came along. He was in town to see Andy in a play and invited me to join them for dinner. I didn't want to pass up the opportunity to see him again, so despite the apparent awkwardness of meeting one of his parents so soon, I went for it. Over enchiladas and beer, Andy's dad asked about my childhood, my parents, and my career. The conversation flowed freely and easily. The most remarkable part of the night was how unremarkable it all seemed.

Looking back, I don't think either of us thought for a moment we'd end up marrying each other. I don't think either of us even thought at the time that marriage would ever be an option. I still remember the first words out of my mom's mouth when I came out to her just a year earlier: "You still want to have kids, right?" I didn't know how to answer that question. A future in which a gay couple could get married, raise a family, and live happily ever after seemed out of reach—not just for me, but for countless gay and lesbian people across the country.

Of course, this wasn't for lack of trying. As early as the 1970s, in the wake of the Supreme Court's decision striking down interracial marriage bans in *Loving v. Virginia*, same-sex couples began fighting for the right to marry. Many of these plaintiffs were laughed out of court, but most were ignored altogether. Some, like Tony Sullivan and Richard Adams, got the worst of it. When they petitioned for a spousal visa following a private marriage celebration in 1975, the U.S. Department of Justice informed them on official letterhead: "You have failed to establish that a bona fide marital relationship can exist between two faggots."

Marriage equality, or "gay marriage" in the shorthand of media punditry, seemed a lost cause throughout the 1990s. It wasn't until 2004 that Massachusetts became the first marriage equality state in the nation, joined a few years later by Connecticut in 2008 thanks to the leadership of civil rights lawyers like Mary Bonauto eager to build momentum in the courts.

In this context, it's no wonder that unlike so many of our straight peers who had been in long-term relationships, Andy and I never talked seriously about getting married. What was the point of making an impossible plan?

Nonetheless, by the time the 2008 presidential campaign rolled around, our relationship had progressed—and despite the odds stacked against us, the possibility of marriage had started to take root in my mind. Still, it felt like a silly proposition: sure, we could trek up to Andy's home state of Connecticut and have a wedding ceremony there, but what was the point if our marriage license was worthless at home in the District of Columbia?

That June, just weeks after moving in with Andy, I was deployed from the Democratic National Committee, where I had been working as a political fundraiser, to Chicago to work out of Obama campaign headquarters. The next few months were a whirlwind of campaign events marked by long hours and a handful of quick weekend trips to see one another. But we both felt it was worth it, and on election night, we each celebrated Barack Obama's victory—me just steps away from the President-elect in Grant Park, and he with a raucous crowd outside the White House. When Barack Obama took the stage to declare victory, it felt like the political status quo had been momentarily upended. It felt as though anything might be possible in America.

But then the news came in that Proposition 8 had passed, prohibiting same-sex marriage in California. Our joyful celebration morphed into complete shock. On one hand, America had done the unimaginable by electing its first black president; on the other, California had done the unthinkable by passing an anti-gay initiative in one of the most progressive states. In Grant Park that night, LGBTQ campaign staff shared knowing looks that conveyed conflicting feelings: victorious yet demoralized.

In that moment, we all wondered: *Will Barack Obama help us fight back?*

And I found myself asking: *Will I ever be able to marry the person I love?*

* * *

By the following year, I had joined many of my campaign colleagues in the Obama administration, landing—of all the improbable places—at the Pentagon. Given the President's pledge to end "Don't Ask, Don't Tell," I hoped being at the Department of Defense would allow me the opportunity to be a part of history. Despite campaign promises, however, the early days of the administration provided little reason for optimism among LGBTQ advocates. A few gross missteps by the Justice Department in legal briefs concerning the so-called Defense of Marriage Act, or DOMA, provoked many LGBTQ movement leaders to privately—and increasingly publicly—question whether the Obama administration would get the job done.

Among the network of LGBTQ appointees, we did our best to stay positive despite mounting pressure from our community. Perhaps it was genuine confidence in the President and his team, or perhaps it was self-preservation. It was easier to believe that he saw the big picture and had a plan to get us there. Whatever it was, we continued to reassure one another, read the tea leaves in the best possible light, and assume good intentions all around.

In the midst of all this uncertainty, the President held his first LGBTQ Pride Month reception at the White House, throwing open the doors of "the People's House" to hundreds of LGBTQ activists from around the country. A decade earlier, these men and women were greeted by White House police wearing gloves; in 2009, they were honored guests.

And in that way that only Barack Obama can, he weaved together the varied histories of civil rights and social justice in America, telling us:

> I know that many in this room don't believe that progress has come fast enough, and I understand that. It's not for me to tell you to be patient, any more than it was for others to counsel patience to African Americans who were petitioning for equal rights a half century ago. But I say this: We have made progress and we will make more. And I want you to know that I expect and hope to be judged not by words, not by promises I've made, but by the promises that my administration keeps.

It felt like a nudge and a wink in our direction, but one that left our most pressing question unanswered: *When?*

* * *

By 2010, Andy and I could no longer wait for the law or public opinion to catch up. We were going to *make* "happily ever after" happen.

After more than five years together, and with shared custody of an affectionate and food-motivated rescued beagle named Penny, it was clear our futures involved each other. And since the District of Columbia had recently adopted marriage equality, joining six other states, we took comfort that the act of getting married would at least have some legal standing.

Nevertheless, tying the knot still felt like radical activism in that moment. Accordingly, our wedding was thick with symbolism. We had one friend read from a statement by Mildred Loving—of the landmark case *Loving v. Virginia*—in which she placed the freedom to marry in the context of our nation's ongoing march to a more perfect and equal union. Two more friends sang k.d. lang's "Simple," and its refrain—"Love will not elude us, love is simple"—rang across the rooftop overlooking the Capitol Building, packed with friends and family wearing white ribbons to represent their support for our marriage.

A few days before the big day, we sat down with a bottle of wine to write out the wedding program and draft our vows. While we could have thrown out the script and written something new, fresh, and fabulous, it felt important to stick to some tradition. So when it came time for our vows, we uttered the same words that countless couples had repeated before us: *love, honor, cherish. I do.*

In retrospect, ours was a fairly traditional path: boy meets boy, boy falls in love with boy, boy marries boy. Indeed, the next morning, between unwrapping gifts and packing up the car, my new father-in-law not-so-subtly asked: "So, when can we expect grand-kids?"

In his eyes, and in the eyes of our friends and family, we were just like any newly married couple. But in the eyes of the federal government, and in forty-four states, we might as well have been complete strangers.

* * *

The very next month, President Obama held an interview with a group of progressive bloggers who pushed him on a range of issues. Most of his answers were unsurprising, but when asked about mar-riage, he ventured further than he had before, adding, "Attitudes evolve, including mine."

There it was: "evolve." Evolution: a word that suggests change, or growth, usually from a lower state to a higher state. Did the President just show his hand?

That December, Andy and I were invited to a White House holiday party. We're normally not ones to hold hands walking down the street, but that night I clutched his hand as we walked through a beautifully decorated East Wing and took an embarrassing number of photos and selfies. I wanted everyone to know: *We're here, we're queer, please hurry up and legalize our marriage.*

A few champagnes later, it was time to line up for a photo with the President and First Lady. From my campaign experience, I knew that we'd have just a few moments with them and each one had to count.

The military social aide greeted us and, without any hesitation, asked, "Partner or husband?" to ensure he announced us correctly. I proudly replied, "Husband," and that's just how we were introduced to Barack and Michelle Obama. We quickly shook hands with the President and First Lady and smiled awkwardly. The camera flashed. I somehow managed to stutter out, "Have a wonderful evening!" and the President replied wryly, "We'll try," knowing full well they had a few hundred more handshakes and hugs to get through.

And then Michelle Obama turned to my new, mostly legal husband. She gripped Andy's elbow, stared into his eyes and then mine, and said, "You two take care of each other."

We melted.

It felt like something was stirring. Words were changing, hearts were opening.

* * *

And something even more important was about to happen: the repeal of "Don't Ask, Don't Tell." My wish had come true: I had spent the last year on the Pentagon's repeal working group, directing outreach to organizations and advocates for and against the repeal. Following one particularly vitriolic meeting with opponents of repeal (it was either the one where someone compared homosexuality to bestiality or the one where someone speculated about sodomy parties on the battlefield; it's hard to keep track), an important realization suddenly dawned on me. Many, if not most, social conservatives weren't actually that concerned about gays in the military. Rather, they were concerned about gay military families.

In a nation where the sacrifice of our military families is held so sacred, our opponents correctly anticipated that once gay and lesbian troops could serve openly, DOMA would prohibit their spouses and dependents from receiving the full range of military family benefits. The public would neither understand nor honor this kind of discrimination.

The repeal of "Don't Ask, Don't Tell" would force the American public to understand, and empathize with, gay troops and their families, whose stories made the point perhaps better than anyone else: *We're just like you.*

* * *

After spending a year working on "Don't Ask, Don't Tell," I had developed strong working relationships with many of the LGBTQ movement organizations and leaders. Perhaps it was because of that experience that, in mid-2011, I got a call from Brian Bond, President Obama's liaison to the LGBTQ community and one of my longtime mentors, asking if I'd have any interest in replacing him at the White House that October.

My impossible dream was coming true: I was going to work for Barack Obama.

I imagined myself as Sam Seaborn from Aaron Sorkin's *The West*

Wing, walking the halls of the White House with purpose and passion, changing hearts and minds with monologues about idealism and patriotism. I was going to be a part of hope and change; I was going to be in the room where it happens.

I wasn't completely naive, though. I knew stepping into such a high-profile job—one that required balancing the community's interests with the administration's interests—would be challenging. In the intervening months, the Department of Justice had taken the incredibly important step of dropping its defense of DOMA, effectively signaling to the courts, "Bring it on." And yet, the status of the President's evolution seemed unchanged.

Just weeks after starting my new job, I participated in an LGBTQ community roundtable in Dallas. It was a standard public engagement trip; our goal was to hear from community leaders about their priorities and needs, and share what the Obama administration was doing on a broad range of issues ranging from international LGBTQ human rights to bullying prevention.

What we hoped would be a relatively friendly conversation turned into a heated exchange. It was clear that community leaders were unhappy with the slow pace of the President's evolution, and they wanted us to hear their frustration. Lawyers raised the broad set of legal issues associated with DOMA, while LGBTQ-friendly faith leaders talked about the positive message it would send to gay youth—many of whom experience family rejection and discrimination in schools and churches—to hear the President of the United States fully affirm and validate their identities and relationships.

And then one activist pointedly asked me: "How can you—an openly gay married man—work for someone who doesn't value and support your marriage?" I had no good answer. When pushed, I tried to pivot to a policy argument: "By directing the Justice Department to no longer defend DOMA in the courts, the President has already done what we need him to do."

But as the weeks and months passed without any announcement, I was having an increasingly difficult time answering that question while negotiating my personal misgivings. *Was I doing enough to push internally? Could I balance competing loyalties and priorities: to myself, to my community, and to my boss, who happens to be the President of the United States? Could this get so toxic, professionally or personally, that I should consider resigning?*

Without proof of progress, there were days I thought about quitting. There were days when I imagined taking my frustration and storming out the door, leaving behind righteous indignation and a terse letter of resignation.

But one thing stopped me from walking out: I believed in Barack Obama. Not just as president, but as the man who had spoken so eloquently of hope and change eight years prior in Boston. I believed on faith then what I later grew to know from experience: that this is a man who leads with integrity, sees around the corner, and has a deep understanding of what Dr. King called the arc of the moral universe.

I tried to reassure myself that I was making an impact. I shared what I was hearing from advocates and activists on the ground, trying to convey both the strong legal rationale as well as the raw emotion behind their argument. Knowing that a change in the President's thinking would also require a change in messaging, I worked with my colleague Shin Inouye in the Communications Office to suggest positive language around "loving, committed couples" for the President's speeches and proclamations. And as the President traveled the country to speak about his agenda, I worked with local community leaders to ensure that wherever he went, he would see and meet those couples, and more importantly, their kids. I couldn't *make* the President evolve, but I could do everything in my power to prepare him and his team for the moment he got there.

So I stuck around, which was the right call because things were about to get far more interesting thanks to the rapid progress marriage equality was making in the courts and in the states.

Strong lawsuits—*Gill v. Office of Personnel Management, Pedersen v. Office of Personnel Management, Hollingsworth v. Perry,* and *United States v. Windsor*—were steadily moving through the system and building case law along the way. At the time, we didn't know which one would reach the Supreme Court first, but we knew it was imminent. At the White House, we refocused the staff working group that Brian Bond had pulled together around "Don't Ask, Don't Tell" to meet regularly on marriage equality and other LGBTQ issues, tracking these court cases and trying to game out which had the best chance of getting heard by the Supreme Court and resulting in a positive ruling.

Meanwhile, the smart legislative strategy laid out by Evan Wolfson and other advocates was producing results faster than anyone had anticipated. In the summer of 2011, New York State passed its marriage equality law, and Maryland soon followed suit. And then in February 2012, the freedom to marry came to my home state of Washington.

Just a few days after the Washington bill passed, the President was scheduled to speak at an LGBTQ fundraiser at the home of Karen Dixon and Nan Schaffer, a married lesbian couple. As the event got under way, I wondered how the President would react to the unavoidable question about his evolution on marriage. Perhaps hoping to nudge him along, Karen and Nan had slyly placed a large photograph from their wedding—the two of them, radiant in white wedding dresses, walking down the aisle—on the wall immediately across from where the President was to stand.

Shortly after the press was ushered out of the room, the President took questions from guests. Appropriately, it was another trailblazer—Jim Hormel, the first openly gay person to serve as a U.S. ambassador—who raised the issue indirectly, asking the President for his reaction to the Washington State marriage equality bill. Instead of ducking or redirecting the question, the President paused, tilted his head slightly, and spoke slowly but deliberately. He said he thought the law was a positive development, that it represented a step in the right direction, and he hoped other states would follow a similar path.

Having closely followed the President's every statement on marriage over the past year, I was surprised—and moved. Not just because it was his most forward-leaning statement yet, but also because it was delivered with such care and purpose that it clearly signaled a change in his political thinking, and perhaps even a change of heart.

I left the event inspired and hopeful. For the first time, it felt like my long-held hope of seeing President Barack Obama lend his full support to the freedom to marry was within sight.

* * *

And then Joe Biden "got over his skis."

On Sunday, May 6, Andy and I were having brunch with my college roommate—he had been my best man at our wedding, and I at his—and his wife. We naturally had *Meet the Press* on in the background, but only gave it our full attention when the Vice President came on the screen.

About halfway through the segment, in between comments about the 2012 campaign and national security, the interviewer, David Gregory, raised—seemingly off the cuff—"social policy" in the context of the election and asked the Vice President about his views on gay marriage.

In response, Biden gave a surprisingly impassioned answer that placed the debate squarely in the context of a fundamental value: love.

Who do you love? And will you be loyal to the person you love? And that's what people are finding out is what all marriages, at their root, are about.

He shared a story that he has since told many times, about speaking to a gay couple after meeting their two children: "I wish every American could see the look of love those kids had in their eyes for you guys. And they wouldn't have any doubt about what this is about."

I thought to myself, *Well, that is going to complicate things.* As it turned out, I was right.

Just two days after the Vice President's interview, on May 8, 2012, the people of North Carolina voted for Amendment One, amending the state's constitution to prohibit same-sex marriages and civil unions. It was a crushing blow, particularly since it was a landslide anti-LGBTQ vote in a state that, four years earlier, surprised many by voting for Barack Obama. Nearly four years had passed since Proposition 8 and election night. In so many ways, it felt like we were making progress—but here we were again, losing our freedom at the ballot box.

That very night, I was with President Obama at a national dinner celebrating Asian American and Pacific Islander Heritage Month. I was the lead staffer for the event, and I remember greeting him, introducing him to a small group of community leaders backstage, reviewing his remarks with him, and waiting with him backstage before he went on.

With every minute that passed, I was keenly aware that I had a unique opportunity—protocol be damned!—to ask about Amendment

One. To tell him about my husband, explain why his support mattered, implore him to speak out.

Instead I stayed silent. If Joe Biden and Amendment One weren't enough to move him, what could I possibly do? I felt demoralized and defeated, resigned to the possibility that we would need to wait many more weeks, months, perhaps even years to see this evolution complete.

* * *

The wait turned out to be less than twenty-four hours.

At ten o'clock the next morning, Wednesday, May 9, 2012, I was sitting at my desk in the Eisenhower Executive Office Building when I got a call from Valerie Jarrett's assistant with a terse message: "Valerie needs to see you right away."

I gave my office mates a panicked look. In addition to overseeing our entire team, Valerie was the President's most trusted senior advisor. An urgent summons to her office meant something was happening. I grabbed my notebook, ran across the street to the West Wing, and darted up the stairs to Valerie's office. I opened the door to find members of the President's senior staff—from White House counsel to press secretary—seated around Valerie's table. I must have looked bewildered, because Valerie gave me a reassuring smile and told me: "Later this afternoon, the President will give an interview in which he will express his support for marriage equality. We have to get ready for it. You need to make a rollout plan, but you can't tell anyone. Go."

In a daze, I somehow made my way back to my desk. My mind was racing through an endless list of priorities—advocates who would need to be called, the alerts we'd need to send out, the importance of getting the framing just right—all without knowing exactly what the President would say or how he would say it.

The next few hours were a blur as I made lists of LGBTQ

movement leaders and marriage equality advocates who we'd need to engage, many of whom had worked years, even decades, for a moment like this. I tried not to think about it too much. I knew that if I allowed myself space to reflect, my emotions would catch up with me—and I had a job to do. My office mates must have known something was going down, because they gave me a surprisingly wide berth through the late morning and early afternoon.

Sometime around two thirty p.m., our entire team—the Office of Public Engagement and Intergovernmental Affairs—was called over to the West Wing. My boss, Jon Carson, wanted us to witness this historic moment together.

While the team huddled inside Carson's office, I sat outside his and Valerie's offices. I borrowed a coworker's workstation to coordinate our outreach after the interview and respond quickly to questions from community leaders and advocates the moment it ended.

The interview began. Across the second floor of the West Wing, everything came to a standstill. Every television was tuned to ABC News, and staff from every office and every level of seniority tuned in to watch President Obama talk to Robin Roberts.

And then Barack Obama made history. The President of the United States finally said the words so many loving, committed same-sex couples and their allies had been longing for:

> For me personally, it is important for me to go ahead and affirm that I think same-sex couples should be able to get married.

As soon as the interview ended, I hit "send" on an email blast to community leaders and LGBTQ staff across the administration. We decided to keep it simple—a quick message and a link to the transcript—to let the President's words speak for themselves. It was a message I had spent months waiting to send, sharing news I had always wanted to hear. I thought to myself, *The President of the United States doesn't just see us, he sees our love. He sees in my relationship with Andy evidence of the same love and commitment that he finds in his marriage.*

I had a hundred calls to make, but my shaking fingers dialed a number I had memorized seven years earlier. I called Andy. I don't remember what I said, or what he said, but it ended with me sobbing uncontrollably at that borrowed workstation for all in the West Wing to see and hear.

As my colleagues trickled out of Carson's office, many of them stopped to give me a hug or squeeze my shoulder. I knew then that the President's evolution on marriage was a victory for every single one of us who believed and worked for change, even when it seemed too audacious or improbable. Because in that moment, Barack Obama did more than just affirm his support for marriage equality. He did something far greater: he created possibility—rooted in the kind of audacious hope that animated his campaign and his presidency—for countless Americans like me.

* * *

The impact of President Obama's support for marriage equality was swift and significant. Within weeks, polls of black voters in Maryland and Pennsylvania showed double-digit bumps in support of marriage equality. That November, as the President cruised to reelection, voters, for the first time in history, proactively affirmed the freedom to marry at the ballot box in Maine, Washington, Minnesota, and Maryland.

And the momentum continued. The very next summer, the Supreme Court handed down its landmark decision in *United States v. Windsor*, striking down DOMA. Three years later, the court finished the job with *Obergefell v. Hodges*, finally bringing marriage equality to every state in the nation. The White House was bathed in rainbow lights.

I've been asked whether the timing of the President's evolution on marriage was genuine or political. I honestly don't know the answer to that question. What I do know is this: intentional or not, the undeniable by-product of his very public evolution on marriage was that countless Americans evolved with him. He gave permission to large swaths of Middle America—regular folks who knew gay people, but weren't sure how they felt about "gay marriage"—to change their minds, to do so with grace, and to come out on the right side of history.

* * *

When staff members leave the White House, the tradition is to take a departure photo with your immediate family and the President in the Oval Office.

This time around, I introduced Andy as my husband without a second thought. And as we lined up in front of the Resolute Desk to take a final photograph, President Obama gestured Andy over. "Hubby, come over here."

When it came time to leave, I turned to the President of the United States and spoke words that echoed the ones he'd delivered a decade earlier on that stage in Boston: "Mr. President, my story—of immigrating, coming out, marrying the person I love, and serving the highest office in the land, not in spite of who I am, but because of who I am—that story is only possible in America."

"It's because of young people like you guys," he said to me, "who are working so hard."

Hearing these words brought home to me the scope and sweep of the journey we had each traveled in our own way; that change doesn't come easy or fast, but the good stuff is worth fighting for.

And here's what Barack Obama taught me: in America, change—even the most improbable and audacious change—is possible.

A young man's idealism can allow him to live fully and authentically and follow his dreams all the way to the White House. A society's capacity to learn, grow, and change can take an issue from politically toxic to common sense within a generation.

And a president's evolution can change the course of history.

BECOMING A MAN

Michael Strautmanis

Potential. That was a word I heard a lot growing up. I had potential. As a black boy in Chicago, potential was a big deal. It meant opportunity, but it also meant responsibility, because if you had potential, you could do that one thing that every adult in your life who loved you wanted you to do—"make something of yourself." One of those phrases that's defined by the negative space around it and begins to slowly reveal itself. Growing up in the black community in Chicago, I saw people who were not making something of themselves. And there, in that darker, quiet, distant blank space, was my absent father.

In that reality, how do you become a man?

* * *

On September 24, 2009, Derrion Albert was making something of himself. He was an honor student at his neighborhood public school in Chicago, Fenger Academy High School. One day, Derrion was walking home from school when he walked past a massive cross-neighborhood fight, got snared in it, and was beaten to death. One more young black life snuffed out.

But this time was different. Maybe it was the fact that someone caught it on video; maybe it was the fact that Derrion was a model student, one of the good kids. This time, the community cried out for a response. People began to ask important questions and, more importantly, began to demand different answers. National news outlets arrived, and the modern American media machine began to churn.

And something else was different. Barack Obama, an African American man who had spent his adult life residing in, working in, and representing the South Side, was President of the United States. At the time, I was serving as the President's deputy counselor. I read the story, saw the clip, and felt sick to my stomach. This was our hometown, and I was convinced that we had to bring the power and spotlight of the administration to the issue of youth violence. Valerie Jarrett agreed, and she brought our recommendation to the rest of the senior staff. The decision was made to send two members of the cabinet to Chicago, the attorney general, Eric Holder, and the secretary of education, Arne Duncan. When she told me, I felt a surge of satisfaction and pride. Even though Barack himself couldn't make the trip as I'd initially recommended, we were acting; we were really leaning in. We were taking Derrion's death seriously. Things were going to get done.

And then Valerie gave me a look that I came to know well: she was sending me, too. *Wait . . . what?* I wasn't a member of the cabinet, I was behind the scenes, a fixer. The one who quietly listens and tinkers. Why was I going? And what was I going to do? She made it clear: I knew Chicago, and I knew the issues. I was going, and it was on me to make sure it went well.

During those early days of the administration, I was often doing two things at the same time. I was in the room, in the moment, working and engaging and making decisions. But at the same time, I was also listening to the part of me saying, *Can you believe this? We're in the Oval Office! Barack is president! Look at him, he's sitting in the chair. That's the bust of Dr. King. I didn't realize the Oval was so small, but kind of feels bigger now that we've been here for a while. I wonder who else sat on this couch? Did Gorbachev sit on this couch? We're in the White House. Why is Pete Souza taking my picture?* It was exhausting. I wanted to tell that guy to shut up because I was trying to concentrate, but instead, often in my head I would answer, *I know, right?!*

That day, though, I knew I'd have to be up to the task. I had just spent two years in a presidential campaign, working in communities all over the nation, rich and poor, urban and rural, with all races, creeds, and religions. I knew that the problem of youth violence was pervasive, and that it ate at the soul of communities. People wondered anxiously how they could protect their children, and what all this violence said about our society. After decades of using only the inefficient, aggressive tools of the War on Drugs, it was time to see if another approach would create safer communities and better lives for our children.

Together, Eric Holder, Arne Duncan, and I decided on a few goals for the trip. Offer comfort to the Fenger community; talk to the mayor and discuss the perspective of the local government; and more than anything, listen to the voices of people on the ground to help point the way to solutions.

When we arrived in Chicago, we spent a very long day in meetings—with the Mayor's Office, with faith leaders, with students and parents—listening and talking about solutions. And as the day wore on, I realized that this was a problem that was not going to be solved overnight, and I became convinced that we had to do more than just visit after notable tragedies. Americans needed the support of their federal government in a way that would be more nuanced and focused than just the blunt force of the police state.

Young men—most often, they were men—who were both victims and perpetrators of the violence plaguing neighborhoods in Chicago and across the country, were dealing with a tidal wave of challenges that stacked the odds against them: the education system, the economy, a pervasive absence of custodial fathers, the drug trade, gangs, the list goes on. Too often, the media painted a picture of these young people as problems, or to use a loaded term from the era of the War on Drugs, as predators. I saw, and President Obama did, too, that if we could flip that narrative and see these young people as assets, as citizens, we had a chance to empower them to address challenges within their own communities.

One day, when Barack was a junior senator from Illinois considering running for president, we were walking together outside on Capitol Hill. I was talking to him about how grueling a presidential campaign could be, both physically and mentally. How mud might be slung and lies might be told about him. It wasn't much of a pep talk, but looking back on it, I think we wanted to be clear-eyed about the downsides of a campaign, and the reality that he might lose. He looked away and shared a conversation he'd had with a friend of his about how much a serious run for president might impact the worldview of a young black child watching the campaign unfold. He realized that just running alone could change a child's life, change that child's idea of what was possible. He turned back to me and said, "That would be worth it." And I had to agree, "Yep, that would be worth it."

There is so much talent out there in overlooked communities, so many undervalued people. I've heard it said before that one of these young people could have the potential to one day discover the cure for cancer. That may be true. But I also know from my own life that one of these young people could one day work in the White House.

* * *

I met Michelle Robinson when I was twenty-two years old. I had just graduated from college and had been accepted to the University of Illinois Law School. I was petrified. I hadn't been a particularly good student, but I really intensely wanted to do well in law school and be a lawyer—in part because I was inspired by stories about civil rights and the law, and in part because I was inspired by Blair Underwood in *L.A. Law*.

I had two months to soak up everything I could as a paralegal at Sidley & Austin, one of the biggest and most prestigious law firms in the city. Of the three hundred lawyers at Sidley, there were about four or five black lawyers. One of them was Michelle. One day, I approached her and told her my story. She was, as she is now, down to earth and approachable. So it's no surprise that when I came calling, she invited me into her office, showed me what she was working on, and over the coming weeks talked with me about law school and what it was like to practice law in that firm.

That meeting, and the relationship that grew from it, truly changed my life. It gave me a confidence and a conviction that I didn't have. From that moment on, I knew that I had a mentor in Michelle, and she has supported and advised me throughout my professional and personal life. And my relationship with her got even deeper when I got to know Barack.

Back then, Barack Obama was the hotshot young lawyer everyone at Sidley was talking about. After my first year of law school, I was back at Sidley as a summer associate. We were at a picnic of some kind and people were playing basketball; and that's where we met, on the

basketball court. He was left handed, confident, fun, and a pretty normal guy—unexpected, coming from the president of the *Harvard
Law Review*.

As we got to know each other, Barack and I realized that the similarities ran even deeper. Like him, I had an absent father who left the
family before I was born. My mom remarried when I was about five,
and I was adopted by her new husband, a Latvian immigrant, who
moved us from the projects of the South Side of Chicago to the
wealthier—and whiter—North Side. So, like Barack, I had the
chance to see life from many sides of the racial divide. Despite my
parents' best efforts, I never quite forgot that I was a black kid in that
interracial family. Even at a young age, my race was always present.
I'll always remember that everyone was always asking me to dance.
Looking back, I remember feeling excited about the attention, and
cringing a little inside, because I didn't quite know where the line was
between having fun and being on display. It all felt like it had the tinge
of a minstrel show. And when they divorced years later, when I was
about ten years old, I was once again forced to cope with the absence
of a father in the home.

I'm lucky: my story has a happy ending. But tragically that has not
been true for others in my life. I have a cousin who is three days older
than me who lived and grew up around my grandmother's house in
Chatham on the South Side, a central point for our entire family. But
where I caught some lucky breaks, from growing up on a few stable
blocks on the North Side to a young lawyer taking an interest in my
future, he got caught up in the drug trade, received a severe federal
sentence, and went away for a long time. *There but for the grace of
God* . . .

As a result, it's always been abundantly clear to me that despite
the progress we've made as a nation, opportunity still isn't equally

distributed. Not everyone has the ability to take advantage of their talents and gifts to pursue their hopes and dreams. It makes me angry, and that anger drives the immense sense of responsibility I have always felt to do something about it. Once I got out of law school, I joined the board of Jamal Place, a boys' home in Chicago, and while I studied for the bar I volunteered at the Public Guardian's Office representing kids who were in the abuse and neglect system. I was often one of the few African American men in these organizations. I felt a special responsibility, if not sometimes a burden, to fight for these kids and not allow them to be painted as problems to be solved, but as assets worthy of our investment.

After practicing corporate law for a few years, I felt like something was missing. I knew there were other things lawyers could do that were more fulfilling. Michelle Obama left the law firm to work in city government, and then left behind practicing law altogether, becoming the first executive director of Public Allies in Chicago. Barack went to a civil rights firm, and every time I went by his office, he would describe his work pursuing housing discrimination remedies, pushing for a more just society.

Barack and I also started talking about our interest in politics as a way to make a difference on the issues facing our city and the nation. I was always grateful that when I talked with him about politics, it was okay to be both clear-eyed about what was necessary to win and idealistic about the good that could be done through our system. A few years later, I was standing in a storefront office in the South Shore neighborhood in Chicago, supporting Barack as he launched his campaign for the state senate.

I found myself drawn to national politics and moved to Washington, DC, to work in the Clinton administration on international aid and development issues. After the 2000 election, I spent a few years as a legislative aide in the House of Representatives and then began working on civil justice issues for the Trial Lawyers Association. One day in 2003, Barack called me to let me know about his decision to run for the U.S. Senate. I was thrilled for him but a little worried as well. He had just lost a race for Congress to Bobby Rush, a campaign in which he was painted as "not black enough." It made me angry to think that had happened to a man who had done everything that we were told we should do by the elders in our community: excelled in school, got married, had a family, gave back to the community. He made something of himself. I had gone all-in on his congressional campaign and I took the loss hard. I also knew that Michelle was just about done with the life of a political spouse. Barack had the pedigree to secure a position that would bring home more money and allow him to be home more often. Running for the Senate didn't seem wise.

I quickly found out that Barack was in "up or out" mode. He was convinced that he had the opportunity to do more at the federal level, and he thought there was a real path to victory. He had put together a solid plan, gathered some real talent around him, and was willing to leave politics for good if he lost. Not for the first time and, as it turned out, not for the last time, I made an easy decision: if he was all-in, I was all-in.

During both the congressional and Senate campaigns, I had the chance to spend more time with him than I had in a while, and I watched those campaigns make him a better candidate and a better politician. He was more clear about what he wanted to accomplish. And we shared a sense of urgency about many things. There were the key issues that were being debated at the time: opposition to the Iraq War and a broken economic policy tilted to the wealthy and powerful. But there was something else. We both felt imperatively that there were an overwhelming number of young people who were not being given the tools and opportunity to reach their potential. He was passionate when we discussed the policies that could change the odds for communities that were left behind, and a new kind of politics that could bridge divides and reunite our country.

After he was elected to the Senate, I settled into a role as his chief counsel, responsible for a broad portfolio of key issues. We hired a young minister named Joshua DuBois as a legislative correspondent. He was ambitious, brilliant, and had a deep spiritual background. Joshua and I were searching for an issue that was authentic to the senator, where he could make a significant impact even as a junior senator and connect himself to the faith community. We pitched then senator Obama on the issue area of fatherhood. After all the time we had spent together, Barack knew that it was personal to me and I certainly knew that it was personal to him. We had both seen so many children, children who looked like us, children who could have been us, left to figure out the path to manhood without a consistent father in their lives. It was a silent cancer eating away at our community, leaving so many young people—particularly young men—without a sense of structure or a future for themselves.

We had the opportunity to make a difference for scores of children and their fathers. It was a no-brainer. We began to support policies that strengthened the opportunities for fathers (custodial or noncustodial) to make a difference in the lives of their children, but we also knew that there was a cultural element to the issue. He had the opportunity to spark a conversation—especially in the black community—about what it meant to be a father. And by 2008, he was running for president, which meant he had an even bigger platform to deliver this message.

That June, he decided to go back to Chicago and speak at Apostolic Church of God in the South Side, a large African American church. On a Sunday morning, Barack talked about what happens to the entire community when fathers don't step up, and offered his own message on being a man. "Any fool can have a child," he said. "That doesn't make you a father. It's the courage to raise a child that makes you a father." He talked about how the absence of fathers can create young people "who have a hole in their hearts"—a hole that can't be filled by government programs but that needed communities and particularly men to step up.

It was a bit of an out-of-body experience. Sitting in the pews of Apostolic Church I suddenly stopped being a political staffer and felt the impact of the moment. This was one of those issues that "we"—in the black community—only spoke about privately. I'd heard the "fathers need to step up" sermon before from preachers, often given to a congregation of mostly women. But to hear it spoken about by a presidential candidate, by my friend, was like hearing my truth spoken out loud for the first time. It was a new experience for me, and I'm sure for many others, and it was one of the reasons why his candidacy was so important. I knew how much he understood it, too; we were both trying to be the best fathers we possibly could, admittedly both spending a lot of time away from our children in the middle of a presidential campaign.

Of course, not everyone loved the speech or appreciated the message. Fatherhood can be a loaded issue, and in many ways, the broad image of absent black fathers is false. Recent studies have shown that the black dads are more involved in their children's lives than most, despite the many barriers created by overpolicing and the criminal justice system. And we heard many complain that he shouldn't shine that kind of light on the negative aspects of our community. They asked tough questions: *Why are you using your platform to say these things? Who are you to lecture us?* In fact, just days after his speech, Reverend Jesse Jackson was caught on a hot mic blasting the senator for "talking down to black people," and exclaiming, "I wanna cut his nuts out."

But Barack Obama has never been silent just because it might rub some people the wrong way. His perspective has always been this: I want what's best for my community, I know these issues have affected me and others in our community, and we need to talk about it.

* * *

A year later, we were in the White House. Barack Obama was now President Obama, and he carried the weight of the world on his shoulders. The gray had begun to fleck in his hair, and he had a really cool office. But he was still the same man. I started to believe that it was relaxing to him when he saw me. I was a friendly and familiar face. I didn't want anything from him, and I knew his thinking and his values.

I knew that during my time in the White House, however long it lasted, I was going to have his back. Often that meant making sure that issues I knew were important to him were handled well, even if he didn't have the bandwidth to deeply focus on them himself. Because of my personal experience, my long-standing relationship with the President, and the seniority of my role, I could speak for him.

After our trip to Chicago in the wake of Derrion's death, we created an interagency task force on youth violence that led to the National Forum on Youth Violence Prevention. Joshua DuBois became the director of the White House Office of Faith-based and Neighborhood Partnerships, and through that office, we continued our work on fatherhood and healthy families with a national campaign encouraging men to "take time to be a father." We also launched a mentoring initiative designed to recruit more people to step up to serve as mentors to young people, even creating the first-ever White House mentoring program, which paired up senior officials as mentors with boys and girls in Washington, DC. The head of the girls' program was the First Lady, Mrs. Obama; I was the head of the boys' program.

Throughout the first term, it felt like we were making progress. But then in January 2013, just a mile or so away from the Obamas' home in Chicago, a young girl named Hadiya Pendleton was shot and killed by gang members just one week after performing with her school marching band at the President's second inauguration. It had been four years since Derrion Albert died on the streets of Chicago in strikingly similar circumstances—and we had to do something about it.

This time, the President decided to go himself. He planned a speech to announce new federal investments in improving outcomes for young men of color. By this point, there was a team working on these issues, including the President's Domestic Policy Council, and they found the perfect program to lift up as a national model. An organization called Youth Guidance, based in Chicago, was producing extraordinary results through a program it ran in the South Side called Becoming a Man (BAM). Of all the efforts and programs to improve outcomes for boys and young men of color, this one had the best metrics and results. It provided a cognitive approach to improving decision-making skills for these young men by giving them social and emotional support and teaching them how to create space between stimulus and response. This might sound complicated, but it's the kind of thing that young people learn in supportive, stable environments. There is a stimulus—a teacher yells at you—and there's a reaction—you get angry. But we need to learn that there can be space before a response. And that space allows young people to think—*I don't want to get in trouble, maybe the teacher has the problem, is there another way to handle this?*—before they choose to respond. Teaching these skills was having a profound impact, reducing levels of school suspensions and violence, as well as engagement with police.

Before the speech, the President was scheduled to meet with a cohort of young men participating in Becoming a Man. I had been told a few days earlier by Alyssa Mastromonaco, the President's deputy chief of staff, that he didn't want a lot of staff in the meeting because he really wanted to interact with the young men. But, aware that I had worked on these issues for so long, she and Valerie Jarrett both knew that I needed to be in there, so I was assigned to the trip.

On a cold, sunny day in February, I took a cab down to Hyde Park Academy High School in Chicago. Going into the meeting, I was emotional, almost overcome with anticipation because I knew in my heart that he was going to be great in that moment.

I have experienced Barack Obama as a mentor. I remember talking to him about my career when I was working for him in the Senate. I was thinking about going to a public policy graduate program at Princeton. He didn't give me any advice right away. Instead, he asked me a lot of questions about what I was looking for and what was driving the decision. He has a focus on self-examination—on relentlessly examining and testing yourself, coming up with conclusions about what you're good at and what you need to improve, and then taking steps to improve yourself. In that conversation, I realized that I was feeling inadequate because I had gone to my state school, the University of Illinois, and I was surrounded by people with Ivy League educations. After that came out, he let me know that he respected me and my intelligence, and that I didn't need an Ivy League degree to work for him and move ahead. It was a great skill to learn—that level of self-examination. I knew that he would pass that on to these guys, and that he would listen, make a personal connection, and share his own story.

There was another observer at the meeting: Cornell McClellan, the President's personal trainer. Cornell was also my personal trainer. In the first year at the White House, the President simply informed me and a few other senior staff, "You're going to work out with Cornell," noticing I had gained a few pounds since he first saw me on the basketball court. Over the first term, Cornell—who split his time between Chicago and Washington—and I had spent a lot of time talking about these issues, and about young men, violence in Chicago, and the dysfunction we saw in our communities.

When the President arrived, the group was seated in a circle with an empty chair for him. He walked in, gave me and Cornell a nod, and then made his way around the room, giving everyone some dap and a hug before sitting down, taking off his jacket, and rolling up his sleeves.

Marshaun Bacon, a BAM counselor, and BAM founder Anthony Di Vittorio were there. Marshaun opened things up by talking about the program, what they do, and describing a ritual they call "check-in," where the members of the cohort share how they're doing physically, emotionally, intellectually, and spiritually. One guy who's on a football team might talk about getting injured; another guy might share that he had a fight with his girlfriend and they're trying to patch things up. They end by saying, "And with that, I'm in." It's an important ritual, one that gives the counselors an opportunity to build connections and gives the guys a moment to be vulnerable with each other and connect.

When it was time for the President, he started by nodding to Cornell. "Well, I worked out this morning so I'm feeling pretty good. And I just had Valentine's Day with Michelle so we had a nice chance to be with one another and connect."

Tears were in my eyes as I saw him immediately reduce the

distance between the most powerful man in the world and these young men from Chicago.

"Intellectually, the job really challenges me all the time. And spiritually, you know, this job is really forcing me to go deep. And with that, I'm in."

He continued to tell his story—one that is well known by now—about how, as a young man, he got into trouble. At one point, he mentioned drinking and smoking weed. One of the big kids, a football player, shot up his hand and blurted out, "Are you talking about *you?*"

The President responded, "Yeah, I'm talking about me." He then went on to make an important point: that even though he made mistakes, he grew up in a more forgiving environment than the one these young men found themselves in. He had a support structure around him so if he made a mistake, people talked to him, counseled him, and gave him the tools and support he needed to make different decisions.

He added, "You're in a less forgiving environment than I was—and that's just how it is for you guys right now. You are going to have to be tighter even than I was because, unfortunately, no one's really going to feel sorry for you. It's unfair but it's real. You have to step up."

There are very few people with that kind of authority who would have come and sat down with these guys, and even fewer would have had such a bracing message for them. But that was Barack. He has high expectations for these guys because he sees the similarities between him and them, a sense of: *If I can do this, you can do this, too.*

Obviously, he has a high opinion of himself. After all, he decided that he should be President of the United States. Throughout his life—from going to the prestigious Punahou School to being the first black president of the *Harvard Law Review*, from getting elected to the Senate to winning the Nobel Peace Prize—there have been moments in which he could have accepted that he is exceptional, different, and that he just doesn't have much in common with others.

But he's never done that. Instead, in that moment, with young men who were in so many ways so far away from his daily experience, he found common ground and empathy. That's the kind of leader, and man, that Barack Obama is.

Going into that meeting, I knew he would have an impact on those young men. What I didn't know, but hoped, was that they would have an impact on him.

There is so much about being president that is broadcast to the public, which means the moments that allowed him to forge genuine personal connections were all the more important. I also knew he enjoyed being a mentor, especially to young people, and hoped the experience would help feed his soul, and sustain him through the work that remained ahead. Afterward, I remember him talking about how bright and engaged they were; how they weren't intimidated or shy, didn't try to posture, and how present they were throughout their time together.

When you're president, the impact of so much of what you do is so downstream or diffuse or complicated by our federal system that you may never see it directly. But that day, I knew he felt he made an impact.

* * *

And that impact would be felt for years to come. The new investments the President announced later that day were the beginning of something much greater. In 2014, President Obama announced an initiative to build upon the work that began in the days after Derrion Albert's death. It was called "My Brother's Keeper" and it consisted of both an inside strategy, an administration task force that focused and leveraged the work of federal agencies, and an outside strategy, working with a group of philanthropic partners to create the MBK Alliance, a nonprofit organization to bring together the private sector with community-based organizations to move the needle on issues facing boys and young men of color.

But it was going to have to happen without me: my time in the Obama administration had come to an end. By the time of the trip to Hyde Park Academy, I had already decided to leave the White House and move on to another adventure. A few reasons stood out, but among the most important was my commitment to my family and especially my children. While our oldest son, now a college freshman, was in high school, I was busy with the 2008 campaign and the first term. Valerie Jarrett, supported by the President and Mrs. Obama, worked hard to create a working environment that was sustainable for parents with children at home, but I wanted to be a more present dad for my two youngest children. Our middle child, Jori, had been diagnosed with autism at a young age, and as he reached adolescence, his challenges became more profound, and new, sometimes frightening behaviors presented themselves. And our youngest, Nia, was starting elementary school and showing us just how much we would need to do to keep up with her. My wife had done so much to raise our children without me present, and I desperately wanted to rebalance my life.

I began to realize during my White House years that because of the influence and scale of the federal government, if I could move the ball forward a yard, it was massive. Frankly, most of the time, I was trying to keep bad things from happening or fixing something that had gone off track in the process. It was complicated, at times frustrating work. But every time I worked on reducing youth violence, or fatherhood, or any of the issues that turned into MBK, I didn't wonder whether all of the hours were worth it; I knew I was making a difference. This was both a unique opportunity and an obligation: I knew that if we didn't do *this* work for *this* president at *this* time, it wasn't going to get done. I knew that I probably would never have that chance again.

It's sort of like being a dad. We have these children and time passes. We don't know how long we'll be together on this side, and each stage of their life is limited and fleeting. If I'm not filling the role of father in their life, it's not going to get done. And if I'm not there, I may never have the chance again.

Working at the White House, I know that I got some things really right. I know that I got some things very wrong. But I'm satisfied that I did my best to make the biggest and best impact on the world that I possibly could.

I guess that's as good a definition of manhood as any.

IMAGINE JOEY LUCAS

Leah Katz-Hernandez

2000

It was hot, sweltering summertime in Connecticut. I was at sleepaway camp, a little place tucked away in the Berkshire Mountains
set on an island in the middle of an almond-shaped lake.

When viewed from the neighboring mountains, Camp Isola Bella
takes on the shape of an iris in an eye. The symbolism is fitting: the
island is owned by the American School for the Deaf, which uses it as
a retreat and camp space for deaf children and families to use year-
round. After all, deaf people are "people of the eye." We are uniquely
dependent on our eyes in our navigation and approach to the world,
except in the cases of deaf-blind people, whose understanding of
sound transfers to other senses in the human body.

It was at that camp that I met Ari. She was Jewish, like me, and
she came from an upstate New York family. She and I had formed an
especially close bond years earlier and looked forward to reuniting on
the island every summer. We were deaf, like all children on the island.

Ari had large, heavy-lidded eyes full of soul and she carried herself
with poise and a deeper understanding of the world. She was always

intellectual and curious and pointed in her comments. We were both playing on the floor of our cabin when I asked Ari to name her favorite TV show. "*The West Wing*," she quickly answered.

I had never heard of a show called *The West Wing*. My parents couldn't afford cable so I was accustomed to hearing about shows on Nickelodeon and the Disney Channel that I wasn't able to watch.

Ari went on to explain, "It's a really funny show about the White House, and it's just really witty, and I like it. There's also a deaf woman on it."

I looked at Ari, more amused about the fact that she had used the word "witty" and barely registering her mention of a deaf woman on this TV show. Ari looked at me softly and then she sort of spaced out, looking off into the distance.

"A deaf woman at the White House . . . It's a good show."

2002

I was sitting at the kitchen table at the Katz-Hernandez family house, stuffing my face full of food—probably cheese. My father was asking me what I wanted to do in the future, when, out of the blue, he eagerly suggested, "You could become like Joey Lucas and work at the White House!"

"What? Who's Joey Lucas?" I asked back.

"She's the deaf woman from the TV show *The West Wing*."

I remembered Ari mentioning a deaf woman on her favorite TV show. I relayed the story to my father and he confirmed that it was the same show.

"Hmm, I'm not sure," I replied. "What does she do?"

"Joey does polling—she helps people understand issues," my father answered, his eyes eager and hopeful. "She works at the White House. Joey is deaf."

I shrugged.

2004

Attending a deaf state school is like attending Hogwarts: you travel across multiple school districts to arrive at a completely unique school—sometimes on a historic campus with 1800s-era school buildings and dormitories—where you are among peers until graduation. Following the founding of the first school for deaf children in the United States in 1817, government-supported educational institutions for the deaf sprang up across the nation in the 1800s and early 1900s. Even with the current trend of mainstreaming—sending a deaf or hard-of-hearing child into the regular school system with an individualized plan for accommodations—deaf state schools continue to be considered by many as a prestigious, culturally competent, and accessible choice for education.

There is a large tree on the campus of the Maryland School for the Deaf, which was founded in 1868. Deaf high school students like me and my friends often liked to hang around beneath the stocky tree branches, in the shadow of the fat, napkin-sized deep green leaves. We would drift slower beneath this tree, with our fast-moving hands stretching the clock's hands as much as possible.

At the age of seventeen, I was a ready debater with anyone who dared cross my views politically. It was beneath this tree, as I walked back and forth from lunch hour to classes, that my arguments often reached their climax.

One day, my argument was about the apathy of deaf people in

politics. A friend had argued that it was meaningless for deaf people to get involved with politics because we were almost always excluded and left out of the political process. I disagreed vehemently, quickly listing out a variety of examples in which marginalized communities successfully won advances by engaging with elected officials.

My friend abruptly stopped as we reached the edge of the tree's shade, turning to me with a serious yet sly look in his eyes. "You're so good at explaining politics . . . Tell me, what's next? When will we deaf people get power?"

I choked. I didn't quite have an answer other than repeating my trope that people needed to engage in order to bring about desired results. Throughout that afternoon, I thought about what my friend had said, but I had no easy answers.

2007

I looked around for my father in the dark ballroom. We were at a fundraiser for the Mexican American Legal Defense and Educational Fund, one of my father's favorite nonprofit organizations. Growing up as a biracial foster child in Los Angeles, my father put himself through college, and, after many years of work, was able to obtain a PhD and a stable job to support his family. Being involved with this organization was my father's way to stay connected to his own roots.

This was my first time attending a Washington, DC, reception. Driven by my father's incessant questioning of what I wanted to do for my career, I had decided on the possibility of getting into government and communications. This prompted my father to bring me along to this event where I could meet with Latino professionals in these fields and ask them about their careers.

My father sidled up to me and, with a smile on his face, informed me that Senator Barack Obama was in the room. "A surprise visit!"

My eyes adjusted to the glowing figure in the center of the room. There was a single central light in the reception area and the senator just happened to be standing in the middle of it. A soft white light encircled him, the rest of the room dimly lit.

"Come on, you need to talk to him!" I felt my heartbeat quicken.

My father strategically planted us near Obama and when the senator had concluded his conversation, my father instantly started talking and signing at the same time, telling him I was a college student at Gallaudet University. From the expression on Senator Obama's face, he recognized my university, a federally funded institution serving the deaf and hard of hearing. Our university's charter was signed by Abraham Lincoln after the dozens of state schools for the deaf had produced droves of alumni who were ready for college-level education in the 1800s.

Senator Obama asked me about recent campus protests surrounding the selection of a new university president. I didn't expect him to know or ask about what was going on at my university, but I quickly gave a summary of the events and he responded thoughtfully.

We took a picture together and after a pleasant handshake he thanked me for my explanation. As I watched him move on to speaking to other people in the crowd, a strange stillness entered my mind. I had a feeling that was deeper than hope—a feeling of real opportunity and a preview of the future. I knew I wanted to work for him.

2008

I woke up very early in the morning and immediately hit the snooze button.

My alarm clock was a special type sold only to the deaf and hard of hearing. It had two cords that attached to the lamp by my bed and to a brick-sized piece of vibrating machinery shoved under my mattress. When the alarm clock went off, my whole bed shook like there was an earthquake and the lamp next to me flashed like there was a massive lightning storm. This was how I had woken up by myself ever since I stopped having my mother rouse me.

Instead of going back to sleep during the snooze period as I normally would have, like any regular college student, I lay there on my bed in the dark. My eyes were wide open.

I looked up to the ceiling and thought to myself on loop, *This is it. This is Election Day. This is it. This is Election Day.*

Adrenaline flooded my body and I continued lying there, thinking back on the past several months.

I thought about how I had relentlessly chased down and talked to every single deaf person who I knew in a battleground state. How I had even gotten back on friendly talking terms with my ex-boyfriend, in large part because his family lived in Ohio and I had hoped to persuade his swing-voting family members to vote Obama.

I thought about how I had traveled to Denver for a thrilling once-in-a-lifetime chance to experience the Democratic National Convention with a group of Gallaudet government majors. Once I got there, I saw so many exciting things that I tired of writing emails back to my family and friends and instead set up a blog with videos in American Sign Language. Suddenly, my blog took off and, in a very short amount of time, comments came in from deaf people all over the nation and the world, followed by inquiries from mainstream news organizations finally taking notice of the voting power of deaf people.

I thought about how I had returned to Gallaudet University's campus for the fall semester and went to work registering fellow students to vote on campus. I turned my blog into a clearinghouse of information on voting to help the deaf and hard-of-hearing community, with regular updates on my journey volunteering with the Obama campaign and videos of me canvassing in battleground states with a smile on my face.

I thought about the vast audience of deaf and hard-of-hearing people, both domestically and internationally, who watched my journey through the blog. For them, the barriers for deaf people were still there, but the doors and windows were cracked a bit open against the backdrop of a historically different presidential candidate campaigning on an upbeat, thudding message of "Yes, We Can."

I thought about how, despite knowing the history of the disenfranchisement and marginalization of the deaf and hard-of-hearing community, I still felt hopeful. Over the past several months, I went to bed every night amazed at the shifting winds of progress in the United States. And last night, I had prayed—simply and deeply—*Please, let him win. Please, let our vote mean something.*

The alarm went off again, a cacophony of rumbling and flashing lights in my bedroom. I got up and looked at the dark outside. It was four thirty a.m.

I got dressed and ready for the day, preparing to head to my local polling place to help the local precinct captain. Throughout the day, I would update my blog and keep the audience beyond my computer screen informed. Then, at last, I would head back to Gallaudet University to anxiously watch the election returns with the campus community.

I went outside and felt the chilly, early morning November air hit me in the face. I softly closed my eyes with one more slight prayer. I breathed in the cool air and imagined what a win would feel like.

I would know exactly what that felt like, eighteen hours later.

2010

Delighted and terrified, I filed into the auditorium across the street from the White House with about eighty-five other interns. When the White House internship director came out on the stage with her brown polka-dot dress, smiled brightly, and said, "Welcome!" all of us cheered and laughed at the same time.

President Obama—*President* now!—and his team were in the second year of their administration. There was a feeling of blazing optimism and steely determination to bend the course of the nation's trajectory toward a more equitable future full of opportunity for everyone. Each one of us, young interns in our cheap, new, straight-out-of-college clothing, were exhilarated at the opportunity to be part of this historic administration.

It was overwhelming for many of us. Coming to work at the White House is like jumping on board a moving train. Hoping to impress our White House bosses, many of us aspired to move faster every day, trying to anticipate our supervisors' needs and complete tasks before they were even assigned. The "White House intern work ethic" pushed all of us to work at a breakneck speed.

I quickly learned that much of my work was unglamorous but critically important to the success of the Office of Public Engagement. From managing the official White House in-boxes that received emails from the public and managing outgoing responses on behalf of the White House, to researching and "vetting" candidates to be invited to public events, to helping write briefing memos on a broad range of events, I supported my supervisors with whatever they needed to coordinate and accomplish their goal: engaging the American people. And since my internship took place in the fall, we were in full swing planning for the winter holidays. For the interns, this meant that nearly every day, we wrestled with massive spreadsheets that we updated daily with names, addresses, and special notes for invitations to holiday receptions and mailing the White House holiday card.

Among days of dizzying scrambles around emails and computer tasks, I ran back and forth between offices, escorted and directed guests arriving for events, carried boxes full of programs or cards or printed spreadsheets to various locations on the White House grounds, and heaved cases of soda to staff in perpetual need of sugar or caffeine.

My favorite moments often happened when I was walking down the iconic hallways of EEOB—the Eisenhower Executive Office Building—with its endless black-and-white-checkered floors. I frequently walked laps around the hallways simply to memorize the locations of various offices so I would not be lost if I was ever called to one of these offices at a moment's notice. Out of the corners of my eyes, I would watch passing staffers carefully, memorizing their faces and the offices that they had walked out of. I tried to remember who was most likely to walk down certain hallways during certain times, who seemed the most approachable, who seemed most harried, and—especially—who acknowledged my presence as a deaf, petite woman and smiled at me.

On one of those walks, I looked sideways to my fellow intern, Ben, with whom I had already grown incredibly close. As he met my eyes, he smiled. "Has anyone told you that you're just like that woman from the TV show, Joey Lucas?" I laughed and answered, "Yes, but I'm not . . . I'm an intern!" I answered.

Though it was nice to imagine a deaf woman in the West Wing, I felt some amusement about comparing my career to a fictional person from a television show. Amusement and frustration, because I knew that real life is far more difficult than what we see on television. Even for a hearing person arriving at the White House as an intern is an accomplishment. Working on the White House staff—let alone in the West Wing—was more than I could ever imagine for myself, especially as a deaf, mixed-race woman. On many days, I quite simply didn't want to think about the potential challenges ahead.

Yet, I knew Joey Lucas had a pull on people's imagination. I wondered, What was it about her, other than her deafness? What did she represent to hearing people?

2014-15 Winter

Following my internship, I worked on the President's 2012 reelection campaign (where he once signed "thank you" to me at an event!) and his second inauguration. Then, by a stroke of luck, a former supervisor became chief of staff for First Lady Michelle Obama. She knew my work ethic, and I was hired into the First Lady's communications team and continued my intense work schedule—only, this time, in the East Wing of the White House.

My very first week on the job, I met Mrs. Obama. I was prepared to be starstruck, and I was completely blown away when she signed to me in complete sentences. I later learned that she had attended Whitney Young Magnet High School in Chicago, a school that was also well known for having a robust mainstream program for deaf and hard-of-hearing high school students. As a high school student, Michelle Obama learned sign language among her deaf classmates. To this day, she retains some knowledge of sign language. The moment that I saw the First Lady's welcome expressed through her graceful signs, I knew I'd arrived to a great place to work.

When I passed the six-hundred-day mark, I stopped counting. I stopped keeping track of how many hours I worked each week. I stopped keeping track of how early I woke up to edit and send out the daily news clips to my team and the First Lady herself. I stopped counting the hundreds of public events that I helped plan and execute for the First Lady, some even with the President.

I stopped counting the moments that touched me, brought tears to my eyes, and took my breath away. All the moments when I stopped in the middle of the hustle and bustle of a busy day—such as the day when Anna Wintour passed me by, or when I had my breath taken away upon seeing the White House flower shop's gorgeous creations for the French state dinner, or when a world-famous reporter recalled his memories ducking the bullets at Tiananmen Square—to silently think to myself: *This is real. I'm working in the White House, for First Lady Michelle Obama.* There were too many of these moments.

By the time I passed my six hundredth day in the White House, it had all snowballed and rolled together into one fantastic, incredible, extraordinary job. My daily life was a constant, unyielding roller-coaster ride of staff demands and an incredible amount of emails received and sent through my official White House email address.

Finally, I took a weeklong Christmas vacation to New Mexico to see my best friend and her two children, to whom I was the all-important aunt in their lives. It was my first vacation in a long time, and I luxuriated in it. I set my "out of office" message and, in the relative safety of the holiday break, allowed myself to enjoy the rambunctious chattering of my five-year-old niece and two-year-old nephew. I regaled them with stories from the White House and drilled the five-year-old on American presidential history.

As they sat on the floor and looked up at me with their curious eyes, I described pulling off the Puppy Bowl on the South Lawn of the White House, a complicated task that involved getting twenty-two adorable puppies comfortably through a security screening process that included K-9 dogs, ensuring they didn't escape from the South Lawn (while answering emails on my BlackBerry at the same time), and keeping Bo and Sunny, the White House dogs, "on script."

I described the world and its time zones to my niece and nephew, neither of whom had ever traveled outside of the United States. I told them that when the First Lady flew to China, I had to keep Chinese hours—a twelve-hour difference from Washington, DC—and stay up all night working to support the members of the communications team as they traveled.

In their remote region of New Mexico, surrounded by burnished reddish gold mountains and steely-cold blue skies, cell phone service was scarce. Nothing was more peaceful than having no emails arrive all day . . . until I went into "town" and the little electric rectangle hanging in my back pocket started to vibrate endlessly, receiving hundreds of emails. During the holidays, most emails were press releases or news clips, but some emails still required a response—even on a holiday.

A single email stood out among the rest. It urged me to call an internal White House number as soon as possible. The best signal in town was in a thrift store, so once there, I quickly situated myself on a yellow velvet sofa and called the number using the video relay service app on my phone, which enables me to video-call with an interpreter who speaks with me in sign language and translates for the hearing person on the other end of the line. When I finished the call, I walked over to my friend, who was checking out the selection of children's shoes.

I stared at her and started to gasp out in sign language the results of the call.

"I've been promoted to a job in the West Wing. This is really happening," I said, dumbfounded. "I will be working on the same floor as the President of the United States."

My best friend was holding a child's boot. Laughter spread across her face like the opening of a parachute and I instantly joined in—both of us, two deaf women, in a New Mexican thrift store, laughing hysterically in glee and shock.

Late 2015: The West Wing

Each day, as the dawn's light shone behind the White House's east side, I passed through the doors of the West Wing and entered the lobby to begin my day.

As West Wing receptionist, my job was to receive and greet the President's guests, making small conversations wherever appropriate, and sometimes giving a heads-up to other staff that certain people were in the lobby. I received CEOs and billionaires who passed through to discuss trade and economics. Over time, they grew to know me on a first-name basis; one even insisted on taking a picture with me. I saw a litany of celebrities, including musicians whose beats I had moved my body to throughout high school and college. A common misconception is that the deaf don't listen to music, so as I recognized and warmly greeted musicians, I showed them, and my colleagues, that the deaf do love music. Fighting back tears, I greeted civil rights legends and military veterans who had risked their lives for this country and its ideals.

The writers were always the ones who made me starstruck. I deeply admired those who had taken the power of language into their own hands to entertain, challenge, and mold the human mind for generations. One such writer was Ta-Nehisi Coates, who later wrote about the people who he had met in the West Wing in his article for the *Atlantic*, "My President Was Black":

> I was introduced to a deaf woman who worked as the president's receptionist, a black woman who worked in the press office, a Muslim woman in a head scarf who worked on the National Security Council, and an Iranian American woman who worked as a personal aide to the president.

Just a couple of weeks after I started my job, several news articles covered me and my position, noting that I used sign language to communicate with the President and the First Lady and describing my mixed background as the daughter of a Jewish mother from the East Coast and a biracial father from the West Coast. As I sought to remain in my lane and focus on being a dedicated, hardworking staffer, I also grew to understand that in many ways, I was not an ordinary receptionist. As I greeted people in the West Wing, my sign language indicated my deaf existence. I was thrilled when people didn't even react to my signing at all; to me, that meant they acknowledged my existence as an equal.

I eventually realized that I had viewed myself as less human than my hearing counterparts all my life—until the Obama White House experience taught me otherwise. For my whole life, I had internalized the message that because I couldn't hear, I was valued less as a human being. Throughout my career, I had sought to work even harder than my hearing peers just to simply prove that deaf people "could do it." In the West Wing, that self-perception changed because of how people responded upon seeing me in the lobby. My being there was simultaneously ordinary and extraordinary—just like the Obama administration itself. I was welcome—and in turn, I welcomed others.

Every day, I met visitors who shared with me that either they or an immediate family member had a disability. I wasn't surprised. There are fifty-seven million people with disabilities in the United States today: one out of every five people. As I like to remind people, if you don't have a disability yourself, the chances are high that you know someone who has a disability, either in your family or in your community.

Still, every time a visitor signed back "hello" to me in the lobby, I couldn't help but react with wide-eyed shock, followed by a warm greeting and a series of quick exchanges around how they knew sign language. Nobody minded in the least that the first face they would meet before they saw the President or his top advisors would be that of a deaf woman of color signing away at them with a sign language interpreter.

Sometimes people asked me, with genuine curiosity, how I got to the White House. Even though I had worked hard and had enough experience to compete with other qualified, hearing candidates, I knew my story didn't begin there. So I would tell these guests that I was a product of the American public deaf education system and a proud graduate of a deaf school and a deaf university. I would tell them about the laws that protect the rights of people with disabilities in education and employment, and how these laws allowed someone like me, a young woman with a visible disability, to work in the White House.

What I had once imagined, and what countless others had seen on television, was finally a reality: a deaf woman working in the West Wing.

So it was only fitting that, just a few months later, I had the chance to meet and thank Joey Lucas.

* * *

In November 2015, my friend and colleague Maria Town, who served as the White House's disability liaison, brought the razzle-dazzle of Broadway to the White House for a celebration of disability in the arts. But Maria didn't just bring any show; instead, she brought an acclaimed deaf production of *Spring Awakening*, a rock musical full of provocative themes and focused on young people coming into their own.

The cast was a mix of hearing and deaf actors, and featured some longtime Hollywood and New York theater heavyweights. Following a performance from the show, as the musicians and cast took their seats, I went up to the stage and looked out at an audience full of disability advocates and trailblazers who had fought for our representation on-screen.

And right there in the front row was Marlee Matlin, the very same Oscar-winning, hard-of-hearing actress who played Joey Lucas in *The West Wing*. As she racked up acting jobs in the years following her 1986 Oscar win for the movie *Children of a Lesser God*, Marlee had also become an advocate for the removal of accessibility barriers in the entertainment industry, both online and in the real world.

I was suddenly struck by the fact that the fight for representation on the television screen had eventually led to representation at the White House in real life. So naturally, I started with, "Maybe some of you have seen the show *The West Wing*. If you did, you know who I'm talking about. So many people kept mentioning this fictional character, Joey Lucas. This role was played by our own Marlee Matlin." I looked at Marlee and could see her barely contain her great joy. "Thank you. Thank you," I said directly to her.

"Now, in real life, there's a deaf woman working in the West Wing. It's not fiction anymore. That's the power of people with disabilities in arts and that's the power of #deaftalent."

Before an audience of people with disabilities in the arts, I was deeply proud to address them as a real-life deaf woman representative of the Obama White House.

I was reminded of all the people that I had encountered over the years who mentioned Joey Lucas to me, and how their perspectives of me as a deaf person were influenced by seeing a fictional deaf woman working in the West Wing on television. In that moment onstage, I understood that imagination is intertwined with hope and opportunity. Imagination pushes the boundaries of human advancement. Imagination enables people and culture to get ready for change. Just like so many American movies featured a black president long before we elected a black president in real life, we first need to imagine what is possible—even if such a scenario doesn't seem possible at the moment—before it can happen.

Even as I shrugged off Joey Lucas references, I failed to recognize that those people were *ready* for Joey Lucas to exist in real life. Standing before an audience of entertainment industry change makers who advocated for greater representation of people with disabilities, I realized that those very same people were the ones who first brought forth the idea of a deaf woman working in the West Wing—and by the time I got there, everyone in the building was ready for it.

We have reached the White House, but there's more work to do. Only when we have full representation—in our political system but also in our culture—will "all barriers begin to crumble and fall," as Agatha Tiegel Hanson, the first deaf woman graduate of Gallaudet University, said in her 1893 valedictorian speech.

2016

It was another hot summer day, but instead of idling away the day at a sleepaway camp I was at the White House, where I had agreed to take a friend and her seven-year-old deaf daughter, Sheila, on a tour of the West Wing.

Sheila had a lot of imagination and ambition for her future. Her mother was determined to show her the White House to make sure she knew that she could work there one day if she wanted to. I was honored to play a part in giving her such a formative experience.

At the end of the tour, we exited the north doors of the West Wing lobby. As the sun set, the building took on a soft glow—one much like the light in which I met President Obama nine years earlier—and Sheila began to twirl around and dance on the asphalt outside the White House Press Briefing Room. I smiled at the sight. I loved it every time I saw deaf children at the White House. I spun my blue White House badge in the air to get her attention and she came over, her bright blue eyes shining.

Like my father did many years ago, I asked Sheila what she wanted to do when she grew up.

Sheila looked straight at me in the eyes and described a career field that, I knew based on historical facts and the present statistics, is extremely hard for deaf people—and women—to break into.

And yet, I had no doubt she could do it. Because that summer day's reality was much different from when I was a young girl at camp with Ari. In the intervening sixteen years, the imaginary became real. The ground had shifted for that conversation.

What will we imagine—and make real—over the next sixteen years?

LAUGHING BETWEEN THE FERNS

Brad Jenkins

My grandfather, Oscar Jenkins, was a simple man. He loved his six children. He loved his wife. And, more than anything, Oscar loved to make his family laugh. It filled a room. It was infectious. And it happened to come from a black man working at an all-white country club in segregated Oklahoma City.

Despite the government's efforts to dehumanize Oscar—to treat him and his family like second-class citizens—he was defiant in his laughter. On special days, he would bring his six-year-old son Walter to work and the two would end the day by going to the segregated movie theater downtown. Oscar would fall asleep midway through the film and wake up to the sound of his son's laughter. Two black men, father and son, would laugh together in the dark, empty movie theater.

At the age of forty-two, my grandfather passed away during a routine hernia operation. The last photo of my grandfather is of him laughing the night before his operation, his son on his lap, the two of them cheesing for the camera. There was no good reason that in the greatest country on earth, my grandfather couldn't get the health care that he deserved. The care that was available to some, but not all.

In the summer of 2011, I called my father to tell him that I had been hired to work in Barack Obama's White House. The first black president. I got emotional even before making the call. I wondered how much this was going to mean to him, given how far his family had come in just one generation. How proud he would be. I picked up the phone and told him the news.

"What?! You're going to work at the White House?" *Laughter.* This is not at all what I expected.

My father wasn't laughing because he was proud. He was laughing at the sheer absurdity of what I was saying. His son working at the White House? Comical! Ludicrous! His laugh was so loud that I had to wait a few beats before continuing.

"I know. It sounds crazy, huh?"

Laughter. "What the hell are you going to do at the White House?" *More laughter.* He is not convinced this is a real thing.

"I am going to work in something called the Office of Public Engagement. My old campaign boss in Chicago, Jon Carson, runs the office with Valerie Jarrett. Do you remember Jon?"

"What is that? Office of Public Engagement? That sounds like some BS." *More laughter.* Not infectious in the least.

"Okay. Well, anyway. I just wanted to call you and tell you the good news. The FBI may be contacting you for my background check and security clearance."

"What should I tell them?"

"Just be honest. I have no idea if they'll actually call you. But I had to give them all of your information."

The laughter finally stops. "Wait. You gave the government our information? I don't trust these people."

"Dad. It's just protocol. Can you just answer their questions if they call?"

"Okay, Brad. Good luck."

I never imagined that I would be lucky enough to make a call like that. To call your father to tell him that you are going to work at the White House. And while it's true that my father escaped poverty and oppression by ignoring the government—by not allowing them to define his worth—it still would've been cool to hear him excited about his son working at the White House.

Walking up to the security gate on your first day at the White House is a surreal experience. You approach the Secret Service officer with your photo ID in hand, slide it underneath the glass window, and do your best to convey "I am a serious person and deserve to be allowed entrance into this historic complex" while waiting for men in uniform to confirm your existence.

"You're not on the list."

"Excuse me? Um, can you check again? It's my first day. I work here now."

"You sure about that?" The Secret Service officer wasn't laughing. Over the past year, I had heard horror stories of people starting at the White House and being fired for not passing their FBI background checks. This must be it. I don't deserve to be here. My dad was right.

"Okay. I'll, uh, call my boss," I stuttered out.

The officer handed my driver's license back and motioned for me to move away from the entrance. My hands started to get clammy and cold even though it was eighty-eight degrees out. I pulled out my phone and called Jon Carson's assistant. I was trying my best not to panic.

"Hey! Victoria! It's Brad. I, um, I'm outside the gate and they said that I don't work here . . . Do you know if I passed my background check? I never heard back on whether I did or—"

"Oh, Brad! No. You're good. I just forgot to put your name in WAVES. Sorry. It will be a few minutes."

Every day, the White House welcomes hundreds of political

leaders, everyday heroes, CEOs, and even the President's political rivals. Every single one of them is processed by WAVES (Workers and Visitors Entry System). And if you enter your information incorrectly (or not at all) you will inevitably be stuck outside the gate until it gets remedied by some helpful human on the inside. In other words, WAVES is the worst. But what are you going to do? You can't let just anyone inside the White House. Especially the son of a crazy old man like Walter Jenkins.

Once I was finally allowed entrance that morning through the metal detectors, the bomb-sniffing dogs, the second gate of metal detectors, and the second Secret Service officer checking my ID, I became a legit White House staffer. I was given a badge that allowed me to walk anywhere on the White House complex. A generation ago, my father could only drink out of Colored Only water fountains or be seen by Colored Only medical professionals. And here I was, walking into the most secure facility in the world without anyone batting an eye.

One month into the job, my father called and asked me how it was going.

"It's good, Dad. I have been given two engagement portfolios. Progressives and the creative community."

Laughter. "What the hell does that mean?"

"I do outreach for all of the progressive political groups. I do meetings, phone calls, strategy with senior staff and sometimes the President. And I guess I'll do that for the creative community, too. I haven't really done much with that portfolio yet."

"What's the creative community?"

"Artists. Celebrities. Writers. But no one is really focused on celebrities right now. We're organizing groups around the debt ceiling battle."

"And what are you going to do with them?"

"We're going to explain to the American people and members of Congress that we can't let the government default on its debt."

"Why would anyone trust these progressive groups? This is why government sucks, Brad. You should get those writers and celebrities to do the debt ceiling stuff."

"Okay. I have to go. Thanks for the tip, Dad."

A year before I started at the White House, President Obama signed the Affordable Care Act into law. Now it was 2013. The President had just won reelection, and in October his signature legislative achievement was finally about to become available to every man, woman, and child regardless of where they lived or how much money they made. And, speaking of children, my first child was due to be born two months before the start of the open enrollment period. It was shaping up to be a big year. The White House Office of Public Engagement and the Jenkins fam had our most important campaigns in front of us: the ACA and Baby Jenkins.

The stakes were high. The Congressional Budget Office estimated that six million Americans needed to sign up in the first year of enrollment for the health care exchanges to function properly. Independent analysts expected that the millions of families who desperately needed the ACA were going to sign up as soon as the exchanges opened. What was less certain were the young uninsured millennials out there. In order for the risk pool to be balanced, our office was tasked with getting as many healthy young Americans as possible to sign up for health care.

When we spoke with consumer experts, they were honest with their assessment: this was not going to be easy. Our target uninsured demographic was extremely hard to reach and even harder to influence. My dad's early advice was proving annoyingly true on the enrollment campaign. Political groups were not the messengers that we needed. Instead, our team focused on trusted influencers around the country: doctors, nurses, community leaders, business and faith leaders. And my portfolio, the creative community, became absolutely essential to the ACA's success. We hunkered down with my former colleague the actor Kal Penn and other Hollywood friends to figure out: How do we get the biggest stars in the world to promote health care and turn their support into a runway to success? And how do we make it feel as genuine as possible?

Almost a year before the October enrollment kickoff, our draft plans were due. Because Baby J was due right before enrollment began, I was obsessed with ensuring that everything was ready months in advance. Our plans contained comprehensive, week-by-week enrollment strategies focused on the regions of the country with the highest uninsured rates. In order to make the creative plan a reality, we met with all of the key Hollywood players and kept a tracking sheet of commitments. By the time October first rolled around we had over two hundred celebrities confirmed to participate in our outreach. Every new name that I added to the tracking sheet I thought of as possible Baby J names. Pharrell Jenkins? Gaga Jenkins?

And then it was game time. Baby Jenkins—Sadie—was born on August 2. And on October 1, two hundred celebrities, artists, writers, musicians, and creators were primed and ready to post #GetCovered at Healthcare.gov to hundreds of millions of followers. Lady Gaga and Pharrell were joined by Kerry Washington, Diddy, Snoop, Connie Britton, Katy Perry, and more. The list went on and on. We were set to inspire hundreds of thousands of young Americans to believe that government can and should work for all people.

Ten minutes after Lady Gaga posted her first #GetCovered photo to sixty million fans, I received an angry phone call from her camp.

"Brad. The fucking website is not working."

"What?"

"Healthcare.gov. It's not working."

"Wait. Hold on." I typed in the URL on my government-issued laptop and a message appeared:

> The system is down at the moment. We're working
> to resolve the issue. Please try again later.

"Brad. What the fuck is going on? Should she delete the posts? This is awful."

"No. Don't delete it. Look, it's just early morning hiccups. It will be working by the afternoon."

I had no idea what was going on. After I hung up, John Legend's team called. Then Pharrell's. Then Rashida Jones herself sent me an angry email. This was a nightmare. Rashida Jones hated me. And it was only nine thirty a.m.

By eleven a.m., our team was finally let in on the news: the website was completely inoperable. Seventy celebrities and dozens of mayors, CEOs, community leaders, and members of Congress had already posted to their accounts. They were all furious after finding out that they had promoted a nonfunctioning government website for the Obamacare thing that Republicans had already primed everyone to hate. Hundreds of thousands of Americans tried to sign up that first day and were denied, thanks to stereotypical government incompetence. The Tea Party had warned the American people that government could never be a force for good. The launch of Healthcare.gov was proving them right. On cue, my father called around one p.m.

"Hey. Your shitty website isn't working! What happened?" *Laughter.*

"Dad."

"You guys better get that thing working. This is life or death for those families. You said it yourself."

We *were* in trouble. Jon Stewart, Stephen Colbert, and Rachel Maddow dedicated entire segments to the disastrous launch. Thanks to the government shutdown, many Americans believed that inaction in Congress was to blame. In reality, it was federal bureaucratic malpractice. The government spent three hundred million dollars on a website that didn't work. This was my father's idea of how government operates. It was a tragedy.

When the government shutdown finally ended on October 17, only three in ten people were able to get through to the website. While the President held daily meetings with his chief of staff, cabinet, and senior staff on how to fix the website, I was receiving angry phone calls from agents and managers—even while changing diapers in the middle of the night—and I had to apologize to each and every artist on behalf of the White House.

It took two months for senior staff and a dozen of the best Silicon Valley engineers in the country to fix Healthcare.gov. It was a miraculous feat. Think *Ocean's Eleven* for website infrastructure. But our original public engagement plans were thrown out the window. We were no longer unveiling a shiny new product. We were now rereleasing the most poorly damaged brand in internet history. How the hell were we going to get young people to Healthcare.gov after this? It was ludicrous, comical even. But if heroes from Silicon Valley could fix Healthcare.gov, I believed we could find heroes from Hollywood who could get people to use it.

The president of production at Funny Or Die was a believer like me. While I believed in the power of democracy, Mike Farah believed in the power of laughter. He joined Funny Or Die in 2008, the same month that I moved to Chicago to join the Obama campaign HQ.

Farah was a producer, the Hollywood version of a community organizer. He found ways to get shit done. Whether it was financing a web series with love and spare change or connecting an unknown writer to an A-list celebrity, Farah made comedy dreams a reality.

In planning our health care campaign, most of our efforts were spent trying to convince anyone and everyone to help the White House. But Funny Or Die came prepared with video ideas that they were going to execute whether we were involved or not. One involved using the stars of *Step Brothers* to reach uninsured men. Another was a satire of Kerry Washington's *Scandal* aimed at reaching millennial women. As Farah put it, if the Koch brothers could spend hundreds of millions of dollars trying to scare people, they were going to spend hundreds of dollars and make millions of people laugh.

One of the most popular Funny Or Die series was a program that Farah executive-produced entitled *Between Two Ferns with Zach Galifianakis*. It was an intentionally low-budget, public-access-style interview show created by the comedian Zach Galifianakis and director Scott Aukerman to point out the absurdity of the Hollywood bubble and the artificiality of the talk show format. *Ferns* followed the talk show format to a T: an A-list celebrity is forced to sit down and make vapid small talk in order to pitch their movie, album, or whatever entertainment they were currently hawking. Natalie Portman, Bradley Cooper, Will Ferrell, Ben Stiller, Jennifer Lawrence—the biggest names lined up to join Zach between those ferns. Each episode racked up tens of millions of views, turning Zach into a star.

Months earlier, Zach and Farah had pitched *Between Two Ferns* to Valerie Jarrett and the OPE team in person. While Valerie loved Zach, she was still not convinced that the platform was appropriate for the President. But much had changed in the two months since the enrollment launch. President Obama was furious with how things were going. Healthcare.gov was finally working, but enrollments were well behind the CBO's six million target. We only had three months left. The President demanded that we shake things up. Shortly after a tense Roosevelt Room meeting, Valerie knew that we needed to act. Yohannes Abraham, her chief of staff, called me.

"Brad. Can you talk *Ferns*? Are you free?"

"Yes!"

I ran to Yo's office. Marlon Marshall, the President's director for enrollment outreach, laid out the problem. Our biggest fear was that millions of people would wait until the last minute, right before the March 31 enrollment deadline, to enroll. After all, every tax professional told us that the busiest days for filing taxes were always the last few days. The problem with Healthcare.gov was that the website was currently held together with the electronic equivalent of duct tape. If too many people waited until the last few days, the traffic would overwhelm the system. We needed to drive a surge of traffic weeks before the deadline and we especially needed to convince men aged eighteen to thirty-four (who were less likely to have health insurance). That was exactly the demographic of Funny Or Die's organic audience. We needed *Between Two Ferns*. And just like that I was given marching orders to prepare a decision memo for the President.

Every night before he went to bed, President Obama was handed a binder of documents to read in the residence that night. Some of the materials were briefing documents. Some were decision memos. Typically, the Office of Public Engagement didn't send up a ton of memos, but the success of the President's signature legislative achievement wasn't resting in the hands of policy wonks or legal scholars now—it was in the hands of Valerie Jarrett and her scrappy team of community organizers. During this crucial moment of enrollment, OPE was sending up decision memos daily. Which CEO should POTUS call to help get the word out: Zuckerberg or Cuban? Can we get a "Google Doodle" for enrollment? How about LeBron—can POTUS call LeBron next week?

Decision memos are short. They are meant to lay out the different options for the President to consider, with pros and cons and the office's suggested recommendation. For *Between Two Ferns*, we made the case that no other company in the world could help us more than Funny Or Die. And no other web series was better suited than *Between Two Ferns* to drive massive online enrollment.

The decision memo went up the ladder. In the meantime, I called Mike Farah to let him know that we were pushing for this to finally happen.

That evening, my father called. Again. By now, he wasn't laughing—he was really concerned about how I was holding up.

As you can probably tell, my father is not that hip to what millennials are watching. He is a baby boomer, an army veteran, a Fox News–watching, black Republican (who calls himself an Independent). But that evening, after I sent him a link, he learned that he loves *Between Two Ferns*.

"Brad, this is really funny! He's going to do it?"

"We are going to try. Yes."

"Why?"

"Because millions of young people will watch it and hopefully click on Healthcare.gov."

"This is the best thing you've done since you started working there. People are going to click on that. That is hilarious."

My father was actually excited about something that I did at the White House. This was a good sign.

The following week, I received an urgent request from Valerie to set up meetings with celebrities coming to the White House for the

France state dinner. Bradley Cooper, J. J. Abrams, Mindy Kaling, Stephen Colbert, and others were set to arrive, and all of them could help with Healthcare.gov outreach.

Bradley and his date arrived shortly before the dinner so they were already dressed to the nines, ready to party. He was excited to help, laser focused on the challenge of reaching young people, but he also admitted that he couldn't do much himself since he wasn't on social media. But, then he exclaimed: "Hey! Have you guys heard of *Between Two Ferns?*"

Valerie smiled at me and answered him. "Yes. We have. What do you think of it?"

I don't believe in fate. Or God. Or divine intervention. But I do believe that Bradley Cooper being invited to the France state dinner, and then turning into the greatest Funny Or Die pitchman in history, was not just mere coincidence. Thank you, Jesus.

Bradley continued, "Oh, man. Those *Ferns* videos get millions of views. Actually, maybe *tens* of millions! It's all about Zach. He is brilliant. He would definitely do this! Do you want me to call him?"

Valerie laughed. "Now?"

"Yeah! I'll call him. He'll pick up. He's probably just hanging out on his farm. His wife just had a baby. He's probably changing diapers."

I finally chimed in. "Let's do it!"

Bradley dials Zach on his cell, puts it on speaker, and lays the phone on Valerie's desk. Zach answers after the first ring. "WHAT?!"

"Hey, man! It's Bradley."

"Yes, I know! What do you want?!" Zach is feigning anger. You can tell he is happy that Bradley, his *Hangover* costar, is calling.

"Zach, I'm here with Valerie Jarrett at the White House. Do you know who she is?"

"YES! I do, Bradley." Zach again answers angrily/jokingly.

"Okay. Well, hey. I was just talking to Valerie and her team and I recommended that the President go on *Between Two Ferns* to promote Obamacare. And they love it! What do you think? Can you do it next week? They need it ASAP!"

"Yes! I am totally in."

The rest of the state dinner, Bradley Cooper pitched every senior member of the White House on *Between Two Ferns*, including the President. Valerie went to bat as well. The decision memo that had sat for the past four days in someone's email box was approved early the next morning. The President was finally in.

A lot of things could have easily derailed this project, but a producer like Farah knew how to make all of the pieces fit without destroying the vision. Zach and Scott did *Between Two Ferns* for one reason and one reason alone: to make people laugh. The White House cared about *Between Two Ferns* for one reason and one reason alone: getting people to sign up for health care. This was all going to come down to balance.

The first draft of the script was essentially a series of jokes with "OBAMACARE PITCH" written near the end. Cody Keenan, the President's chief speechwriter, worried about getting the President's senior advisors to sign off on a script that had such a late, and incidental, Obamacare pitch. But when Farah replied that it needed to feel genuine, not artificial, both Cody and Valerie believed him. Prior to the shoot date, we did a quick preproduction call with Farah, Zach, and Scott Aukerman. All three seemed unconvinced that this was actually going to happen. Zach even asked if we would actually let him say awful things to the President, to which Cody answered, "Yes. That is how much he cares about getting people signed up for health care. Let's not screw this up."

February 24, 2014, was the big day. While FOD producer Rachel

Goldenberg drove forty miles outside of DC to secure the only ferns available in the metro area, Zach, Farah, and Scott arrived at the White House for lunch before the taping. I patiently waited at the same gate where I was denied entrance on my first day, nodding to the very same officer who didn't let me in. Zach, Mike, and Scott were all laughing. The officer looked at their IDs and said to me:

"They're not on the list."

Zach looked at me and Mike. "This isn't going to happen, is it?"

"No. You guys are good. Just give me a few minutes."

With their WAVES correctly reprocessed, we entered through the metal detectors, the bomb-sniffing dogs, the second gate of metal detectors, and the second Secret Service officer checking IDs, and down to the Navy Mess for lunch with the senior staff.

During lunch, Zach asked thoughtful questions to the WH staff on how enrollment was going. He wanted to get a sense of how quickly we were going to have to turn everything around in order to have the most impact. His seriousness quickly turned to confusion when the navy officer brought over the menus for the day.

Zach pointed to the dessert name.

"Chocolate Freedom?"

Pause. We're not sure where Zach is going with this.

"That's what you guys all call the President, right?"

We erupt in laughter. The table to our left and right overhears Zach's joke and erupts as well. I had eaten in the West Wing Mess for years and I had never heard laughter like that before. It was unbridled. Genuine. The tables that didn't hear the joke were looking over in curiosity. My stomach turned over in excitement. We were going to fucking save Obamacare.

Later that afternoon, we waited for an hour and a half in the Diplomatic Reception Room. Zach went over his jokes quietly, only once reprimanded by an usher for sitting in a chair that was over two hundred years old. Residence staff kept popping their heads in, seeing Zach, smiling, and walking out. The room was electric.

Normally, the President rolled with an extremely small staff for tapings like this. But on this day, everyone wanted to be there. Early on, Farah had warned us, "*Ferns* doesn't work if you have a big crowd watching. It needs to be intimate. You have to keep the room as small as possible." I looked over at him for signs of concern—but he couldn't care less who else was in that room at this point. Zach and Scott were in the zone. They were about to make comedy history to get millions of people some health care.

When President Obama finally arrived in the Diplomatic Reception Room, he clapped his hands and yelled out, "Two Ferns!"

Before we started rolling, Zach apologized in advance for the horrible things he was going to say. The President laughed it off. It was an Oscar Jenkins kind of laugh. Everyone in the room started to giggle; it was infectious. But I could see that Zach was still nervous. This was all very odd. Ten minutes into the shoot, the President stumbled on a response, laughed at himself, and yelled to the director:

"You know what? Let's run it back! Let's do it from the beginning!"

Zach's eyes lit up. He finally realized that the President was really fired up about this. He wasn't just going through the motions. Up until this moment, we were all concerned about time. The President never has free time in his daily schedule. But something happened along the way: Barack Obama started having fun. We expected to get through this just once, but the President wanted to make sure that we got it right. Zach's confidence grew.

"I have to know, what is it like to be the last black president?"

"Seriously? What's it like for this to be the last time you ever talk to a president?"

Zach broke character and laughed. We all knew even before we looked at the footage that this was something special.

That night, the full crew, Zach, Scott, Farah, and I celebrated at a friend's home. We sat in her living room, taking turns describing what each of us had witnessed. The common refrain from the evening? "I can't believe we just did that."

Two weeks later, on March 11, Funny Or Die released *Between Two Ferns* with President Obama. The evening before it released, I was a nervous wreck. The video was set to post at five a.m. ET with a *New York Times* exclusive. There was no guarantee that this was going to be a success. No guarantee that people were going to love this thing as much as we all loved this thing. I woke up at five a.m. and kept refreshing *NYT*, Twitter, and Funny Or Die. The first tweets reacting to the *NYT* article started to trickle out. Pulitzer Prize–winning reporters were losing their collective minds. In a good way! There was no other urgent news driving the morning. No scandals. No domestic humanitarian disasters. *Between Two Ferns* was already the biggest story of the day. Holy shit. This was all happening. But would people go to Healthcare.gov?

I showered, got dressed, and changed my baby's diaper before heading into the office. Baby J must have been as nervous as I was, coughing up some vomit all over. I was too filled with adrenaline to get upset. I laughed, rushed to the bathroom to get cleaned up, kissed my wife, and jumped in the car.

When I arrived at my office, the view count was already in the millions. In a couple hours, it was up to tens of millions. My phone rang. It was Yohannes, Valerie's chief of staff, again. He called to inform me that Valerie wanted me to give the President a briefing on the success of the video.

Now, look: I know I played a role in making *Ferns* a reality. But I also knew there were so many other people who could've given that report directly to the President. In fact, there were dozens of senior officials who could have broken down the exact metrics—the earned media success or the real-time numbers of enrollment. That briefing could have come from cabinet secretaries, the WH press secretary, or of course Valerie Jarrett herself: the woman who really made it all happen.

But instead, Valerie and Yohannes gave me the opportunity to tell the President the great news. I was humbled. The only hitch was that I was set to brief the President in the Oval Office in just forty-five minutes. I texted my father immediately.

"I'm going to brief the President on *Ferns*. It's a huge success, Dad."

He called back immediately.

I was expecting a laugh. I was expecting his usual smart-ass joke. But somehow, in the midst of all this madness, out of all the things that I could have done in the White House, making my father laugh was the thing that ultimately made him cry. There was silence on the other end. His voice cracked. "I am proud of you, son."

"I love you, Pop." I hung up, took a deep breath, and pulled up a new Word doc to write a recap for the President of the United States:

Mr. President, you have set a record for Funny Or Die for most views in 24 hours. You have just hit 30 million views. But, what is most incredible is the surge in traffic. As you may have seen, traffic to healthcare.gov has increased by 40%. The hard-to-reach millennial demographic is soaring thanks to your video. 90% of the people who are clicking-through to healthcare.gov from Funny Or Die have never visited health care.gov before. The video is doing exactly what we set out to do. And, we were able to do it weeks before the last days of enrollment. This is a huge win for the millions of families who are counting on government to work. Congratulations, Mr. President.

I ran over to the Oval Office, bullet points memorized, sweaty, and nervous. Valerie teed up my remarks with: "Mr. President. Brad was the mastermind behind all of this." To which the President jokingly replied,

"No way, Valerie. You're all about those Ferns!"

After I rattled off my prepared facts and figures, the President reached out to shake my hand.

"Brad, great work. Let's make sure we keep doing things like *Two Ferns*. This was great."

We shook hands. Valerie thanked me again and I slowly walked back to my office.

Yohannes popped his head in:

"Congrats, B."

"Thanks, man."

"How was it?"

"It was . . . comical."

"You know you have baby vomit on your sleeve."

I laughed and refused to look at it. "That sounds about right."

"You think we can get Zach on the phone in the next few minutes? The President wants to thank him."

"Hell yes. Calling him now. He's probably changing diapers."

One year later, my son, Oscar, and my daughter, Sadie, made the first black president laugh out loud in the Oval Office. I like to believe that my grandfather Oscar was somewhere laughing along with them.

AMAZING GRACE

Heather Foster

You never left early when working at the White House. Leaving early was seven p.m. Important meetings could be scheduled at six p.m. I often joked that four p.m. was our noon, the time of day when you might finally sneak out of the building for an afternoon walk. There were no such things as half days, part-time, or even "working hours," for that matter.

We worked around the clock in the White House Office of Public Engagement, commonly known as "the front door to the White House." Our team was responsible for representing the President to the American public and all its communities. In my role as director for African American affairs, I was the President's liaison—in some ways, an ambassador—to the African American community. It was not an easy job, but with steady prayer and patience, over several years I built a program to engage and inform national and regional leaders. Every day, I worked to provide African Americans across the country the same feeling they had on November 8, 2008, when Barack Obama was elected.

The job came with few, if any, breaks and I was always working at a breakneck pace. At any moment, anything—from a natural disaster to a viral outbreak—could happen and I had to be prepared to inform and influence the President's thinking.

The afternoon of June 17 in 2015 was different. I took off early from work because my aunt was having brain surgery in Atlanta and I was nervous for her results. My stomach had been in knots and I felt the usual pang of guilt that I wasn't at the hospital with the rest of my family. A few weeks earlier, my aunt had given me a wide smile when I left Atlanta. She, and my entire family, loved that I worked at the White House—more importantly, that I worked for Barack Obama, our nation's first African American president.

My mother and father immigrated to the United States from Jamaica in the summer of 1968. They arrived to a country reeling from the death of Reverend Martin Luther King Jr. and stricken with riots fueled by growing impatience with inequality for African Americans. Nevertheless, they decided to stay and start a family, teaching me and my siblings the value of hard work and determination. My mother watched over our self-esteem like a hawk, reminding us weekly to carry ourselves with pride because we represented many generations across a wide range of cultures. As a teenager, I rolled my eyes at her speeches, but as I became an adult I grew to value the pride she instilled in me, particularly as I started to experience racism and sexism in all their pernicious forms.

Every morning as I approached the gates, flashed my badge, and nodded hello to the Secret Service agents, I felt the pride of my family and approached my work with that sense of dedication.

When I joined the Obama administration, I invited my aunt to visit me in Washington, DC. Worried about my health, she cooked meals that I could freeze and reheat later on days when I had to work particularly long hours. After she had been diagnosed with a brain tumor, my mom planned a family vacation over the Memorial Day holiday where we all piled into a four-bedroom condo for a weekend of laughter, stories, and beach volleyball. Every now and then I would see my aunt humming her favorite gospel songs and smiling, showing no fear of her upcoming surgery.

As I prepared for bed the evening after her surgery, I called my mother. She told me my aunt had slipped into a coma but they expected her to awake in the morning. We said a quick prayer together. Then, like any other night, I climbed into bed, leaving my BlackBerry and laptop on the nightstand—just in case something happened and I needed to respond quickly.

I closed my eyes—but then heard a buzz and popped one eye open, groaning. The red light of my BlackBerry flashed. I reached for it, entered my password, and thought to myself, *It never fails . . . something is always happening.* I reviewed the messages, mainly news clips and some inquiries from civil rights leaders on an upcoming meeting. I sighed, but then noticed a number of new texts on my personal phone. I worried instinctively that it was about my aunt.

I sat up and read, "Have you seen what happened in Charleston?"

Dread immediately filled my body. Because of my position in the White House, over the past two years I had on *several* occasions given advice on how the President and his administration should respond to the deaths of young black men killed without provocation. Trayvon Martin's death in 2012 prompted a national conversation, which reached a fever pitch the next summer when the State of Florida failed to press charges on George Zimmerman, the man who admitted to killing Trayvon. Riots and marches could erupt over how to solve these complex issues rooted in systemic racial bias. And in the courts, too often the judicial process resulted in charges not being filed or a failure to convict, leaving all of us to grapple with what to do, and leaving families and communities with pain and anger at the government.

Because the country was faced with the ongoing debate of how to reckon with these tragedies, I never really slept deeply.

Not surprisingly, black community leaders expected a lot from the first black president. Making a statement wasn't enough; they wanted him to fix the problem—and there was no way President Obama could do that on his own. Once, before meeting a group of activists, the President asked me if I thought people truly understood his role in these moments. I shook my head emphatically in reply. This was my daily predicament. Black leaders believed the election of the first African American president should have meant an end to these injustices, but instead there were even more questions—and they always came to me for answers.

When I saw that text about Charleston, I jumped out of bed. I pulled out my laptop and turned on the local news station to see a headline that brought chills to my bones. I sent texts to my contacts, informing them that a shooting happened during the Wednesday night prayer service. That a white man joined the service of African American parishioners at Mother Emanuel Church and, after taking part, gunned them down.

At this point my phone rang, and when I picked up I heard the familiar voice of Reverend Al Sharpton, a longtime civil rights advocate with whom I had worked closely during the Obama campaign and at the White House. "Heather, did you see what happened? Reverend Pinckney is dead." I was officially awake at that moment. I knew Reverend Clementa Pinckney was a prominent state senator and pastor who had worked tirelessly to elect the President in 2008, particularly in the lead-up to the pivotal South Carolina primary election.

I immediately called Rick Wade and Anton Gunn, former colleagues in the Obama administration who now both lived in Charleston, South Carolina. They had not yet heard the news. Alarmed by my notification, Rick and Anton promised to start reaching out to community members and keep me apprised. They knew that in situations like these, having accurate information was imperative so that the President could make the right decisions. I scanned the news, read my texts, and made a few more calls. Then I carefully crafted an email describing the state of events in Charleston to senior White House staff. Given the state of racial tension in the country, if there was a disruption in the African American community I was immediately the lead staffer on the issue. I knew this email would be forwarded through the entire White House network, and I had to be careful and thorough. Even though the shooting had only happened a few hours before, reporters would be looking for a response from President Obama.

Ten hours later, I found myself standing in Starbucks on four hours of sleep. On top of everything, I had also spent half the night worried about my aunt, who was still in a coma. As news spread of the tragedy, more of my friends started to send notes about how distressed and worried they felt, wondering how we could live in a time that yielded such horror. One friend texted, "Why do African Americans have to always live in fear? I can't go to work today because I can't stop crying." I felt the familiar numb sensation that came upon me during these times: another tragedy under this president and this time fueled with racist hate.

The ring of my cell phone snapped me out of my reverie. I picked up to the terse voice of our chief of staff in the Office of Public Engagement. In times like this—and we had been through too many—we ignored greetings and pleasantries. "Do you think you can go to Charleston today? You can come back tonight." I didn't even hesitate: "Yes."

I bolted from the Starbucks with my iced coffee and headed into the building adjacent to the West Wing where my office was located. My fatigue would have to wait. I needed to make sure I was ready to confront what happened in Charleston.

As I slid behind my desk, I saw a new number pop up on my phone, one that I knew belonged to a representative of the African Methodist Episcopal, or AME, Church. The AME Church has an outsized importance for African Americans. In the late eighteenth century, freed slaves were prevented from joining the Methodist church. In response, Richard Allen broke away to found the African Methodist Episcopal Church, which basically followed the same creed and rituals as Methodists. Mother Emanuel was a particularly significant AME church, one full of history from the days of Reconstruction and the civil rights movement in the Deep South. I picked up and silently thought to myself, *Here we go.*

"Heather, nine dead!"

"I know," I said calmly. "I am on my way there."

"Good. When is the President going?"

That was always the question immediately after a tragedy.

While people were happy to see a presidential statement in these kinds of moments, everyone always wanted to physically see and hear from President Obama—particularly in the African American community. I knew that I received twice as many invitations for the President and First Lady than my colleagues who worked with other constituency groups. The media carefully watched the relationship between the first African American president and the community to which he belonged and which championed him with unparalleled loyalty.

I looked wearily at the calendar. Time was ticking. I had two hours to dig into the mountain of unread emails waiting for me and cancel my meetings to travel to Charleston. I quickly dictated two emails to my intern and told her to man the phones all day in my absence. She gave me the familiar look that conveyed, "I never imagined my internship would be like this." On any other day I would smile back wryly, but today, I simply stared back and asked, "Any questions?"

My phone rang again: the van was leaving for Andrews Air Force Base. As I packed up my things and frantically looked for two matching pumps in the shoe box I kept under my desk, I continued to answer calls from other colleagues and community leaders and reassured them that we were monitoring the situation. At this point, no one had been apprehended for the murders and I could tell tension was rising in the African American community. I jumped into the black escort van with several civil rights leaders who were on the same flight and headed to Andrews. Melanie Campbell, president of the Black Women's Roundtable, looked at me and shook her head silently. "It hasn't even been twenty-four hours; the city has to be in shock." I could only imagine what was waiting for us.

When we landed in Charleston, I ordered an Uber. The driver was a young white man who looked anxiously at us. He said, "Y'all here for the shooting, huh?"

Silence filled the car as I looked up from my BlackBerry. "Yes, we are here to visit with everyone today."

Our driver was a young white man. He anxiously looked in the rearview mirror at a van full of African American civil right leaders and said, "Charleston just isn't like that. I don't know what that boy was thinking going into that church. Folks are heartbroken today." By the time we landed, news had emerged that twenty-one-year-old Dylann Roof had attended the church service and opened fire on the parishioners afterward. The fact that the victims had prayed with their murderer was shaking the nation—including our driver, who told us how difficult it had been to talk to his son about the shooting.

Upon arrival in downtown Charleston we went straight to city hall to meet with the mayor. The faces of his staff—somber, with swollen eyes—let us know quickly the mood that day. When we met with Mayor Riley, a spry older man, the leaders shared their desire to help the city recover from the shooting and defuse the racial tensions. The mayor also expressed his deep concern for the residents of the town, and said, "Right now we just have to take this day by day and find out why this young man felt the need to do this."

I then took the group to lunch at a local diner so they could meet with the people of Charleston, most of whom were still shocked and upset over the shooting. We heard more stories of Reverend Pinckney and the members of Mother Emanuel. The same theme kept coming up: the spirit of Charleston meant faith, hope, and grace for everyone, including strangers from the nation's capital.

We finally made our way farther outside of the city to a community prayer night hosted by a prominent church. As we walked in, I was approached by a local elected official. "White House, right?" I nodded. He asked, "Can someone speak?" I thought about it, but quickly realized I didn't have enough to say yet, so replied, "I think one of our faith leaders should speak tonight, perhaps Reverend Lee."

I turned to Reverend Tony Lee, an AME pastor who represented a coalition of faith leaders who worked closely with me on various public policy issues. He squeezed my shoulder and walked confidently to the podium. Standing before the audience of community leaders, he spoke about hope even in the midst of darkness. The church attendees leapt to their feet as he finished his words and I looked around, amazed. Despite the tragedy in their community, these people, like the driver, the mayor, and the residents at the diner, still had hope.

On the plane ride home, the civil rights and faith leaders thanked me for traveling with them. I nodded, knowing that taking the time to be available and present for them was part of the reason why so many trusted my counsel despite my relatively young age. I started drafting my nightly memo, describing the events of the day and what I had observed. I knew that my report could potentially be read by the President so I wanted to make sure that it reflected the tenor of the day. That night, I sat in my bathtub soaking away the stress of the day and thinking about the individuals I met in Charleston. They all felt the pain from the shootings but still held on to hope that mankind is not naturally that brutal or evil. It's a feeling of hope I remembered so well from my own childhood and especially my own church.

My parents always worked multiple jobs with the hope of providing enough for me and my two siblings. We lived in a working-class neighborhood in a split-level house and attended good schools—but we never had a rainy-day fund. My dad had periods where he was laid off from the technical work he did at several telecommunications companies in Atlanta. To make ends meet, he would take part-time work or short-term projects in other states. Later, when my sister started college, my mom took a part-time job at our church for additional income.

Through all this, we would make the drive to downtown Atlanta every Wednesday evening for church. It didn't dawn on me until much later in life how tired my mom must have been: driving sixty minutes round-trip with my brother and me after working a full day as a high school teacher, starting at four a.m. On those Wednesdays, my brother and I would count out change to convince her to stop at McDonald's to get our weekly cheeseburger and French fries for eighty-nine cents. It was a welcome departure from the West Indian rice and peas that we normally ate for dinner during these tough periods.

At church, my brother and I would sit in the Wednesday night prayer service, sometimes doing our homework unnoticed, but often listening to the sermon and prayer requests, learning lessons on love, hope, and God's unmerited grace. Anyone and everyone was welcome. I embraced church during adolescence as a place of hope and safety at a time when I started to question the world, and the racism I encountered in my neighborhood, at school, and even on television. So I immediately understood why the horror of Dylann Roof entering that Wednesday night service was so heartbreaking for both parishioners and the members of that community.

As I lay in bed that night I knew that the White House would need to provide a significant response beyond a presidential statement. I was struck by the similarities between President Obama and the Reverend Clementa Pinckney: a state senator who was deeply committed to changing and shaping his community, a devoted husband and father of two young girls. In so many ways, Reverend Pinckney walked the same path as President Obama, yet his destiny was cut short. I also knew that Charleston was a community with a history of complicated racial history. A shooting in a community besieged by hate with a history of complicated race relations reflected the complexity of the national challenge that we had been dealing with. During my time at the White House I had seen mass shootings happen across the country and realized that while there was no way to erase the grief of the community, the President had a unique way of providing some peace to those grieving.

The following days were a blur of meetings as we learned as much as we could about the shooting. The shooter had been arraigned and the FBI had gathered information on the victims and their families. Civil rights leaders were calling for the Confederate symbol, which was a part of South Carolina's state flag, to be taken down because of its history of association with slavery and racial oppression. I knew that we would soon have to recommend whether the President should travel to Charleston to attend any memorial events. As I spoke with other members of my staff to get their input, my colleague and friend Ashley looked at me and, without hesitating, said, "He needs to go." I nodded in agreement.

That Saturday, I was at a barbecue with the "Kick It Crew," friends from various White House offices who got together on Saturdays to let loose and detox from the week of stress. We debated the week's events, cooked, laughed, and did our best to dance away the weight of our jobs. That Saturday when I arrived at the barbecue everyone knew I was carrying the events of Charleston. I was just starting to unload my thoughts and share stories from my trip with them when I heard the familiar ping of the BlackBerry tone that I had assigned to senior advisors to the President. I quickly scanned my phone, and there it was: the request from senior staff for my thoughts on the President's further engagement. I typed the response that I had been thinking about for days, that he should attend the memorial service of Clementa Pinckney and give remarks. I returned to the barbecue, wondering what would be the final decision when they brought the recommendation to the President. I knew that it was a good idea to enjoy the night because the next week might be even busier.

Early the next week, Valerie Jarrett, the President's senior advisor, called to let me know the President had reviewed the options and wanted to attend the funeral services of Reverend Pinckney.

I sat back at my desk. I knew right away this would be a major moment, even if that wasn't necessarily clear yet to all my colleagues. For many of us, the White House was often a tough place because we had to compartmentalize our jobs just to stay sane. We often joked that literally everything happened at once. International conflict, major domestic policy debate, meetings with members of Congress—all on the same day and sometimes even at the same time. Each staffer dealt with three or four important issues that often made it to the evening news, so stress was high and time was always of the essence. African American leaders had been calling me all weekend to see if the President would travel to Charleston. I gave my usual response that I would let them know when I had an answer.

I paced by the window and thought of my aunt. She had been moved from ICU over the weekend but wasn't responding like the doctors had hoped. She was fortunately still alive, but I would not be able to head home anytime soon. My mother had reassured me earlier that morning that my aunt would be proud of what I was doing with the President.

I had two or three hours of peace before all the questions about attendance, location, and logistics would come my way. But before the President's visit was announced publicly by the White House, Valerie and I needed to call Reverend Pinckney's widow to check if she approved of the President participating in the funeral service.

After hearing Reverend Pinckney's wife cry soft tears and thank us from the bottom of her heart, I knew that President Obama had made the right decision. I also knew my mother was right.

What I did not know was how crazy things were about to get in Charleston.

A few days later, I boarded myself on an American Airlines flight to Charleston to join the President's advance team. When I met up with them, they already looked weary as they worked around the clock to do in three days what they usually do in at least a week. Preparing for the arrival of the President of the United States is the production of productions. And this was no exception. After the White House announced President Obama's attendance, ninety members of Congress also committed to attending the funeral, as well as Vice

President Biden and Dr. Jill Biden. Security measures make everything more complicated, and the staff was stressed with the quick turnaround to manage the arrival of a sitting president, first lady, and vice president, the cabinet, and so many members of Congress. And because Mother Emanuel Church was too small to host such a large crowd, the services had been moved to the Charleston Convention Center.

After landing, I found an airport shuttle van driver and asked him to take me to the convention center. I saw his curious stare as I managed my two phones, one nestled between my head and shoulder and one in my hands as I typed responses to emails. The shuttle driver chuckled. "Oh, I see . . . you Olivia Pope. We been waiting on you White House folks. I can't wait to hear from President Obama. He always comes through in times like these."

Arriving, I saw a middle-aged black man pacing nervously outside of the convention center. I knew that would be Reverend Pinckney's best friend. I turned the corner to run straight into Yebbie Watkins, chief of staff to Congressman James Clyburn, one of the most senior African American members in the House of Representatives and whose district covered Charleston.

He smiled. "You know what is about to happen, don't you?" I took a seat in the large convention center, which was lined with chairs. Yebbie continued, "You know everyone thinks they need to be at this funeral."

Any large event with the President of the United States is complicated, but in this case we had to consider several additional factors: the family of Reverend Pinckney, the families of other victims who I had notified would be meeting President and Mrs. Obama, local elected officials, senior government officials, influencers, civil rights leaders, the AME Church, and of course the local community. In addition, we were eighteen months from a presidential election and the entire world was watching the rising tensions between blacks and whites in America, what some thought was a backlash to electing the nation's first black president. I looked at Yebbie and said, "We will figure it out. That's what we always do."

As the afternoon came to an end I took a walk to Mother Emanuel Church, a few short blocks from the convention center. I had been in back-to-back meetings since arriving and knew that I had a short window to see the church before I became too busy. I approached the white facade slowly, taking a moment to look at the diverse crowd, and at the teddy bears and signs encouraging love. I couldn't help but think back to the Obama campaign when I would see people of all races working together in campaign offices, organizing rallies and making sandwiches to keep people in line at the polls.

As I looked at the tape blocking the physical entrance of the church I was reminded of the faces of Dr. King's children watching President Obama take the stage at the Lincoln Memorial almost fifty years to the day since their father's iconic speech; the Tuskegee Airmen standing in their red coats to greet him at the White House; the Bloody Sunday marchers who shed quiet tears when they saw Barack Obama's motorcade drive over the Edmund Pettus Bridge in Alabama.

My throat ached and my eyes watered. I looked around and thought, *How did we get here?*

* * *

Twenty-four hours before the service, the convention center was buzzing with construction, security, and staffers from congressional offices who were anxiously trying to figure out where their bosses would sit. I had stayed up all night reorganizing the seating chart and communicating with the victims' families on the day's logistics. By this point, I had come to feel as they did: sadness mixed with some anticipation.

All that remained was preparing the President's remarks. Our office typically received drafts of the President's speeches twenty-four to forty-eight hours before an event, giving us enough time to offer edits and feedback. But this was an unusual situation. This was the same week of major Supreme Court decisions on health care and marriage equality, so it was anything but slow around the White House. In addition, Cody Keenan, the President's director of speechwriting, told Valerie and me that the President wanted to write these remarks himself, so we should expect little time for turnaround. I had too many other issues to tackle so I put the speech out of my mind.

The next morning, when I arrived at the convention center with several of my coworkers, I stared in disbelief. It was six a.m. and lines were already wrapped around the building. The doors didn't open until nine a.m. and the President was scheduled to arrive at one p.m.

I checked my BlackBerry again—no speech. I wrote Valerie a quick update and she responded rapidly, "Let me know if anything comes up."

My BlackBerry was humming with questions from my colleagues at the White House and various African American leaders who wanted to attend at the last minute. I looked at my personal phone, which already had over one hundred unread text messages. I could tell this was going to be a long day. I shook my head, trying to remember that the only thing that mattered on "game days"—as we called them—was the President and his message for the American people.

Despite all the logistical challenges, my biggest fear was that the distraught families would forget the careful instructions I had given them the day before to help them navigate Secret Service security measures and prepare for meeting the President, First Lady, Vice President Biden, and Dr. Biden. I started calling the families, one by one, and directed them to a backstage room with their names so they would have privacy amid all the public attention. Our advance team had already met with Reverend Pinckney's wife and placed her in a separate backstage room with her daughters. The little girls tugged at our hearts. They knew that, despite all of the cameras and flurry, it was still their father's funeral.

Meanwhile, the convention hall was filling up fast. Shortly after ten a.m., I heard a cheer in the auditorium: "Love won!" The marriage equality decision had been announced by the Supreme Court. Our team high-fived. Triumph and sadness mixed together—par for the course at the White House.

I ran back to my makeshift station behind the stage. I had what I needed for the day: the President's briefing memo, the list of families, granola bars, and pens. My BlackBerry buzzed—the speech. I scanned quickly for names and triple-checked for anything important that might have been missing. I could tell it was a heartfelt eulogy for a man who'd lived a life that President Obama understood, and he had been able to weave in the emotions of African Americans who were struggling to reconcile this shooting. I took a deep breath and realized it was game time.

It was an all-hands-on-deck moment. Our entire team was scurrying around to put out fires: seating issues, leaders who wanted photos, and other last-minute logistical issues that were inevitable during presidential events. As the President's liaison to the African American community, I was the face of the White House staff. I felt the usual surge of adrenaline and nerves but tried to replace it with calm because I knew that this moment could become emotional quickly.

As we neared the President's arrival, I got one last email from Valerie: "He's ready."

As President Obama and Mrs. Obama took their seats, the crowd cheered—an awkward thing to do at a funeral, but most funerals aren't attended by the president. In many ways, Reverend Pinckney's funeral had turned into a praise, worship, and community meeting rather than a somber funeral service. The AME leadership stressed that it was how he would have wanted to be remembered.

Moments before President Obama was supposed to start the funeral, I learned that one of the families was missing. I ran through the back hall and straight outside to see a cabdriver arguing with a police officer about entering the convention center. I stepped in between them and flashed my badge. Melting in my black dress in the summer heat, I escorted the last family backstage, and as I did, my colleague Ashley texted, "Get in here. You have to hear the speech."

The convention center grew quiet as President Obama took the stage. He began his speech by acknowledging the deep pain that many African Americans feel—not only because we are too often victims of hate violence, but because too often such attacks go unaddressed. He reminded the grieving families that their grace, the grace of the victims who left us on June 17, and the grace of the Charleston community would help the country move on. His tribute to Reverend Pinckney and to the city of Charleston held a healing quality that I knew only Barack Obama could share. His eulogy was powerful, and it wasn't long before I saw tears running down from the eyes of the men and women around me. And then he stopped speaking. I looked up. I didn't remember a pause written into the speech. The room was eerily quiet.

And then the President of the United States started singing "Amazing Grace."

I was startled—this was not in his speech. But there he was, the leader of the free world, the first African American president of a nation that once practiced slavery, bowing his head and singing as he might at any church service. Within moments, the AME pastors onstage with him jumped from their seats and burst out into song. We all started singing.

In my time in the White House, I had witnessed so many inspiring and heartbreaking moments, but I felt a chill run down my body as we all came together singing. I couldn't help belting out the words, realizing it really was amazing grace that brought us all together to heal and celebrate in the aftermath of such tragedy.

As the President returned to his seat the audience erupted into applause. He stopped to hug Mrs. Pinckney and her daughters. He hugged the First Lady—and then he turned, looked straight at me, and smiled.

I learned early on that it wasn't helpful to view Barack Obama as a rock star, or as a transformational leader whose election changed how black people were viewed in America, but as any other manager who you wanted to perform their best. Our interactions needed to be professional and serious; the gravity of his position and the intense pace of my job didn't usually allow the time or space to reflect upon his leadership or legacy.

But when I saw him smile, I knew his singing and remarks had been, and would be, a healing moment for our country. Once again, Barack Obama was able to channel the pain of an entire community into a moment that thousands could relate to, one that would inspire Americans to be better.

After the service, I escorted the President and First Lady to meet the families of the Charleston Nine. Stories, tears, and hugs were exchanged as families shared their agony. I watched him take it all in.

Vice President Biden and Dr. Jill Biden, still grieving from the recent passing of their son Beau to brain cancer, also visited and grieved with the families. As things wrapped up, I stood with my colleagues and members of the senior staff as the President walked over. We gave our usual hugs to the President and First Lady before they left in the motorcade and I looked at my colleagues. We had survived forty-eight hours of disagreements over seating charts, negotiations between the funeral home and church leaders, caring for grieving families, and even finding that our car had been towed from the convention center. None of this was easy, but it was worth it.

The first email I read after the President's departure from the convention center said, "Heather, I have been crying in my office all afternoon. That speech was amazing. Grace is amazing and I could tell that my President knows my pain and my experience. Hopefully the world will see it as well." I looked around the empty auditorium and teared up for the first time in weeks. And then I got a note from my mom: "Praise God your aunt is awake."

The next morning, bleary-eyed, I was walking through the Atlanta airport en route to a speech I was giving to black elected officials in San Diego. It was seven thirty a.m., but as I approached my connecting gate I saw people crowding around a television screen. As I got closer I realized they were watching President Obama's speech being replayed from the day before. I stopped in my tracks when I saw the faces of the people crowded around the screen, because it was the same expression that I had seen from the mourning families the day before, from the clergy onstage at the funeral, and from the community members that leapt to their feet during Reverend Lee's remarks that first day after the tragedy. I recognized that expression.

It was hope.

WORTH IT

Cecilia Muñoz

The *Washington Post* headlines were ugly. In 2011: "Activists say Obama aide Cecilia Munoz has 'turned her back' on fellow Hispanics." Somewhat more gentle, in 2014: "White House immigration advisor Cecilia Muñoz is taking the heat for Obama." At least they learned how to put the *ñ* in my last name by the time they printed the second article. One blogger called me a "Latina spokesmodel for Obama's immigration policy," which my daughters found hilarious—no teenage girl thinks of her mother as any kind of "model."

Years later, it's still a little surreal. I can't claim that it didn't sting to see those headlines in the morning paper, but I knew that the criticism would come the moment Barack Obama asked me to serve.

I first got to know Barack Obama in 2006 when immigration reform was under consideration by the U.S. Senate and he was a new senator trying to get up to speed on the issues of the day. I am an expert on immigration. I have worked on a lot of issues over my thirty years in the civil rights movement, but immigration is my thing, the issue with which I am most identified. It's not just that I developed extensive expertise in this area over twenty years at the National

Council of La Raza (the largest Latino advocacy organization in the United States, now called UnidosUS); it's also because I come from a big immigrant family. My parents arrived in Detroit from Bolivia in 1950 so that my dad could finish his degree at the University of Michigan. Things in Bolivia were difficult, and soon my dad had a job in the auto industry, and we were welcoming more family members to Detroit. My big, bilingual family is the center of my world. I married an immigrant, too, from India by way of Kenya and the UK, so my daughters have also grown up with a boisterous, multilingual family.

Immigration isn't just what I do. It's who I am.

So when Senator Obama invited immigration policy experts to brief him in 2006, I was one of the people sitting around the conference table in his small Senate office—the cramped offices they typically give to the freshmen. He peppered us with hard questions. "I understand that immigrants are good for the economy, but how do I explain that to people in southern Illinois, who aren't inclined to believe it?" And he listened carefully to the answers. As the Senate debate advanced, he would call with additional questions by cell phone.

I remember thinking this was a senator who was interested in getting it right, and in making sure he was truly representing the needs of his constituents. It's why I became a supporter when he began his long-shot run for president.

But I never expected to work for him. So when I got a call from John Podesta a week or so after the election in 2008, I was shocked. John had been President Clinton's chief of staff and was now helping lead President-elect Obama's transition, and he was inviting me to interview for a White House role with the incoming chief of staff, Rahm Emanuel, and his deputy, Jim Messina.

Half of Washington was waiting for a call like this, but I wasn't. I wasn't angling for a job and I wasn't interested in working in government. I figured that the country needed good people on the inside of a new administration, but also needed good people as advocates outside of government. I was sure I was one of those "outside people." I couldn't imagine leaving a job of twenty years—one that offered me challenging work that I cared deeply about, along with precious flexibility to be available to my family—to take on a role in a notoriously family-unfriendly workplace. The recent death of my mother had focused me on balancing my work and my family, and on being the best mother I could possibly be.

Even so, I was curious. Rahm had a reputation for being hostile to immigration reform, and I wanted to see how the incoming administration was thinking about the issue. I figured it would be a low-stakes interview. I didn't want the job; I wanted information.

Rahm did most of the talking during my interview, laying out a clear vision for how immigration reform could get done in a new administration—and dropping a lot of foul language along the way, which is pretty much the way he talks all the time. I was impressed with his strategic vision, but I was also honest about not wanting to disrupt my family. Rahm kind of scoffed at that—he had already planned to move back to Washington, leaving his family behind in Chicago to finish out the school year—so my fears of upheaval for my family, which would involve no separation, no move, and no change of schools, must have seemed small to him. But it felt huge to me. So when Jim Messina formally offered me a job on the President's senior team, I found it easy to say no.

The next day, I got the call. It was a busy Friday afternoon and I was doing carpool duty for my daughter and her classmate. My phone showed a Chicago number, so I pulled into a parking space and answered. It was Rahm, promising me that he would build a family-friendly workplace, and that the President needed me to help lead the discussion on immigration. Then he asked me to hold for a minute.

The next words I heard were, "This is Barack Obama. I want you to help me change the country. Hillary couldn't say no to me and neither can you."

The President-elect of the United States then merrily threatened to call my husband and children, to come to my house, to make it as embarrassing as possible to say no. He knew he was offering a once-in-a-lifetime opportunity, and he was enjoying the challenge of overcoming my resistance. I was flabbergasted. My husband, normally a skeptic, burst into tears when I told him. After a major family meeting, at which he and our daughters enthusiastically agreed to make whatever sacrifices it would require of all of us, I took the job.

I took it knowing the challenges that lay ahead and the criticisms I'd inevitably face, even from within my own community. Our country has an immigration system that everybody knows is broken. There are eleven million people who live and work here without immigration papers, and we have been locked in a debate over it for almost twenty years. No matter how you feel about how they got here, undocumented immigrants are interwoven into our communities and our economy, in some cases going back decades. It is in our collective interest for them to get on the right side of the law rather than to maintain the status quo, which means keeping them in the shadows, or attempting to deport them all, which is harmful to families, to communities, and to our economy.

Yet, even as we deal with the question of undocumented immigrants, we also have to enforce the existing laws, which brings us into territory that is really uncomfortable for the Latino community: immigration enforcement at the border and in the interior of the country. Hispanic Americans, whether we are immigrants or not, have a long and troubling history with immigration authorities. Many of us, especially in border states, have stories of harassment by immigration officials, regardless of whether or not we were born here. Some of the uglier moments in our nation's history involve attempts at immigration enforcement, including the historic "Operation Wetback" of the 1950s under which thousands of people were "deported" without due process of law, including native-born U.S. citizens who were assumed to be here illegally because they "looked Mexican."

This isn't just for the history books; it still happens today in states like Arizona and Texas, the latter of which recently passed a law that encourages local police to check the papers of anybody they suspect of being here illegally. In a state that is 40 percent Latino, this means that a lot of people will get asked to prove that they belong in their own country. It happens all the time.

When I said yes to working for President Obama, I knew that I would give my all to reforming our immigration laws, legalizing undocumented immigrants, and making changes in the way immigration enforcement is conducted—but I also knew that we were never going to arrive at perfection. And I knew that anytime someone was harassed by an immigration agent, or the enforcement process separated a family, the President would own that outcome. And because I was the person the President appointed to work on the problem, I would own it, too.

The challenges started almost immediately.

Early on, the biggest source of frustration, inside the administration and out, was how to deal with Dreamers, young immigrants who were brought to the United States without papers as children by their parents, grew up here, and in many cases had no idea that they were undocumented until it was time to learn to drive or apply for college, when they would discover that they had no Social Security numbers. They were named Dreamers for the DREAM Act—the Development, Relief, and Education for Alien Minors Act—a bill which would legalize their immigration status.

Some of the most compelling work I have done in my career has been with Dreamers. I was part of the effort that led to the drafting of the prototype of the DREAM Act, initially called the Student Adjustment Act, which was first introduced in 2001. It was the result of young people courageously telling their stories to members of Congress from both parties, who introduced a bill to help them get on a pathway to becoming Americans. When he served in the Illinois Senate, President Obama was the sponsor of a related bill.

In 2010, a small group of intrepid Dreamers walked all the way from Miami to Washington to bring attention to their plight. Valerie Jarrett, the President's senior advisor, and I wanted to meet them but couldn't invite them to the White House. White House staff—even the President himself—are not supposed to interfere with the judgment of law enforcement officers, which meant that we could not tell the Secret Service to refrain from contacting the Department of Homeland Security if we attempted to bring undocumented immigrants into the White House. We couldn't ask the Dreamers to take that risk, so instead of inviting them to visit us, we met with them at a nearby church instead.

It was an emotional meeting. One by one, each of the Dreamers who had made that long journey on foot told us their stories. Like so many others around the country, they had been brought to the U.S. as very young children by their parents. They grew up seeing themselves as American. They had done everything right. They studied hard, got good grades, dreamed of college and career, only to find their pathway to driver's licenses, financial aid, and a bright future blocked. Being deported back to countries they barely knew was unthinkable.

Valerie and I were so moved by their courage and commitment. And like them, we were frustrated by our inability to fix the problem right away. We couldn't order DHS to ignore the law when it came to Dreamers or any other undocumented immigrants. Fortunately, though, DHS was already moving in the direction of establishing new enforcement priorities focused on removing immigrants with criminal records rather than people like the Dreamers, who pose no harm to the country. We could continue to encourage DHS to do a better job with these priorities, and continue to push Congress to pass the DREAM Act. But neither of these felt like enough.

Frustration at the slow pace of change boiled over to Capitol Hill. I have a long history with the members of Congress who care about immigration issues, particularly the Hispanic Democrats in Congress (also known as the Hispanic Caucus). The President invited these members in groups, large and small, to meet with him at the White House throughout his two terms. I attended all of these meetings, and as the caucus grew more and more frustrated, the meetings became more and more uncomfortable.

One meeting with the entire Hispanic Caucus took place in the State Dining Room, one of the large formal rooms of the actual White House mansion, because the West Wing's meeting rooms were too small. A couple dozen members of Congress were seated around a hollow square so that the President could see everyone. I sat at one side of the square with a few of my White House colleagues who were there to follow the discussion. Staff were rarely called upon to do anything in these meetings; we would send the President detailed memos in advance, and since he remembered even the wonkiest of details, we were largely invisible at these meetings.

At this particular meeting, however, frustration was high. New Jersey senator Bob Menendez, who I have known for many years, pointed to me and said something like, "Cecilia knows that we're right. If she weren't sitting on that side of the table, she would be just as angry as we are. She can't speak her mind now, because she works for you."

In response, the President did something I rarely saw him do: he got visibly angry. His voice became sharp, and he responded forcefully, "Don't go after Cecilia. I love her and I'm very protective of her. If you want to go after anyone in this administration, go after me."

As grateful as I was for the President's support, I wanted to crawl under the table.

Senator Menendez had no idea what I was doing behind the scenes, but I had hoped that he knew me well enough to know that I was doing my job forcefully and well, including speaking my mind. As we walked back from that meeting, I tried not to look shaken. I must have failed, because as we walked back along the colonnade next to the Rose Garden, the President stopped me on the small ramp that leads up to the West Wing. It is one of my favorite spots because, on one of my many walks along that colonnade, I realized that the ramp was built to make the route from the West Wing easier for someone in a wheelchair. I thought of it as FDR's ramp.

Right there, President Obama gave me a pep talk that I will never forget, reminding me not to "let them mess with you." I remember it with some discomfort, actually, not because of anything that he said, but because I was so aware that the President carried the weight of the world on his shoulders. My job was to support him in his work, not the other way around. But that was the kind of president, and the kind of boss, Barack Obama was. Throughout my time in the White House, he would send notes, check in, and demonstrate concern and empathy that move me to this day because they are the marks of a generous and kind man.

The frustration of the Hispanic Caucus continued to grow as it became clear that the DREAM Act was not going to pass. So by mid-2012, after numerous attempts at refining the DHS enforcement priorities, Secretary Janet Napolitano reached the conclusion that we needed to do something more forceful to ensure that we weren't expending enforcement resources on Dreamers—a population whose ties to the U.S. were so compelling that most of the country supported allowing them to stay. She came to us with a proposal to defer deportation for Dreamers who met specific criteria and to provide them with work authorization that would allow them to study and work without fear of deportation.

Without her knowing, we at the White House had separately reached a similar conclusion. My team at the Domestic Policy Council was working quietly with the White House Counsel's Office to develop some options, but we hesitated to take a big, ambitious proposal to DHS because we feared that the agency would never succeed in implementing something that had been suggested by the White House. I was relieved that they brought the proposal formally to us.

To be clear, this proposal was a very big deal. Hundreds of thousands of Dreamers—we estimated as many as a million—might qualify, which made this an enormous undertaking. They would have the opportunity to step forward and as long as they had clean criminal records and otherwise met the criteria, DHS would agree to "defer" their deportations for two years at a time, which meant letting them stay in the country they called home. Aside from temporarily removing the fear of deportation, this would transform the lives of

Dreamers, allowing them to work, go to college, and come out of the shadows that had dominated their lives.

This was also enormously risky. We knew that DHS supported this action, but could they implement a brand-new process and withstand a possible flood of applications? We knew that nearly all Democrats and a large number of Republicans supported the DREAM Act, but would that support transfer to the President doing something similar on his own without Congress? Would Democratic senators facing tight reelection bids in conservative states support him? For that matter, would voters support him? There was no way to know in advance, and we couldn't test the idea with our friends because we knew that if we shared it with congressional Democrats, they wouldn't be able to resist breaking the story to the press.

By that time, I had become the President's domestic policy advisor, and my job was to prepare the memo for his decision. Decision memos typically explain the issues, the pros and cons, and conclude with three check boxes: approve; disapprove; and discuss. As we sent the memo up for a decision, I hoped we'd be successful for two reasons. First, since the proposal had emanated from within DHS itself, it meant that there was real buy-in from across the agency that would be responsible for implementing the change in policy. Second, it was simply the right thing to do.

The memo came back with no fanfare, but when I saw a check mark in the first box, my heart skipped a beat. I sent a brief email to my team—"He said yes!"—and we began to prepare a Rose Garden announcement.

The week of the announcement was unusually challenging for me. In a brief interval between meetings in my office, I got a call from my husband's office to tell me that they had put him in an ambulance with chest pains. He ended up spending two days in the hospital for what ultimately turned out to be a false alarm, but I was so wrapped up in making the preparations for the new policy—making sure it passed legal muster, preparing for its implementation, planning an announcement that people would really understand and embrace—that my husband chose not to bother me when they released him. Instead, he took a cab home. It never occurred to him to complain, but for me, this is exhibit A when I think about the sacrifices that my family made so that I could focus on my job. I still cringe when I think about that cab ride.

I took on another challenge that week by placing a heartbreaking call to one of the most prominent Dreamers, Jose Antonio Vargas. Jose was born in the Philippines, and at age twelve his mother sent him to the U.S. to strive for a better life with his grandparents. He is an American success story by any measure, with a distinguished career as a journalist on a Pulitzer Prize–winning team. I met him just before he "came out" as undocumented—a brave announcement that could have ended his career. Since then, Jose had become a friend, but when we designed the new policy I knew that it would not help him because he was a few months older than the age limit. We had a good reason for that age limit: it was the same age limit in the current version of the DREAM Act, and we wanted to stay as close as possible to a policy that members of Congress already supported. I knew that this was the right way to protect the policy, but it hurt to know that Jose wouldn't benefit, and I knew that my discomfort would pale in comparison to his. He was my friend; I felt like I had a duty to be the one to tell him that, though we were taking this big step that would help hundreds of thousands, I was also responsible for the decision that meant that it wouldn't benefit him.

When I called him, despite his disappointment, he was immediately generous, gracious, and genuinely excited for the people who would benefit even as he was left behind. I have always been grateful for his generosity when he could easily have expressed bitterness that day.

On June 15, 2012, President Obama announced the new policy—DACA, which stands for Deferred Action for Childhood Arrivals—in the Rose Garden. Along with my colleagues, I stood and listened to the President between the columns that overlook the garden. Pete Souza, the President's photographer, snapped a photo of that moment, a framed version of which sits in my office, a gift from my colleagues for my fiftieth birthday later that year. Frankly, we all look terrible, our faces contorted with emotion. I remember feeling pride and anxiety—followed by a lot of anger when Neil Munro of the conservative outlet *Daily Caller* interrupted the President as he delivered his remarks, startling the White House press corps. "Why'd you favor foreigners over Americans?" he asked. "In answer to your question, sir—and the next time I'd prefer you'd let me finish my statement before you ask that question—is this is the right thing to do for the American people," the President answered. As nice as it was to watch the boss shut down the question, I still get angry thinking about it.

After a whirlwind of activity getting the job done, and making sure my husband was healthy and safe, I finally had time to absorb what we had accomplished. The reaction across the country was breathtaking. The news was full of stories of Dreamers in tears, talking about how they could finally go to school, finally take that job, finally begin to plan for the future. Hundreds of thousands of young people who had been living in fear could see a bright future for the first time. People were talking about it everywhere I went, every time I turned on the radio. I heard from colleagues and friends who went out of their way to tell me how much it meant to them. I didn't really have a chance to absorb it all until the weekend—and I spent most of that Saturday in tears.

Two months later, DHS started accepting the first DACA applications. Since then, nearly eight hundred thousand people—the DACAmented, as they call themselves— have received the protection of this policy. It has led to extraordinary success. These Dreamers are students, teachers, lawyers, people shaping their communities and our common future in powerful and positive ways. Thankfully, the opposition that we had feared might emerge from more conservative Democrats failed to materialize, and even the attacks from the usual suspects on the far right seemed halfhearted. I attribute this to the Dreamers themselves. Because they courageously told their stories, they were viewed with great empathy by the public. It became difficult to attack Dreamers without seeming heartless.

I will always remember DACA as a high point of my White House years. The high points are pretty good, but wow, the lows can be rough.

For me the low came two years later, when we dealt with the hardest issue I have ever worked on: the crisis of unaccompanied children streaming across the border.

For years, there has been a relatively predictable pattern of children traveling alone or in the hands of smugglers from Central America to the Rio Grande. In response, Congress passed a law in 2000 to make sure that these children would be properly cared for once they encountered U.S. authorities. The law requires that they go through a removal hearing—they don't just get to stay in the United States unless they qualify for humanitarian relief—but Congress rightly determined that in the meantime they should receive proper, kid-appropriate shelter and be reunited with family or placed in a foster home if possible.

What happened in 2014 was a huge and unusual spike in the numbers of children coming across the border, one that we later learned was fostered by smugglers who were marketing the false notion that the border was newly open to such traffic. We ran out of shelter space, and the migrant children ended up in crowded Border Patrol stations in Texas, which are essentially law enforcement lockups—no place for children. The administration scrambled to set up enough shelter space, while also pushing back on the smugglers' messaging in Central America.

Our immigration laws and procedures at the borders aren't designed for a situation like this. A team from the White House and across the federal government worked day and night to provide adequate care for these children, find volunteer lawyers for their immigration hearings, and address the enormous challenges in Central America which were contributing to their exodus.

I traveled to McAllen, Texas, just north of the border, with Jeh Johnson, the secretary of homeland security, to see the situation for myself and meet some of the children who had undertaken this journey on their own. I will never forget them. A thirteen-year-old boy with huge eyes who rode the top of a train across Mexico by himself, hoping to reunite with his mother in New Jersey. Young teenage girls quietly telling me their story of riding for days in a van with a smuggler. The youngest child I met was eight. I also met mothers traveling with newborns.

As a mother, and as an immigration expert, I found my heart breaking several times a day as we wrestled with what felt like wildly unsatisfying options for addressing the crisis.

In the middle of this debacle, the President met with a group of immigration advocates—most of them people I have been close to for years—to discuss strategy on getting immigration reform through the Congress. We gathered in the Roosevelt Room, just steps from the Oval Office, along a long table. The President heard from everybody in the room in a discussion which amounted to an argument over strategy.

The hardest moment came at the end when an advocate, who I think meant to sound sympathetic about the pressures on the President, said something like, "I don't know how you can sleep at night." In response, the President gave a sharp answer along the lines of: "Sometimes I don't sleep at night. But I don't have the luxury of worrying just about the children from El Salvador. I have to worry about children in Sudan, and in other places. The fact is that we live in nations with borders, and I'm responsible for this one." This was followed by an emotional conversation which to me felt very unfair to the President. The immigration advocates were speaking from a place of emotion rather than reason, asking him essentially to open the border without acknowledging the absolute impossibility of that action. I didn't succeed in controlling my emotions either as a tear escaped one eye and rolled down my cheek.

I actually did a lot of crying that summer, but almost never at the office. The strain of managing my piece of the unaccompanied minors issue along with the rest of my portfolio as the President's domestic policy advisor, which encompasses education, health care, labor issues, and a range of other matters, was crushing. I usually ended up in a puddle as I drove home those summer nights.

So that tear in the Roosevelt Room was an exception. I hoped the President hadn't noticed. I was wrong. Later that day, an assistant came into my office to say, "You have been called down to the Oval." When I got there, Valerie Jarrett, my former boss and good friend, was standing with the President. He invited me in, gave me a big hug, and said, "I just wanted to make sure you're okay." Our options under the law were wholly inadequate to the needs of those kids, but it was important to be able to look the President in the eye and tell him that I knew that we as a team were doing as much as we could.

Things didn't turn out as we hoped or planned on immigration reform overall. We tried mightily to work with Congress to pass an immigration reform bill, and we came tantalizingly close to the finish line on the DREAM Act in 2010, and again after passing a strong bipartisan immigration bill through the Senate in 2013. As I write this, the new administration has made the indefensible decision to dismantle DACA, giving the Congress a deadline to act to protect all of the people who benefited. Unaccompanied children still arrive at the U.S.-Mexico border, and the new administration is asking Congress to change the law that provides for their protection.

Despite the personal and professional risks, I decided that working in Barack Obama's White House would be worth it, because I believed that his administration was in a better position to do good than any of its predecessors, because the President had the right values and priorities, and because he had chosen a team who shared them. I knew that it wouldn't be easy, but I had faith in the man who asked me to serve. He clearly wanted me to apply my perspective and experience to the task at hand, and I believed—correctly, as it turned out—that he wouldn't ever make a decision that I didn't feel I could defend.

I still get the occasional attack by people who are angry at immigration enforcement and see me as someone who defended it. And they're right, I did defend it. I swore an oath to uphold the law, and there aren't exceptions when the law is outdated and dysfunctional.

Whether we like it or not, immigration enforcement is a given, and it is on us to find a way to do it wisely, in a way that better honors our values as a country. We proved that it's possible to accomplish this, even if only temporarily. To make any progress on complex issues in the thorny mess of government, you need people with backgrounds like mine, who know what I know and have seen what I have seen, and who are willing to take the plunge and work in government, shaping how laws—even disagreeable and broken ones—are enforced. DACA is the result of these efforts. One way or another, the work that we did in the Obama administration will shape policy when the day comes that we are truly ready for immigration reform. I find it excruciating to watch what the new administration is doing, but I also know that the arc of history is long, and that these battles aren't over.

President Obama likes to say, "You know, sometimes we can't fix every problem, but we can move the ball down the field, and we can come up with something that is better than what we've got now. I'll take 'better' every time." He's right about that, and if a little criticism is the price for making things better, that strikes me as a pretty good deal.

GO TOWARD THE GOOD

Hope Hall

B arack Hussein Obama. POTUS. 44. The first . . . so many firsts. I offer perhaps a lesser-known first: first president to have a videographer. Presidents have had official photographers in the White House since JFK, but videographers? Flies on the wall in the corridors of power, documenting private moments and meetings, recording audio and action frame by frame? President Obama, often dubbed our first "tech president," was the first to take this brave leap. And for six life-changing years, I was there to help him jump.

* * *

Full disclosure: I've always been a big hippie. Now, I don't exactly mean it in the sense of 1970s central casting—counterculture, flowing skirt, peace flag version (though admittedly this could describe me at times)—but rather as my name Hope asks for. As a small human I took shape in the southern, breezy climes of Mexico, Brazil, and California, and I discovered that the calm I found as a gymnast then ballerina then modern dancer helped me navigate the stresses of my loving, chaotic, blended family. I realized, as a tiny teenager, that I had a choice in how I spent my time and with whom, and that this feeling, the peace I felt and sense of ease in my own body, was what I would follow through life. What rolled onward and flowed from that marker of a moment has been a lifetime of exploration of the inner life, of mindfulness through movement and meditation, and of an openness to the ever-expanding science of health.

I took to photography as a kid, but in my late twenties, I began to shoot motion picture instead of single, silent frames. I considered this move an extension of my life as a dancer. It was all about movement. It was all about relationship. One of my mantras as a filmmaker— and as a human—is that it's all about *who*. Who I get to work alongside, who I collaborate with, who I spend my time with. And that compels me to go toward the good: the good people, the good moments. As my father taught me: smile and say hello, be tolerant, and refuse to be insulted.

This is particularly relevant in the connection between cinematographer and subject. That collaboration is the source of the content you create; the footage is a direct result of the relationship, and that ever-shifting, shared ground between my camera and what it's capturing is a source of endless curiosity for me. And when it's the President of the United States blinking into your lens, and your footage will help tell his story both now and deep into the future, supporting the health and well-being of that relationship is more important than ever.

* * *

The date was May 31, the year was 2011. I know that "never" and "always" are inherently inaccurate words, but I can honestly say that I, Hope Elizabeth Hall, never, never, never imagined I'd ever set foot inside the White House. Yet there I was, on my first day as presidential videographer, being greeted happily by the 44th President of these

United States as he strode in to complete [insert big number] of [insert impossible number] items on that day's schedule. My job was to document the President's day, to capture behind-the-scenes, observational video of him doing his job, from within the inner workings of the White House to the ends of this round earth.

I was quite suddenly a foreign exchange student in a truly unimaginably strange land. I didn't know the language, the customs, the local dress. But I was there to learn, observe, and capture. And the passport to this foreign land? My video camera.

* * *

My mandate was strategic, not archival—my position was housed in the (first-ever) White House Office of Digital Strategy. This meant contributing video, edited or raw, from access no one else had to the endless variety of assignments this team tackled via the hundreds of platforms, accounts, and campaigns we shepherded through the halls of power, from rapid-response to long-term projects and everything in the months days hours and nanoseconds between. Our mission statement took a while to develop, but it eventually formed into: *connecting people with purpose, by meeting them where they are, which is online.* What that meant for me, day to day? Get quick, real quick, at churning out viral vids, all while keeping up with a team of people traveling from said halls of power to said ends of said round earth and back again, and then doing it all over again. And again. And again.

It was early in my time at the White House, and I had just finished filming a scene in the Oval, a handful of kooky kids (red cowboy boots and rockin' outfits to meet the boss? nice choice!) taking departure photos with the President, followed by his call to the coach of the Stanley Cup–winning Bruins. I was about to exit stage left when he called after me.

"Hey, Hope!" he said. That unmistakable voice, from behind that unmistakable desk. I stopped in my tracks and turned around, then froze. I had spoken to the boss directly before but in crowded, roaring backstages on the road during the '08 campaign, then in the clunky bunker of transition and around its edges of wonky policy and staff announcements, and over the first few weeks since joining the White House, but so far these were conversations in chaotic situations, typically interstitial and jocular, and all with crews of other staffers in on the banter.

"Seems like we're filming more stuff," he began. "Is this part of a bigger plan?"

"Well," I stammered, "I . . . don't want to miss anything."

"Okay," he said, "so there is a bigger plan. We're just kind of seeing how it goes."

I talked about documenting his presidency while doing no harm, about not impeding the process, about being conscientious, knowing that the camera changes the room. I explained how I wanted my work to help carry out his mandate of transparency and engagement.

"And I really mean it," I said, trying to gain my composure. "I want to hear if things are not working."

"No, it's working fine," said the leader of the free world, waving away my concerns with a benign arc of his presidential hand from behind the witness to history that is the Resolute Desk, on which his feet may or may not have been plonked.

* * *

I knew from that first conversation in the Oval that I'd have to be ever ready with answers to his questions, and I felt that he was genuinely curious about the evolution of my approach.

Over the ensuing years, the boss and I continued this conversation. We talked backstage while introducers busted blithely—or rebelliously—through the finish line ribbon of their agreed-upon time limit, giving us moments to fill. We talked while I perfected the shot for his Weekly Address, the one piece of my portfolio that afforded me the directorial space to set everything up instead of chasing after the President and sneaking into the scene hopefully relatively unnoticed, forced to accept whatever light/mise-en-scène/audio limitations were present. We talked striding along the colonnade as he asked about my new camera (no detail escapes his notice), and as I mused (read: geeked out on tech specs) about the finer points of my slick update to the decidedly unergonomic dinosaur I'd been lugging around for years, and as he took my camera into his own hands, turned it on me, and interviewed me (read: geeked out) on philosophical specs like the light and shade of my methodology, of the ethics therein. We talked while the motorcade rejiggered itself in San Jose (CR, not CA, but maybe in CA, too—it all gets geographically blurry) to get the fifteen to twenty-five vehicles backed up and lurched forward to line up in the completely opposite direction than they'd been poised to go since the night before, all because the schedule had changed on a dime.

I shared with him how so much of what I do as a documentary filmmaker is explore that elusive element called tone, how motion picture is not just picture matched with sound moving through time but actually the relationship between the two, from synced and humming as one to contrapuntal and tense, and everything in between. I talked about the concept of hot and cold and how it fits into crafting the shape of the relationship between picture and sound. And I talked about how surprised I continued to be that the most oft-asked question I got while on the job was: "So . . . what's he really like?" I saw the core of my job as trying to answer that question through portraiture using hot and cold picture and sound moving through time and space in relationship to each other that conveys in its tone what it might actually might feel like to be him.

* * *

There I am, in the Arabian Desert. Picture me in a starkly postmodern version of a Bedouin tent (replete with marble floors), with no women's room, so I am assigned a watchman when I have no choice but to use the capacious men's room (also replete with marble floors). There I am, navigating access and negotiating who might go where for the bilateral meeting with the king even though we all know that all bets are off once those magic, creaking, two-story doors crack open to let us in. There I am, standing alongside my eight Saudi counterparts (yep, this king had eight videographers) near the end of an eighteen-hour day somewhere in the blur of a ten-day foreign trip, grinning for a twenty-first-century selfie, the only one not brandishing a sword.

Speaking of sand: What I learned quickly is that working in the White House is like navigating a landscape of ever-shifting sand. It's like trying to plan while the clock's hands are swirling in both directions at the same time, without even a shred of a sense of a predictable rhythm. Everything changes, moment to moment, all the time. It's living in the face of the highest stakes possible in an atmosphere that is notoriously risk averse. For me, specifically, it was about trying to make visible the work of this heartfelt, thoughtful presidential endeavor by means of an incredible optical sensor with a powerful directional mic. And doing it with the hope that the kids and the baby boomers and everyone in between would not only feel compelled to register a like to that pithy, authentic, surprising video but perhaps even (here's the brass ring for digital strategy) *feel engaged.*

* * *

I began a typical workday biking down the hill, feeling my molecules rearrange as I swooped along, just a person going to work, walking through Lafayette Square after locking up my bike outside of the security perimeter and moving into a fast walk to get to the Office of Digital Strategy in time for our morning meeting. We'd go around the cramped room offering strategy on obstacles and opportunities, and as the mama of the group, I'd often find a way to insert some sort of announcement centered around work-life balance and mindfulness. We'd talk through that day's coverage, and then it was off to the races, running over and across West Executive Avenue with my camera rig to join the boss in the Oval Office for friendly competition with Spelling Bee champs or signing an executive order or hosting another bilateral diplomatic meeting or honoring NASCAR or World Series or Super Bowl winners. Or maybe it would be policy advisors of any sort in the Roosevelt Room, or a sit-down interview in the Blue/ Red/East/State Dining/Cabinet Room but never the Green Room (because green and video cameras don't get along).

On many days, I was instead racing from that morning meeting to find my spot in the motorcade to ride to Andrews to catch Air Force One to a church service in Charleston, or to a tour of the future (and maybe a drop-by for a sandwich made by thoughtful moms and pops) in Detroit, or to a rally in St. Louis, or to visit a refinanced block in Reno, or to a campaign stop at the manse of—insert name you'd recognize here—in Los Angeles. Never a dull moment.

Back and forth, out of the office, back into the office, filming, editing, meeting, interrupting each and any thing to suddenly do the other thing, more often than not actually sprinting to keep up with a shift in the schedule, running into folks from other offices, passing each other with a big hello if in the midst of said sprint, or hopefully stopping for a hug and a chat if not.

Then there were the international trips, every few months, always looming, every day and night of which were crammed to within an inch of their lives with speeches, meetings, drop-bys, cities, countries, all of which had been diplomatically wrangled for months, if not years. Mustering the insight to figure out what to pack in terms of gear, equipment, clothes. Flying overnight, figuring out when to stop working and sleep, how to sleep in your chair or work it so that somehow you got a precious spot on the floor, and making a real effort to make a memorizable mental note on how to actually pack successfully next time, because you land at six a.m. and the pomp and circumstance lined up on the tarmac means running off the plane in an outfit that hopefully won't make news for its diplomatic insufficiency while lugging bags of said gear and equipment that somehow hopefully go unnoticed despite their uncouth sloppiness. No pressure.

Film while jostling people with gear; pair up with counterpart if I have one; smile and borrow from my tired, addled brain a few niceties in said counterpart's tongue, while continuing to jostle and film, also while Instagramming video with the official White House phone; then scramble to find my assigned van in the motorcade while hoping to find the communications staffer I need to look at said Instagram post to make sure I both cover my ass and don't end up bringing down the presidency with my social media digital strategy video antics. Once in the van, commiserate on how our BlackBerrys won't get cell service here in [insert name of foreign land (hello, South Korea!)].

Film the folks lined up on either side of the motorcade (and wave, and cry, and possibly Instagram).

All day, and often long into the night. Repeat. At some point in the day or night, if I'm lucky, finding a watercooler somewhere for a moment of sustenance and respite, in some forlorn hallway in the Vatican. Lugging my video gear, plus laptop and external drive, searching for an out-of-the-way place with Wi-Fi and 120V sockets where I can edit footage while always keeping a trained ear on staffers' movements so as not to get left behind, or risking it with no power so I can grab some precious quiet and room to edit in the van before everyone else gets in there. Madly BlackBerrying the team back home, working on what to post, if to post, confirming the caption, confirming the hashtag, time change be damned, knowing that regardless of the time difference, there's usually someone in DC addled enough to be active on their work phone while all their neighbors and friends and lovers and pets sleep. Falling into the hotel lobby around midnight, some dramatically comic staggering and laughter and relief, and an eye toward the hotel bar for just enough of a boost and shift in perspective through a conversation to make the time stolen from precious sleep worth it, shared with a dear friend or a new friend, usually someone inside the government bubble but not always. Heading up to a secure floor, which means getting off the elevator a floor or two short, then eyeballing the stair + arrow notes taped to the wall of the hallway, up the stairs with hellos to the Secret Service agents for whom your heading to bed represents some of the last activity they'll see for their night shift in that windowless stairwell, unbroken glow stick at their feet, resignation in their faces. One last BlackBerry check, maybe an encouraging word to or from a friend a few doors or floors down, set that damned phone alarm, and in five or six hours, start all over again.

It's Newtown. It's Cuba. It's the boss heading to dinner early—i.e., now—instead of to that meeting you're lurking at, so he can come back later and do that call from the Oval. It's the Blue Room and a 106-year-old dancing woman changing hearts and minds. Situation Room. Golf now, right now, because his crazy schedule means he basically won't get to be outside and walk where he wants for another two weeks. It's him taking the podium, replacing the press secretary for the day (surprise, press!) in the Brady Press Briefing Room. Situation Room. It's meeting the Dalai Lama, in secret, because . . . China. Situation Room. A shooting. Great Falls with the girls on a Saturday afternoon. A shooting. Another shooting. Obamacare on the verge of being repealed. Another shooting. Situation Room. Putin wants to meet. Mandela is gone. Another shooting. Another. And another.

* * *

Within months of starting the job, while continuing to be convinced that I was having the adventure of a lifetime, I started to feel the drag toward the precipice of that charcoal party trick that is the allure of burnout. Snarling at a typo in a potential intern's resume: out of character. Crying: welcome in my personal life, surprising on the job. And the injuries? Oof, they came fast, and they came hard. A fall and a cracked kneecap in Colombia. An impossible-to-ignore goose egg on the forehead plus two black eyes from running smack into the half-open door to the colonnade. One day while he was prepping Obama backstage right before a speech, Secretary of Education Arne Duncan saw me swaying on my feet and, because I was clearly about to faint, stopped midprep to find me a seat next to a fan, and place a water and a cookie into my clammy hands.

The President's physical therapist and I became buds as he continued to patch me up and send me back into the ring with warm encouragement after I'd finished my thread of advice on how to be the dad he wants to be in the head-scratcher world of stage parenting a ballerina daughter. We talked health, we talked well-being, we talked about the single biggest contributor to both: sleep. And soon, that was what this job became: a math problem. How do I reverse engineer the life I want, one where I show up thriving and capable of delivering the kind of coverage and work that my boss—that incredible human—deserves? Since that work is creative, it comes from within.

What I didn't know was that Barack Hussein Obama would be my unexpected guide in achieving the moment-to-moment mindfulness I sought. I didn't anticipate—who could have?—that one of the greatest gifts my job would give me was the opportunity to learn from my boss about the primary importance of the care and feeding of my own inner life.

Taking my cues from him and parroting back his model for self-care—in his case, that meant room in the most litigated schedule on the planet for desk time, reading time, personal time, time for a workout in the morning, and dinner with the family—I took a look at my life and had to consider: what would be my nonnegotiable self-savers? Once a week: hope time. Once a month: acupuncture or massage. Regularly: yoga. Bike rides—commuting or meandering. Sunday morning thermos of coffee and a trip to the wildness of the woods or the mercurial waters of the Eastern Shore or the Potomac. Sunday suppers with my sister and her family, regularly forgetting the forty-year age difference between my nephew and me and often culminating in a dance party in the kitchen, sometimes my dad joining from the West Coast.

Stress is stress no matter the conditions. While working for the President is an exceptional condition, I would posit that no matter the position we're in, we are living in chronically stressful times. While these times may be deeply interesting and revelatory and full of growth and destruction and everything in between, what humans have been crooning for millennia, in sharp poetry and in lilting prose, is a message that still comes through, if you're listening: it's all about love, and our capacity for it. And the source of that love is singular; it's the only source we have. It's our very own inner lives.

* * *

Four years into the job, my dad became critically ill. The day I got the call that he had fallen the night before, had been found, and had just been admitted to the ICU, everything stopped. I put the camera down, walked out of the White House, hopped a plane at National to try to make it to him before his body gave out, then repeated that trip over and over, for three months, until he finally succumbed. To type that sentence is to work with the throat as it closes and tightens around tears and love and a smile.

Somewhere in that tempest of a time I'm shuffling along some Santa Monica sidewalk not wanting to go up to my dad's hospital room but not being able to get there soon enough—I might have been crying at the palm trees overhead—when suddenly a phrase came to me. I was perhaps talking to President Obama in my mind, as I often did on those days. The phrase came to me, again and again. This life of ours, *it's all about love.*

I returned to the White House after a walkabout of grief involving the Pacific Coast Highway and the California redwoods and whiskey. The day I got back, Obama and I walked along the colonnade and lingered in the outer Oval and talked about life, and about death. I told him his daughters were so lucky to have him as a dad. He told me my dad was so lucky to have me as a daughter. While no photos exist, I know it happened. I know how thoughtful that guy is. Truly, no detail escapes his notice. At some point, I blurted out the phrase that had come to me. And elegantly, assuredly, and with perhaps a knowing nod mixed with a bemused shake of his graying head, he agreed with me. "Hope, take all the time you need."

* * *

My dad's death and my travels along the road leading up to it forced the gentle and blessed hand of sustainability. I had by this point seen many colleagues drop like flies and burn out from the best jobs ever. I started warning the next wave as I saw them careening toward that same cliff. Among the things I most admired about Obama were his crystal clarity and infamous calm, his love of and devotion to taking the long view, his belief in a management style that encourages those he works alongside to do their best work (drawing from the campaign motto: respect, empower, include), and his deep understanding of the value of advocating for the vibrance of his own health. All this was inspiration. All this pointed the way toward living a thoughtful, flexible, generous, playful, kind, useful day-to-day life.

My video colleagues and I formalized our relationships into structures and systems that would support and encourage us to make our work together the best work we could do, the best of the best, as our boss deserved. To this day I like to call this advocating for PQ, Presidential Quality. It works, even at home from behind an unresolute desk.

We hired incredible people. We worked collaboratively. It showed in the work. The Office of Digital Strategy eventually grew to eighteen staffers who were behind the official social media accounts for the White House—POTUS, FLOTUS, VPOTUS, and Dr. Biden—plus campaigns, cabinet members, staffers, and cross-agency efforts. I was the oldest person on the team, in most cases by decades. These were whiz kids, still are, and some of the very finest humans I have had the honor and pleasure of working alongside. Pretty much every day we released at least some snippet of video somehow, despite getting challenged by every variable you can imagine. The edit process made me learn to work quickly—I'd been trained in the art of slowness, subtlety, and nuance—and definitely made me a better cinematographer. Because part of the fun of editing is grumbling at the cinematographer, and . . . see what I'm saying? You learn a lot grumbling at yourself.

We had two constant video products during my six years, the Weekly Address, which is the current version of FDR's fireside chats, and West Wing Week, which was a weekly wrap-up released every Friday and featured what the President had been up to the previous seven days. It ended up having a lovely side benefit: White House staff would catch a glimpse of themselves on the job and be able to show their friends and family a moment from their lives in the bubble. And because staff looked for themselves in it, they also got a sense of the larger picture, the bigger endeavor that they were toiling away at, often in obscurity. And I, too, started to be able to look up and out more and more often. Some space took shape around the words, the feelings, the thoughts, the schedule, the pace, the work. I was no longer alone. I was no longer a one-woman band.

I posted a sign on our office wall that said: "Go Toward the Good." It may sound like an annoying cliché, but I began to think of it as an organizing principle. I started holding brown-bag lunches on mindfulness and the creative process with other White House teams, asking them what they were grappling with, helping them to strategize on everything from getting their morning meditation going to making that leap, you know, that big leap in life, because they're actually happiest when they're climbing rock walls or writing pithy essays or singing arias. Finding time to honor those happy places. I started intoning phrases like, "Our lives—and that includes our work—are only as good as we feel," first at Team Digital Strategy meetings, then beyond. Dear friends dubbed me Soul Doctor Hall. It still makes me smile.

And whenever I got the chance to advise a new hire, I would point out that the single most oft-committed flaw I'd seen take people down in that strange place was arriving and feeling that they had to have the answers to all the possible challenges. "Imagine you're a foreign exchange student," I'd say, and they'd chuckle. "You are!"—I'd get all serious-voiced on them. I'd describe how, as you do when you humbly arrive in a totally foreign place, you give yourself time and space to start learning the language, the landscape, the characters, the backstories. You observe. You ask questions when there's an opening. You take it all in, as much as you can handle every day, and then you retire to rest each evening, calling your loved ones and chatting and joking in your home tongue. Eventually, I'd say, you'll find yourself starting to pass, making a joke at the proverbial checkout counter, and even if it doesn't make the imagined cashier chuckle, at least they'll appreciate that you were trying.

While the rhythm of every day during those six years meant careening from one event or crisis to another, the cycle of those days also began to follow somewhat predictable, repetitive rhythms. A few times a year, President Obama and I would bond in disbelief as we walked away from greeting scientists, artists, philosophers. He'd catch me grinning from behind the camera in the Blue Room as I took in James Turrell (James Turrell!) standing in the light of Linda Ronstadt (Linda Ronstadt!), or Toni Morrison (Toni Morrison!) peering in from the Green Room just before receiving some national medal of awesomeness. So while other staffers BlackBerryed and tended to other logistics, POTUS and I riffed, every time, on our love of and luck in honoring these incredible people. In our own version of interstitial banter, we would take a moment before striding out of the Blue Room to soak it in, together. Can you believe Toni Morrison was here, right here, in the Blue Room? Then, invariably, he'd add a variant on the same sentence, just between us: *These are our people, Hope, the scientists, the artists.* Then I'd add my variant to the sentence: *The thoughtful, reflective people, the critical thinkers, the generous ones.* We'd tap our temples, we'd nod and grin, eyebrows up. And it was my way of knowing that my approach, my unlikely approach, was welcome here. That this artist in residence was welcome here, that I was seen, that I was contributing to good energy in the White House, because even I belonged there.

Just like he used to joke, "You see? I told you I'd bring Hope to Washington!"

Coda

I'll leave you with an image, a top contender for a favorite clip, a butterfly that we're missing now that no one in the White House is doing this job: Charleston. Cameras rolling this big scene live from the back of the church, respectfully sequestered on the riser set up five hundred feet back, at the entrance to the church hall.

Obama used to joke that I was either beaming or crying behind the camera. That day was a crying day. I was the one video camera who could roam from backstage to the rafters behind the hundreds of forlorn mourners—including the grieving children in the front row, white socks and shiny shoes swaying above the ground—to the base of the stage where the boss took to the lectern to deliver his address, and, yes, I was crying much of the time. No room in my camera for anything other than what will save us all: consolation and reassurance and hope.

My favorite angle on his face is a two thirds angle instead of straight-on, preferably the left side from just below. Having glanced over the speech draft, I knew to let myself roam to get details, from rows of military caps in hand to tear lines drawn on faces, but for sure to be as close up as possible on the boss for the end. I'd heard and filmed the banter backstage about singing (not a chance). So when he uttered the phrase "amazing grace" from his prepared words, and then slowly reiterated them in an unprepared way, shaking his head and tilting that graying head down so his eyes could close and he could take a minute, I knew that the risk and the awkwardness of sneaking behind the wreaths to be just at the foot of the stage while staying hidden from the main live shot was worth it.

Because there, in my lens, while rolling, was Barack Hussein Obama, 44th President of these United States, working a decision around his cerebellum, right there in the twitches of that decision in his jaw, his temple. And as he lifted his head and busted through the scripted version of consoling a nation of mourners and began to sing, really sing, that dirge of a beauty that is "Amazing Grace," there is now in the National Archives one frame of his eyes looking into the lens that registers that he knew I was on it, that I was beaming and crying right back, that I had the two-thirds close-up that no one else had, that tears were pouring down in rivulets while I held the shot from just below that stage, crouching behind the wreaths. He saw that I had it, the moment when he was healthy and present and kind and flexible and generous enough to be making that heartfelt and oh so bold decision, and that I had shown up ready to be ready to deliver, too. That we can all, from now until as deep into the history of time as the National Archives stands, watch him decide to risk it all and start singing a song that just might heal us all.

BIG F'ING DEAL

Michael J. Robertson

On a crisp fall day in 2013, I got ready for work as I did every morning.

It was the first year of President Obama's second term. Following a hard-fought reelection, we now faced an even more contentious Congress controlled by the other party and a general public that was divided on his presidency. Perhaps no issue was more divisive—especially to our critics—than the Patient Protection and Affordable Care Act. Passed into law three years prior, Obamacare, as it is better known, was almost ready to go into effect.

As deputy cabinet secretary, and a member of the White House senior staff, it was my job to help move the President's agenda through various federal government agencies. And at that moment, my days were consumed with preparing agencies for the upcoming launch of Healthcare.gov, the online portal where, for the first time in American history, people would be able to purchase affordable health care on their own without worrying about being denied because of their preexisting conditions.

As I got ready—pressed suit, polished shoes, perfected half-Windsor—I tried to plan for the day ahead. My first meeting was the

White House senior staff meeting in the Roosevelt Room with the chief of staff and the President's closest advisors. I knew that the Healthcare.gov rollout would be the focus of conversation that morning, so I tried to anticipate any questions that might arise.

It wasn't easy to focus, though. My head was heavy, my mind was cloudy, and my stomach churned. Imagine the worst hangover combined with the worst post-roller-coaster nausea, then multiply that by a thousand. I knew I needed to get to work earlier than usual so I could snag one of the limited open seats in the room instead of my usual standing spot in front of the small bust of Eleanor Roosevelt. Sitting would help me better conceal how I was feeling.

But before I could get out of the house, I first had to hide the alarm-clock-sized chemotherapy pump connected to a needle and a tube coming out of the mediport implanted just below my right collarbone. I carefully snaked the tubes through the buttons of my shirt, tucked the pump into the inside pocket of my suit jacket, and fastened the tube behind my tie with a little clip. I had lost enough weight by now that the bulges from the pump and tubes were nicely hidden by all of the extra fabric of a suit that was once an exact fit.

I stood there admiring my work in the mirror, feeling pretty slick about it and thanking God I had to wear a suit and tie every day. Then I heard the soft *bzzt* that pushed another shot of the cancer-fighting chemotherapy cocktail directly into my jugular vein every ninety seconds. Moments later, a wave of nausea and dehydration took over. *Bzzt*, it continued. Like fighting through a riptide, I struggled through the haze to find my composure and get clearheaded. And then *bzzt* over and over and over again.

* * *

I was diagnosed ten months before starting my job at the White House. I was on vacation in California with my family and new fiancée. It was her first time joining our nearly forty-year family tradition of spending a relaxing week at the beach in Santa Cruz away from the grind of our daily routines. We planned to spend some of our time on the trip planning our upcoming wedding, scheduled for the following spring.

We also agreed I would use the opportunity to check in with my family doctor about some digestive issues I had been experiencing. Having been through an intense period of work—drinking too much coffee and putting in long days—I anticipated the doctor would check me out and give me a lecture about eating better and sleeping more. At worst, I assumed it was maybe an ulcer or IBS. I was thirty-five years old and had been otherwise healthy my whole life, with no family history of any major digestive conditions. What else could it possibly be?

You never forget the day someone tells you that you have cancer. From the moment those words are said to you, your life can never be the same again.

"You have stage IV cancer."

"Well, how many stages are there? Five, six, ten?"

"There's only four."

I remember sitting there, trying to wrap my head around the reality of balancing fear and uncertainty with wanting to fight, but not really knowing how. I learned that I was a stage IV, metastatic colorectal cancer patient. A cancer that usually afflicts those sixty-five and older wasn't just inside me; it was growing and making its way through my body, spreading from a polyp-turned-tumor to a large tumor in my liver and another one in my lungs.

My doctors explained that from what they saw there was nothing in my genetics or family history or past health history that made me more likely to get cancer. Nothing could have foretold it. They said it's like I was struck by lightning.

* * *

Late one evening, I stood at my desk in my first-floor office on the northeast corner of the Eisenhower Executive Office Building. Out my window, I could see the entrance to the West Wing and the spot known as "Pebble Beach," just off the North Lawn of the White House where reporters reported live throughout the day. This spectacular view is forever etched in my mind, understated yet grand.

In the background, the voice of Senator Ted Cruz, one of Obamacare's most hateful critics, bounced from the TV around the walls of my office like a racquetball. He was on the Senate floor droning on and on in a daylong filibuster aimed at defunding Obamacare and declaring that he was willing to shut down the entire federal government to do it. Initially I had the same reaction to the opposition I usually have in a heated policy debate: Why is it so hard for them to put themselves in someone else's shoes? Don't they have family or friends or community members that need these policies? Isn't there a way to get to agreement instead of destroying everything? How can they only talk about the financial cost and not address the human impact?

That's when it started to sink in that this policy debate was different: he was talking about me. He was holding hostage my future, and the futures of the families I sat next to every other Thursday in the infusion center. They were all real people—children, moms, and dads being treated for catastrophic diseases. Our lives were literally teetering on the edge of politics, policy, and science. None of us deserved this disease and every single one of us deserved a fair shot at beating it. That is what our country can do for us. That is what our country *should* do for us.

This fight was now against me and everyone around me. That's another thing about being diagnosed with a major disease. When you get sick with something like cancer, your wife, your kids, your family, and everyone dear to you gets diagnosed with it, too. On a daily level, it affects their life and work while they take care of you. But in the larger scheme, my whole family was now susceptible to my preexisting condition and we knew that being denied coverage could destroy us. Opponents and critics of Obamacare had the power to upend our life and livelihood. Losing my health care would pose both a financial danger affecting my wife and children, and worse, an existential danger, taking away my right to fight for my life.

I turned to the TV to watch the continued debate—complete with abstract numbers and discussions of dynamic scoring and twenty vs. ten fiscal-year budgets—and caught my reflection in the screen. I saw the face of a youngish man, a husband, a son, a public servant fighting for his life juxtaposed with the cold analysis and hyperbolic doomsday predictions that did not involve the real people affected by this debate. I could also see the faces of the people I'd met in the infusion center—the husbands, wives, and caregivers who chatted with my wife after the chemo dripping into my veins sent me off to an uncomfortable sleep.

I felt stunned and infuriated. There was a hollow in the pit of my stomach. I opened my bottom right drawer and pulled out the canister of roasted almonds and dried cranberries I always kept in my desk for the longer days in the office. As I chomped on a handful of nutty sweetness, one of my favorite memories came flooding back to me.

It was appropriations season on the Hill—spring for everyone outside the Beltway—and it was Senator Obama's first year in Washington. I was deeply absorbed with the massive spreadsheet of appropriations requests from constituents back in Illinois. It was part of the important and never-ending support work of a junior Senate staffer. I heard a rowdy *crunch* and swiveled my chair around to see who had dared interrupt my concentration. There stood the junior senator from Illinois, staring nonchalantly back at me next to the open drawer of my desk, with his hand in my prized stash of roasted almonds and dried cranberries.

"You're running low," he said between fistfuls.

"Yep," I replied. "There's a certain repeat visitor I haven't been able to keep up with." One more smile, another handful of almonds, and off he went. "Thanks for stopping by, Barack," I quipped as he walked away.

Back then, he was just Barack.

That moment seemed like yesterday, but it was a lifetime ago. Long before the campaign, long before the Iowa caucus, long before we made history and Barack became *Mr. President*. It was long before cancer, too, but I began to think about why I and others had started this work. We joined the Obama team in the very early years because we wanted to stand up for those without a voice, because we wanted to make people's lives better.

That's how I first heard of Barack Obama in late 2003 during my final year of law school. Though I loved the study of law, I never planned to be a practicing attorney. I wanted a career in public policy. Since the justice system applies and interprets the law created through public policy, I wanted to work in a job where I could impact policies on the front end to help ensure our legal system is just and equal. Knowing that one way to get into the policy and political environment could be through the campaign of a successful Senate candidate,

I was researching about a dozen Senate candidates when I discovered an early, emotional, and grainy video of then state senator Obama speaking in a church:

> If there's a child on the south side of Chicago who can't read, that matters to me, even if it's not my child. If there's a senior citizen somewhere who can't pay for their prescription and having to choose between medicine and the rent, that makes my life poorer, even if it's not my grandparent. If there's an Arab-American family being rounded up without benefit of an attorney or due process, that threatens my civil liberties. It is that fundamental belief—it is that fundamental belief—I am my brother's keeper, I am my sister's keeper—that makes this country work.

I heard in that video what the rest of the world would hear the next year at the 2004 Democratic National Convention. I found in his words the same conviction I carried in my own heart: that we have a responsibility to one another, that we the people, and our connection to each other, are what make this incredible American experiment in civility and society work. It was the first time I had heard any person in a position of public influence describe personal civic duty and the role of government and public service exactly the way I had always believed it should work.

I didn't come from a politically connected or wealthy family. I grew up a typical American kid, raised in America's agricultural heart. My parents, both teachers, set an example of hard work and dedication to helping future generations live up to their potential. They cared deeply about what they did professionally and had a keen focus at home on making me and my little sister feel supported and loved. They gave back to their community by doing their jobs to the fullest and by raising their family to the best of their ability.

Every August of my childhood, I visited the local school supply store, where my parents, out of their own pocket, would buy school supplies for their incoming students. They explained that not everyone had the same advantages as I did, and I had an obligation to help those who did not. They instilled in me this principle, which is the compass of my life: those of us in the broader community who have more—whether it is money, social standing, power, privilege, or just simple luck to be born where we were—have the responsibility to first recognize the different circumstances of others and then to support them in any way we can.

This is why I knew that, though they might not immediately understand it, they would trust my decision to leave my life in California and move to Chicago to work for free on Barack Obama's 2004 Senate race.

That was the moment I took my first big leap of faith. Most Obama staffers I know share this in common. We all remember that one day, situation, or decision where we let our faith in something bigger than ourselves, our belief in a better world for our families and communities, lead us into this unique moment in time, this movement. It was this leap of faith that would lead us away from the comfort of our lives and communities and, after a long journey, all the way to the White House.

* * *

When you work at the White House, every day is one of those "big meeting" or "big presentation" days where you have to bring your A game. Most of my friends outside the White House couldn't remember the last time they had worn a tie; I couldn't remember the last time I hadn't. The required formal attire was just one of many small reminders of the seriousness, weight, and impact of what you do every day there.

Calling these high-level jobs hard seems trite. Of course they're hard. You are dealing with some of the most complex and difficult decision-making roles in the country. Unlike most other jobs, everything you do directly impacts someone's life. You create policies and institute programs that will directly change the course of the lives of millions of Americans. To some, that's an incredibly powerful and intoxicating part of the job. For me and my colleagues, it was an incredible privilege and honor—and an even greater responsibility.

You don't always get to see the effects of these policies and programs in such an obvious way, but we did on the day Obamacare was signed into law. The legislation had passed a couple days earlier and the magnitude of what happened was now sinking in. We had worked so hard to put the President in a position to create policies like this one and it had actually happened. The signing ceremony was the moment I was finally able to absorb the feeling of what we were able to accomplish over the past several years and appreciate how our work would improve people's lives. Whispering to the President before his remarks, Vice President Joe Biden got caught on a microphone saying what we were all thinking: "This is a big f'ing deal." The Vice President was right. It was a big f'ing deal. What I didn't know that day was how big a deal it was going to be in my own life.

By 2013, I did. I chose to take a job at the White House, leaving my position as chief of staff at the United States General Services Administration, knowing I had this disease. I received my offer letter while I was in the hospital recovering from my biggest surgery to date, removing the source tumor that had started everything. My wife and

I discussed the job, knowing full well the intensity of the work environment, but I didn't want to look back and say that cancer prevented me from working in my dream job and continuing the journey that I had started over seven years earlier.

At that point, opposition to Obamacare was so strong Republicans soon refused to pass a federal budget that did not include delaying or killing it, partially shutting the government down for seventeen days. The same day Heathcare.gov launched, the government shut down. The shutdown meant vital services provided by the government couldn't be available to the people. It also meant that thousands of federal workers would be furloughed, and thousands more would need to work without a paycheck until the government was funded and reopened. I was one of those people, but thankfully, my health care would stay intact during this period.

Because of the seniority of my position, I was deemed "essential personnel" so I went to work to keep the country running. The cavernous halls of the Eisenhower Executive Office Building, with its whimsically black-and-white-checkered floors, usually busy and echoing with footsteps and voices, were quiet and still.

There was so much work to be done. It sometimes felt like one long never-ending day. My frustration began to boil over. I could not fathom how opponents of Obamacare could play this cavalier game of politics with people's lives. Pacing back and forth between my conference table and my desk, I tried to work out the anger I knew I wouldn't be able to tame for much longer. Finally, the fatigue hit me like a brick. I fell into my chair, pulled my keyboard into my lap, leaned back, and began scrolling through the emails I needed to answer.

A loud knock on the door jolted me. I was shocked, because I had no idea who could possibly be around during a shutdown and would come by my office. "Yes," I said, loudly enough to make sure my chemo-hoarse voice made it to the door since my chemo-fatigued body couldn't.

The door opened. Like a ray of sunshine sent down from heaven itself, there stood the only person who could have brought me to my feet in my weakened state: Vice President Joe Biden. "Hey, Mike, how ya doin'?" I stood and moved slowly around my desk to greet him. My tired legs threatened to make my knees buckle. "Mr. Vice President!" I beamed back, gripping his extended hand. "Hi!"

It wasn't a secret at work that I was going through chemotherapy treatment, but I didn't want that to define me or my time in the White House. By that time, I had learned that, intentionally or not, folks around you treat you differently when they know you're dealing with cancer. The White House is a tough place, and I didn't want anyone showing me pity.

As we stood there, slight anxiety rose over me. *Should I offer him a soda? Does my office smell like my lunch?* He smiled and looked directly into my eyes and—poof! just like magic fairy dust—his presence made my silly worries fade away. "I know you're beat and I know this is hard . . . in a lot of ways. I don't want to interrupt you. I know what you're doing is incredibly important. I just wanted to stop by to let you know how grateful the President and I are for everything that you do and I wanted you to know that we are thinking of you. Keep up the great work, son."

It was as if he knew exactly what was happening in my head and what I was going through. When he called me "son," it hit me. He did know. Two months earlier, his son Beau, who was about my age, was diagnosed with brain cancer. He more than knew. He was part of the cancer club, too.

Seeing him and hearing him was everything I needed to get out of the funk of my anger. I let the wave of warmth he left in his wake wash over me. It's miraculous what a few words of appreciation does for the soul. Cancer warriors draw strength from deep within, and just like that I felt replenished and enriched. I never knew if Vice President Biden was aware of what his drop-by did for me, but as I watched him walk out the door I knew what I had to do.

I picked up the phone and called my wife, who worked down the street at a PR firm. We had met on the 2008 Obama campaign and ended up working together in the early days of the administration. We were an amazing team at work. We were an even more amazing team at life. She just got me. Not her version of who she thought I was or should be. Me, my idiosyncrasies, my neuroses—all of it. She loved and supported me for who I am.

After my diagnosis, she became my primary caregiver, my cheerleader, my mind when I couldn't think like myself, and my body when I couldn't do things for myself. I wish she didn't have to go through cancer, too, but I cannot imagine fighting it without her by my side. More than anyone else, my cancer affected her daily life, livelihood, and well-being most acutely. If she wasn't on board with what I had in mind, it wouldn't happen.

"Hi, love, you busy?" I asked.

"I can talk," she said. "Is everything okay?"

I hated that she had to get scared when I called her out of the blue. That's another thing about fighting cancer. It keeps your loved ones on pins and needles.

"Yes, I'm okay. You'll never guess who just left my office." I told her about my visit from the Vice President. She was a huge fan of his and listened enthusiastically, asking me how I felt when he said certain things and asking me to repeat certain parts of the story more than once. I could feel her smiling through the phone and I know she could see the furled brow that led into the silence.

"What's up?" she asked.

"I've got to tell my story. I've got to."

She paused and then replied, "I know. What can I do to help?"

With her blessing, I pulled up my email and fired off a note to the team leading the implementation of Obamacare, telling them I wanted to go public about my personal experience with health care. I hoped that my story could help others understand the need for the Affordable Care Act and convince people to sign up. I especially wanted to find a way to get to all of those young folks who didn't know that having to fight a catastrophic disease is never part of your plans. I wanted them to know that, like them, I spent my twenties and thirties focused on building my life, only I had no idea that a cancer that usually only affects sixty-five-year-olds had been growing in me silently, threatening without warning to tear it all down.

The next day—the final day of the shutdown—the White House's senior communications advisor for health care wrote back thanking me, and suggested I write a post on the White House blog. My wife and I discussed the offer, and she weighed the benefits and drawbacks of going public with my story.

"I know your commitment is deep, Michael, and I support it one hundred percent, but I just want to make sure we both understand what we are doing here," she said. "Once you come out about the cancer you are fighting, that's it. It's out. We can't go back. We are opening the door for people to understand from our personal experience why they need health insurance—but at the same time we have no idea which doors we are closing for your future employment. The Obama administration will end, and then what happens? You're so remarkable. You have refused to let this cancer define you. You have aspirations beyond this. Once we come out, isn't it just going to make things harder?"

I knew she was right. No one wants to hire someone who may not be around for long. Sure, there are laws that prevent discrimination for health reasons, but I knew those wouldn't protect me from a quick Google search that would reveal my diagnosis to future prospective employers. I was truly torn. I was already in an incredibly hard situation, fighting for my life. If I was lucky enough to have more life ahead, did it make sense to make things even harder by putting a scarlet *C* on my chest?

A few mornings later, President Obama stopped into the morning senior staff meeting. It was the first time we had all met with him since the shutdown.

"At any given time something is going to go wrong somewhere. It is inevitable and not always avoidable," he said. "You can't always stop it from happening. So you have to be prepared to react. Then you have to get on top of it as quickly as you can and you have to stay on top of it."

As I sat there listening to him, it felt like he was talking directly to me. I had not lived my life and made it to this moment by constantly worrying about what could go wrong. And when the rug had been pulled out from under me and I became a cancer patient fighting for my life, I didn't let the fear paralyze me.

I knew that if I let the cancer prevent me from doing my work, then I was letting it take control. If I have learned anything about fighting for what you believe in, it's that when things get tough, you don't turn around or get out of the way; you bear down and charge ahead full force.

Sitting there in the Roosevelt Room, I knew that sharing my battle against cancer with the world would probably compromise my ability to get certain jobs after the administration, and unfortunately that did later prove true in a number of situations. But we consciously and knowingly made the decision to come out, and if I could help even just one person get access to health care, it was a risk I was willing to take.

Nineteen days before the deadline to sign up for coverage, my blog went live on the White House website. "It Shouldn't Have Happened to Me, but It Did," we titled it. President Obama tweeted it and it was retweeted hundreds of times. A few press interviews followed. Family, friends, people I hadn't seen in ages and some I didn't even know emailed and sent tweets and Facebook messages. That was it. It was out.

Survival—for Obamacare and for me—is an exercise in repeatedly being pushed down harder than you ever imagined possible and having to scrounge up every ounce of energy with every fiber of your body to stand up and fight again.

To date, there have been over seventy attempts to kill Obamacare. Despite these repeated attempts, the law is surviving. After repeated recurrences of colorectal cancer in my lungs, about a dozen surgeries, three rounds of radiation, two clinical trials, over forty rounds of chemo, and by the grace of God, I am able to fight on, too.

Since then, many other cancer fighters have reached out to me after reading my blog post. They've told me about the impact it had on them as they faced their fights, and that reminds me of why I did it. I will never know if sharing my story helped someone obtain coverage and if having that coverage improved their life, but I know that Obamacare has made a huge difference in the lives of millions of families—and that is what matters to me.

There is no easy remedy in the fight for my life, but as long as I am able I will continue to fight on. Every challenge I work through brings us closer to the next frontier in finding a cure for me and the millions like me. After all, that kind of change—the real lasting kind, which only comes after sticking with the fight through challenge after challenge—is why I went into public service in the first place. And when it does happen, it's a big f'ing deal.

ALASKA

Raina Thiele

t's always a big deal to bring home a special person in your life. I've brought home my fair share of friends and significant others to experience the grandeur of my home state of Alaska. But my favorite visit, and the most anxiety inducing, was bringing home the President of the United States of America.

My state has seen its fair share of presidential visits, but typically these are quick refueling stops at a military base en route to or from the Far East. This trip was different. In fall 2015, President Obama spent three whole days in Alaska. He was the first sitting president to visit our rural tribal communities and the first sitting president to travel above the Arctic Circle. His visit left an indelible mark on Alaskans and a lasting impact at the policy level, including the renaming of America's highest peak from Mt. McKinley to its indigenous name: Denali.

I was born and raised in Alaska. My family has lived in the state for thousands of years. My ancestors, the Dena'ina Athabascan and the Yup'ik, took a punishing subarctic environment and made it home. They built strong communities founded in connection: to earth, to each other, and to the water. That connectedness is found in all parts of Alaska, urban and rural, Native and non-Native, north and south.

I was raised to rely on the land to sustain my body, mind, and spirit. Our diet was dictated by the bounty of the seasons. Spring brought a swarm of small fish called hooligan, the summer brought several species of salmon, the fall brought wild berries and moose grown fat from a summer spent dining on willow bark, and winter brought ice fishing and snow-colored ptarmigan. The land has always provided a reliable feast. I grew up wandering the woods of Alexander Creek, Lake Iliamna, and Bristol Bay, rural regions only accessible by plane, boat, or snowmobile. When my siblings and I didn't want to head home to eat, we used the land as our snack bar. We ate the sweet, soft inner ends of grass; we peeled and ate fireweed stock; and we nibbled on highbush cranberries and rose hips. Alaska's animals and plants have sustained the life of my people for millennia.

When I first learned that a presidential visit to Alaska was under consideration, I couldn't contain my excitement. As President Obama's liaison to tribes and tribal people, I'd first pitched an Alaska visit to the President's scheduling team the year before, but it hadn't caught on. By 2015, however, the White House was paying close attention to climate change and its outsized impact on the Arctic and Subarctic. The United States was chairing the international body known as the Arctic Council, and in recognition of this leadership role, the President had appointed a special representative for the Arctic at the State Department and created the White House Arctic Executive Steering Committee to coordinate government-wide policy. The work was high profile and during the two years of the U.S. chairmanship, the Arctic and climate change had a spotlight like never before.

Despite this focus on the Arctic—and the fact that Alaska is what makes America an Arctic nation—a visit seemed unlikely. A presidential visit has to meet three criteria to make the cut: first, there has to be a relevant policy or political reason for the trip; second, the trip has to align geographically with existing trips or commitments; and third, the destination has to have a favorable logistical and security environment. At that time, Alaska met only the first of those three criteria. As you can imagine, Alaska was not geographically convenient to other existing trips or commitments, and with its limited infrastructure there aren't many places where you can land Air Force One. However, in the true spirit of the Obama administration, the unlikely wasn't the impossible and the Alaska trip made it onto his schedule. Despite some staff concerns about distance, length of the trip, and, well, just about everything, the President himself ultimately pushed it over the goal line. I believe the thought of Alaska's wild, sprawling, open landscapes appealed to him, perhaps as a brief escape from his highly controlled environment within the White House. I also like to think that my conversations with him about my home state painted a picture he wanted to see for himself.

In the lead-up to President Obama's visit, there were some White House staff who were concerned about how a "red state" like Alaska would react. I wasn't worried. I assured them that Alaskans would treat his visit with the welcoming arms that define the people of my state. We are proud of our home and love to show it off. When anyone, and especially the President of the United States, cares enough to visit us we're going to show him an engaged and lively welcome, regardless of political leanings.

I feel more engaged and surrounded by kindness in Alaska than I do anywhere else in the world—even when in the presence of strangers. I was once back in Alaska from DC for the holidays and I was standing in line at the grocery store in Wasilla. I think I had my headphones in when the person in front of me started talking to me.

Somewhat annoyed and rushed, I took out an earbud to find out what she had to say. "Here," she said, handing me a hand-cut coupon. "I noticed that you have apples. I have an extra coupon for that." I immediately felt guilty. I'd forgotten for a moment that I was home and it's different here than in DC. It was a reminder that I needed to respect that and pay attention.

That easygoing hospitality takes special form in Alaska's indigenous, "Native" communities. A few days before President Obama arrived, I landed in Kotzebue—a largely Native community—and met up with the President's advance team. Despite the fact that Kotzebue is a community 556 miles north of my family's home region in Bristol Bay, I recognized their version of hospitality immediately. Our Native cultural values are deeply rooted in sharing, community, and taking care of others. When someone arrives at your home, you feed them and ensure that they are put first. In Kotzebue, we were welcomed like family and celebrated with potlucks, traditional dances, meals, and boat rides.

While our reception was warm, the weather was not. When I arrived, the winds were whipping, the rain was coming down, and the temperature was hovering around freezing. As we walked the road that runs along Kotzebue Sound, the seawall built to protect it was being pummeled by waves; near-freezing seawater was crashing over the wall and down onto the very street where the President was scheduled to do his featured interview for the press. I was horrified. The President doesn't like the cold. Despite having lived much of his adult life in Chicago, I think he still prefers the warmth of the Hawaiian sun. The logistics team was worried, too. They had been in Kotzebue for a couple of weeks and the rains and winds hadn't let up once.

But Kotzebue's city mayor and tribal leadership knew everything would work out. They were determined that, rain or shine, the President of the United States was going to visit Kotzebue, Alaska. I asked an advance staffer, Is there a backup? Not really.

"But," she said, "it'll be okay. John already took care of it."

"Who?" I asked.

"John," she said, referring to one of the community's traditional spiritualists. "He did a ceremony to clear up the weather for tomorrow. We're good."

She was dead serious. This young woman from New England who'd been in Kotzebue for a week and a half already felt a sense of connection to the people so strong that she had begun to see the world through a different lens, a Native lens. That was a powerful moment for me. To see people, who had been all over the world with President Obama, fall in love with our Native people, our values, and our way of life. And her experience there wasn't unique. Every staffer I spoke with later said that their visit to Kotzebue was the best and most unique trip they had ever done. It reminded me of the incredible gifts my Native people have to give the world if others take the time to listen and experience. The people who have occupied Alaska's lands for thousands of years may not always be wealthy in financial resources, but they are rich in knowledge, authenticity, and love. Our cultures derive strength directly from the wisdom and spirit of our ancestors. Our stories, hospitality, calm, and humor can disarm the toughest veneer and inspire some of the strongest human connections.

This story is also a testament to the kinds of people President Obama hired to work in his administration. President Obama chose individuals with deep empathy, and diverse upbringings that brought unique perspectives into his White House. I was one of these atypical staffers. Someone from my upbringing and background doesn't usually get the opportunity to work within the walls of the White House. I'm Alaska Native and was raised in an economically disadvantaged household. However, I grew up with wonderfully loving parents and with a nurturing community of close family and friends.

My family moved every three years or so. When friends and colleagues ask me why my family moved so often, I jokingly respond that my parents were driven by the nomadic instincts passed down from our hunter-gatherer ancestors. We grew up breezing in and out of rural and "urban" communities throughout south central and southwest Alaska. "Alaska urban" would likely be considered rural almost anywhere else in America.

From a young age, I knew we were different from the "Americans" I saw on television. When I was in kindergarten and first grade living in Alexander Creek, my father's home village, we commuted to school via snowmobile on a frozen river in the winter and via airboat when the river ice began to melt, shift, and flow. We spent summers in my mother's home village of Pedro Bay on Lake Iliamna, about an hour and a half flight by small plane from Anchorage. There, we would spend our days setting a fishing net, filleting our catch, and hanging and drying the fish in a smokehouse to preserve it for the winter months, just as my ancestors had for millennia. We'd also venture out onto the tundra and into the mountains to gather wild blueberries, blackberries, cranberries, and salmonberries. My mother would then process our harvest and turn it into *nivugi* (Indian/Eskimo ice cream), consisting of berries mixed with animal fat—or more often Crisco in modern times—and sometimes the shredded flesh of whitefish.

My parents, though very smart, reflective, and intuitive, didn't have the opportunity to attend college. However, their educational accomplishments—high school diplomas and the associate's degree my mother earned later in life—greatly exceeded those of their parents. All three of my Alaska Native grandparents (my paternal grandmother is non-Native) were provided only a few years of elementary school, if that. My mother's parents passed away without ever having learned to read or write. On reflection this is mind-boggling, but growing up it seemed perfectly normal when my grandparents handed me a card they'd received in the mail and asked me to read the loving inscription from a grandchild or niece. I now recognize how hard it must have been for them to integrate into the American economy and American society without the ability to read a utility bill or newspaper, open a bank account, or write a check on their own.

Despite the rocky and inhospitable road my grandparents and parents navigated into an increasingly westernized world, they encouraged me to dream big. So I did. I dreamed of visiting far-off places and being the first female president. In second grade, my mother asked me where I wanted to go to college. She always pushed us to go even though no one in our family ever had. I told her that I wanted to go to Harvard or Yale. She was shocked. She wasn't even sure where I'd heard the names of those schools. We had certainly never met anyone who'd gone to an Ivy League school. But nonetheless, my parents were supportive and I would ultimately earn degrees from both.

It helped that I grew up at the dawn of a new technological era. When I was in high school my family installed dial-up internet, which allowed young people like me, without access to much information or resources, to expand our horizons beyond our small, rural communities. Each day after school, I'd hop on the clunky HP desktop computer we had at home, fire up AOL, and listen to the buzz and static of the slow but reliable portal opening to show me the world.

Sadly, in the seventeen years since I left Alaska for Yale and Harvard, the connection speed in rural Alaska hasn't improved much and many still struggle to get online at all. In fact, even the President's staff had to struggle with the lack of reliable internet in rural Alaska.

Throughout the trip, I attempted to engage with colleagues—both in Alaska and back at the White House—on a spotty and often nonexistent internet connection in Dillingham and Kotzebue, the two Native communities we visited. At one stressful point in Dillingham, I was attempting to simultaneously submit edits to the President's speech, finalize the list of individuals who would meet him in Anchorage, and determine a seating plan for participants in his meeting with tribal leaders. These were all quick-turnaround tasks and I was short an internet connection. Thankfully, I had a little satellite router device that the White House advance team uses in no-connection areas, typically internationally.

Rural Alaskans are not afforded such conveniences and are being left behind. This is not a new trend. In fact, many rural Alaskans struggle to access what most Americans would take for granted as modern essentials, like running water, indoor plumbing, and affordable food. And in a world where internet connectivity has become an integral part of communication and commerce, rural Alaska is once again losing out. It's especially tragic and unfair to young people struggling to access the information and resources they need to learn how to apply to college and secure scholarships.

This disparity in access exists across Native America, on reservations, pueblos, rancherias, and in villages. It aggravates an already marginalized modern existence brought about by Western colonization. This legacy still has repercussions today in the form of racial tensions and stereotypes, something I knew from an early age. As a child, I remember hearing comments that seemed harmless—"Raina is good at art because she's Native"—but I also remember young boys at parties making offensive remarks about "drunk Natives" and doing insulting impressions of Native people.

In the fifth grade, our teachers placed the students in one of three math classes. I was always a top student and my performance in math up until that point had been flawless. However, the teachers placed me in the middle-track math class while my white friends were placed in the higher-level course. I was confused but didn't mind. However, I could tell my mother and father were upset—not with me, but with the system. It wasn't until later that year that I realized that none of the high-achieving Native students had been placed in higher-level courses.

The history of prejudice in Alaska has impacted generations of Native people in my state, many of whom struggled for a seat at the decision-making table only to be met with disdain or indifference. This is changing slowly due to the activism of generations of Alaska Native leaders who have fought to maintain their right to self-determination in the land they've called home for thousands of years. This effort was given an unexpected and useful boost during the President's visit when he agreed to host his only roundtable discussion in Alaska with Native leaders. I had the honor of personally overseeing planning of this meeting and I knew then that it signaled something powerful to all Alaskans: that Native people cannot be ignored. They have value and political power, not just in the state but at our nation's highest levels.

As I watched and listened to the roundtable discussion that day, I heard Native leaders give voice to the issues that were most important to their communities: subsistence harvest, protecting the environment, the federal trust responsibility to Alaska tribes, economic development, and cultural preservation. The President listened intently, jotted down a few notes, then, at the end, responded to every comment. His responses weren't scripted; they were thoughtful, and every word he spoke conveyed his understanding of the nationhood of tribes and the trust responsibility held by the federal government. It was a true government-to-government conversation that occurred in our own homeland. A first in our history.

This was not the only barrier-breaking moment of the trip. On the third day, I got to witness the President getting to know firsthand the rich cultures of Alaska Native communities. On that day, I woke up early, hustled outside, hopped into the staff car in the President's motorcade to the military base, and boarded Air Force One for the first time. You can imagine my excitement. Here I was, a homegrown Alaskan girl raised in the woods, and I was flying with the President to one of the communities in my ancestors' homeland. I felt like the past was coming to greet us in the present and that this visit would help lead Alaska to a greater future: one filled with renewed hope, prosperity, and equality.

After landing in Dillingham, we boarded the motorcade while a heavy, chilly rain fell overhead. En route to Dillingham Elementary School, we stopped at Kanakanak Beach. There, elders and community members were waiting for President Obama with gloved hands to show him a preset demonstration of "fish cutting," the ancient and traditional method of filleting the fish you catch in your fishing net. As President Obama visited with the elders, he was shown a salmon that had been freshly removed from the net. "Where are my gloves?" he asked as he stood at the ocean shore. There was a bit of a surprised shuffle at that moment. No one had expected him to want to touch the fish. Thankfully an elderly woman handed the President a pair of gloves and he proudly showed off the fresh catch.

The President next went to the fish-cutting table, where an elderly woman showed him what the fish looked like once it was cut. But when President Obama noticed a whole salmon sitting on the table, he looked over at the nearest Secret Service agent and asked emphatically, "Where's my knife? I've gotta cut up my fish." The Secret

Service agent stared back blankly for a moment, then slowly shifted his gaze, then his entire body, away. What the President didn't know—or playfully chose to ignore—was that Secret Service wouldn't let him or anyone near him wield a knife. "Really, guys?" he asked, playfully but genuinely disappointed.

In retrospect, I realize that at this point—seven years into his presidency—Barack Obama was feeling the limitations to his personal freedom. During his trip to Alaska, he was like a kid in a candy store and loving every moment interacting with Native elders and community members in this wild and new environment. On that day, there was a light shining from within him that lit up rural Alaska. I felt an overwhelming pride for my Bristol Bay relatives and the Native communities where my ancestors had fished and hunted for thousands of years. I also felt great pride for the President himself. On a policy level, he had taken steps to shield the region from mining and offshore drilling. And on this day, I got to see him experience, with joy, the ecosystem and Native way of life he was protecting.

Salmon is one of the most important aspects of the Bristol Bay region and identity. It's in our blood and the blood of our ancestors. My father was, and still is, a commercial fisherman, just like his father and my mother's father. Salmon doesn't just sustain Bristol Bay's residents as a food source, it also sustains the region economically. Bristol Bay is home to the world's largest remaining wild sockeye salmon run, a sustainably managed fishery that had a record run in 2017 with sixty million salmon returning from the ocean to their spawning grounds deep in the rivers, ponds, and tributaries of the Bristol Bay watershed.

If you're from Bristol Bay, your relationship with salmon starts young. The first time I went on a commercial fishing boat with my father I was probably seven or eight years old. At the time, he was fishing in Naknek, a small fishing town on the east side of Bristol Bay, while the rest of my family and I were spending the summer set-net fishing (the practice of running a cork-floated swath of fish net into the ocean from a beach) on the west side of the bay. My dad had flown his small four-seater Cessna airplane—with no roads it's a necessity rather than a luxury for rural Alaskans—over to see us during a "closing," or cessation in fishing, and he let me fly back with him to Naknek to visit. He'd planned to fly me back to the west side later that day, but we were caught by surprise when the Department of Fish and Game reopened the fishery unexpectedly. A serious and somber expression came over my dad's face when he heard the radio announcement. "I have to go fishing," he said gravely. He was concerned about having to take me with him, but I was over the moon—I'd finally get to go fishing with my dad! Even better, our first stop was the convenience store, where my dad, feeling bad that he was dragging me out onto a commercial fishing boat in rough seas, let me pick out a large box full of candy and beef jerky for our journey.

Little did I know, that day was the beginning of the end of my commercial fishing fantasy. Once we got the boat out of the Naknek River, where it was nice and calm, we started rocking and rolling over ten-foot swells. My dream trip quickly turned into a nightmare of vomiting and bemoaning my own existence. I was zero help to my dad fishing. After I'd been sick for about eight hours straight, night fell and my dad—knowing full well I couldn't sleep in the cabin—made me a little bed on the deck. As I stared up at the pitch-black skies and the brilliant stars that night, I imagined I was being rocked in a crib and fell asleep. The next day, the seas had calmed; however, I had lost my desire to be a commercial fisherwoman. Of all my siblings, it's only my dad's youngest daughter, Sara (or "Baby" as we call her), who fell in love with fishing. She started at a young age, around ten, and immediately took to it. Seventeen years later, she still returns to my dad's boat every summer to fish. Like many from Bristol Bay, she finds a kind of Zen out on those beautiful but temperamental waters.

After the President finished his own fishing adventure (sans knife) on Kanakanak Beach, we headed to the local Dillingham school. A few days prior, the advance staff had downsized the event from a large, youth-oriented session to something smaller and more adult oriented. I pushed back, but it's hard to push back against the tough negotiators who make up the President's advance team. But in stepped a local leader named Robin. The culture in Bristol Bay is tough, no-nonsense, and a little rough-and-tumble. Robin is the epitome of this culture. He isn't afraid to fight for something that's important. When it became clear to Robin that the President wasn't slated to interact with the youth of Dillingham, he told the staff lead directly, "Listen, if he's not going to interact with the kids, he might as well not come." I think it was probably the first time the advance team had heard such sharp pushback from a community leader.

It worked. A few hours after Robin's ultimatum, a message popped up in the in-boxes of all of the White House staff on the ground. "We're going to switch the location back and re-incorporate the youth portion of the agenda." Needless to say, Robin and I and the rest of Dillingham were thrilled. For me, this story is a reminder of the strength of people from Bristol Bay. They are both fiercely loving and fiercely uncompromising. Even in the face of a visit from the President of the United States they weren't willing to compromise on what they valued: their youth.

And I'm glad they didn't compromise. I had a going bet with White House colleagues about what the photo of the day would be from the President's visit to Dillingham. The communications staff thought it would be the beach visit with the salmon. I thought it would be the youth dance event. And I was right.

Although the traditional Yup'ik dances of the region have largely been snuffed out by the effects of colonialism, Dillingham has a youth dance group that is working to revive them. This group was slated to dance for and with the President, and sure enough, the photos and video of President Obama dancing with little Yup'ik children dressed in brightly colored *kuspuks* and traditional headdresses captured the day and the hearts of Americans. I know the President was a little hesitant about that portion of the program, having never seen or performed a Yup'ik dance before. However, Barack Obama will do just about anything for young people and kids.

Watching the President take direction from a little girl wearing a bright pink *kuspuk* while she gave him encouraging smiles was a beautiful and powerful moment. It was a moment that pushed back against a century of government-led acculturation and assimilation efforts. That moment held significance not just for Dillingham, Alaska, but for communities all across the state and for indigenous communities across the country. It wasn't just because the President of the United States visited a small tribal community, but because he valued their traditional practices and art forms and decided to highlight them for all of the world.

This was leadership that I recognized: not from Washington, but from my own community.

My maternal grandfather, Gus Jensen, was one of the last traditional leaders of Pedro Bay Native Village on Lake Iliamna. Unlike in Western systems of leadership, an individual there wasn't recognized as a leader simply by assuming a certain title. Leadership was a way of living your daily life. My grandfather was recognized as a leader not because he pronounced himself as one, but because he cared for others. He ensured that every person had a voice and that everyone had what they needed to survive in times of want. Barack Obama was that kind of leader.

I sometimes imagine what would happen if all of our national political leaders did more of this. If leaders earned their roles by caring for others and listening to the voices of people who aren't often heard. I wonder, especially in today's political environment in which so many feel forgotten or ignored, if our country would look different.

A CALL TO ACTION

Lynn Rosenthal

As my car chugged up the mountain road in northern New Mexico, I strained to hear the radio through the static. It was January 20, 2009, and a new president and vice president were being sworn in. As a child of Watergate and the Vietnam War, I had learned to be skeptical of politicians and cynical about the role of government in people's lives. On this day, though, I felt excited for our nation's future. Barack Obama and Joe Biden were the leaders we had all been waiting for, and I was proud of my country.

Like thousands of others, I had volunteered for the campaign. Clipboard in hand, I trudged down back roads and city streets and through fancy new subdivisions. I met hundreds of people, but one man stood out. A few days before the election, I turned down a rutted dirt road, outside Albuquerque, lined with small houses and trailers. At that point in the campaign, most registered voters had been visited many times, as evidenced by discarded campaign paraphernalia and the weariness of residents when they answered the door. But not on this street. There were no door hangers or flyers or yard signs; no evidence that a presidential election was just days away.

When I knocked on the door of a small trailer, I could hear

someone struggling to stand and make his way to open the door. Before me stood a young man, but with a face aged by daily pain. Dragging a walker, he said he hoped this knock was someone from one of the campaigns. He rarely left his home, he said. He had been praying someone would come by and tell him how to get to the polls. He had been waiting, he said. He didn't want to miss the chance to vote for Barack Obama, no matter what it took to get there. As I handed him the voter pamphlet on how to get a ride to the polls, he broke into a big grin.

Every campaign worker had stories like this one. And every campaign worker hoped to be in Washington, DC, for the inauguration. Now Inauguration Day had come, but I was far away from the pomp and circumstance. Instead, I was in a remote area of northern New Mexico on my way to help a small domestic violence shelter stay afloat.

I'd been working for more than a decade to change the way communities dealt with domestic violence and sexual assault, and nothing was more important to me than being on the front lines. Four years earlier, I left a national advocacy job in Washington, DC, first for Florida and then New Mexico, the state of my birth and the place I love more than any other. I became the executive director of the New Mexico Coalition Against Domestic Violence, working to coordinate services around the state.

I was usually satisfied with that decision, but on this day, I wondered why I had taken myself off the beaten path. I wondered why I wasn't in DC, not only for the inauguration but also for all the excitement and progress that would come next. As these thoughts entered my mind, I looked around at the beautiful mountains and thought about the importance of my work in New Mexico. I decided I was right where I belonged and relaxed into my Inauguration Day drive.

For the next few weeks, I threw myself into my work. But then, out of the blue, I received a call from the White House asking me to come to Washington to meet with Vice President Biden. He was interviewing candidates to serve as his special advisor on violence against women. Led by the Vice President, with the full support of President Obama, domestic violence and sexual assault would be at the top of the nation's agenda. This new advisor would coordinate that work across the federal government.

I was surprised to find myself on the short list for this important position, given that I was four years removed from any national advocacy work. I believed others were more qualified, and wondered if I had the skills and experience to do the job. I pondered all this while I sat in the West Wing lobby in my red suit—the one I always wore to special occasions—waiting to be called to the Vice President's Office upstairs. When I went into the meeting, Vice President Biden greeted me warmly and asked what I had been doing since I left Washington. As I talked about my work on domestic violence in Florida and New Mexico, he said my passion for the cause was just what he was looking for. He had asked President Obama to create this position in the Vice President's Office to carry on the work he started in the Senate drafting, and later implementing, the Violence Against Women Act (VAWA). He told me he wanted to hear new ideas, and my recent experience outside of Washington meant that I was in touch with the front lines. He said he was eager to get started.

Within a few short weeks, I was serving as the first-ever White House advisor on violence against women.

*　*　*

At first glance, I was an unlikely person to be serving in the White House. I was not politically well connected. I am not a lawyer or graduate of any prestigious school. I am a feminist activist who once camped out in abortion clinics to keep them from being bombed. I am a social worker who took over a struggling battered women's shelter in 1993 and began to understand experiences of violence in my own life.

In 1994, I came across a report called *A Week in the Life of American Women*, which detailed incidents of violence against women, from severe physical abuse to rape and sexual assault. This stark portrayal, written by Senator Biden's Judiciary Committee staff in 1991, was unlike anything I had read before. In just the one week documented in this report, hundreds of women were beaten by their husbands, raped by boyfriends, assaulted by strangers. In my local shelter, I was seeing bruised and battered women every day. Now this report told the story—one usually hidden away and rarely told in public—on a national level.

With his report in hand, then senator Biden was cajoling his colleagues to support VAWA. No longer could the nation turn its back and pretend we didn't know what was happening. The bill became law on September 13, 1994, bringing funding to states and local communities to coordinate the response to domestic violence and sexual assault. Over the next year, the number of women calling our shelter nearly doubled. By 1995, I was working for the Florida Coalition Against Domestic Violence to implement VAWA. We organized rural outreach projects and legal services for victims, and we mobilized to bring services to all parts of the state. I'll never forget the women we met in rural communities, who told us of driving hours to find a safe place to stay or to have a rape kit exam.

By 2000, I was the executive director of the National Network to End Domestic Violence. I'd been recruited by Donna Edwards (who was later elected to Congress by the voters of Maryland) to come to DC and take her place at the helm of this growing organization.

That's where I first came to know then senator Biden. His understanding of violence against women as an abuse of power resonated with me, and his knowledge of the details of the law amazed me. In 2005, I stood before the Senate Judiciary Committee to share what I had learned about the law in practice, and to encourage them to make it even stronger. Over the next few years I went from Washington to Florida and eventually back to New Mexico. Everywhere I went I continued to do the work, and my admiration for Senator Biden continued to grow.

When I was offered the opportunity to work for Vice President Biden in the White House, it was hard to say no even if it meant leaving my beloved New Mexico and fulfilling work on the front lines. When we met that day in his West Wing office, he talked about progress that had been made since the passage of the law and all the work that remained to be done. He spoke of his vision for bringing about the cultural change that was needed to end violence against women, and the opportunity to use the bully pulpit of the White House to contribute to that cause. That meeting changed my thinking about my next steps in life. Maybe my place really was in Washington after all.

Walking into the White House complex on my first day, I felt a tremendous sense of responsibility. As a grassroots advocate, I knew that fellow advocates were counting on me to make a difference. I knew that survivors were hoping that, through me, they would have a voice at the highest levels of government. I wondered if I would be good enough, if I would make the best use of the institutional power I had never imagined having access to.

In those early days, I was often anxious about my performance. Everyone else seemed so confident, and I was struggling to find my footing. I'd never served in the federal government before, and I

wasn't quite sure how to get things done. Fortunately, I was surrounded by strong colleagues who invited my participation. When
President Obama signed the Tribal Law and Order Act, bringing
new resources to tribes to combat crime on reservations, Jodi Gillette
and Kim Teehee—Native American members of the White House
staff—pushed hard to make sure the legislation reflected the reality
for women, and they brought me in to help with this historic event.
Native American women face among the highest rates of rape and
domestic violence, and tribes have limited court systems and even
fewer resources to address major crimes. This bill attempted to right
some of these wrongs.

Lisa Marie Iyotte, a rape survivor from the Rosebud Indian Reser-
vation in South Dakota, was coming to town to tell her story and introduce President Obama at the bill signing. We arranged for a group
of Native women to meet with Lisa Marie in my office to offer emotional support before her speech, but as the time drew closer, we
learned that she had accidentally arrived at a gate on the other side of
the White House complex. Before we could retrieve her, the Secret
Service called to say that she was being sent around the outside perimeter to another gate on the far side of the building. But once there,
through some misunderstanding, she was sent back around the building to the first gate. On her way to introduce President Obama, she
had now trekked around the White House twice.

There was no time for the important greeting we had planned for
Lisa Marie. I felt terrible as I headed over to the East Wing to meet
her. I ran as fast as I could, weaving my way through the White
House, sweating and waving off the Secret Service as I realized I was
completely lost, having never worked in the East Wing. I finally arrived at the gate, and there was Lisa Marie, in the broiling heat, in full
tribal dress, calm and regal. I felt silly for my panic, having lost sight

of what was most important on this day. We had eight minutes before
the event started, and Jodi took Lisa Marie to the Green Room to
meet President Obama.

As I made my way to the back of the East Room to watch the
event, I was still flustered and breathing hard. Lisa Marie came out on
the stage alone, under the bright lights, and began sobbing quietly.
She couldn't speak. With cameras whirling, we all held our breath.
Then President Obama bounded out on the stage and stood beside
her, his arm around her shoulders. With a deep breath, Lisa Marie
began to talk about the violent rape she had suffered, and the lack of
help that this bill would now address. By then, we were all crying.
Later, Lisa Marie told me what made it possible for her to speak publicly about what happened to her. It was President Obama's presence,
she said. "He got me through it."

That day, Lisa Marie's stunning courage gave me a new perspective on my own work. Her story helped me set aside my own insecuri-
ties and reconnect with my sense of purpose in the White House.

With time, I found ways to make my contributions. It wasn't
always easy, though. From my first day in the White House, I began
to receive calls directly from victims of domestic violence. The stories
were heartbreaking: abusive fathers being awarded custody of children, violent perpetrators being released early from jail, women and
children being threatened with guns. As an advocate, I was used to
jumping into these situations and doing everything I could to find
help. But in the White House, our lawyers advised me that the federal
government could not engage in individual legal cases. It was frustrating to not be able to help directly, but I learned how to leverage federal
policy to make a difference for survivors.

Among the women I heard from were those who were federal employees themselves, or whose partners were, or often both. When

these survivors brought the abuse to a supervisor's attention, they often did not receive the help they needed. Why, I thought, couldn't we require federal agencies to train supervisors and develop policies on how they could help survivors on the job?

Vice President Biden's legal team sprang into action and drafted a presidential memo directing federal agencies to develop policies for addressing domestic violence and sexual assault.

Vice President Biden announced this policy at an event with advocates in the South Court Auditorium in April 2012. As excited as I was, I worried that others in the White House wouldn't appreciate its importance. I thought it might seem like a minor bureaucratic action, rather than an important new policy. But later that day, my phone rang. On the other end of the line was a woman who worked in an obscure office in the basement of the White House. She said we had never met, and probably never would, but she wanted to thank me and Vice President Biden for this workforce order. Years prior, a colleague of hers at another federal agency had been killed by her husband. She hoped that because of these new policies, women like her friend would be saved.

* * *

During my time in the White House, I worked on many efforts, along with amazing colleagues, to improve the national response to violence against women. In response to new data showing the high rates of dating violence and sexual assault experienced by teens and young adults, Vice President Biden reached out to celebrity athletes and actors to get men involved in speaking out about violence against women. David Beckham, Daniel Craig, Benicio del Toro, Steve Carell, and more answered the call and participated in our "1 is 2 Many" PSAs. We started new projects to reduce domestic violence homicides, to reduce the nation's backlog of untested rape kits, and to address the connection between violence and HIV/AIDS among women. After a prolonged fight in Congress, the Violence Against Women Act was reauthorized in 2013, and we—along with national advocacy groups—fought hard to make sure VAWA's long-standing protections for immigrant victims of crime remained intact. VAWA 2013 also brought historic new protections for LGBTQ survivors and further recognized the authority of tribes to prosecute domestic violence crimes.

These efforts required long days and sometimes longer nights, and there were usually two commonalities in the work we did: the stories of survivors framed our thinking, and activists held us accountable for making change.

One night after a long day in 2013, I was mindlessly scrolling through Facebook when I saw an announcement of a demonstration on sexual assault. Always drawn to activism, I clicked on the link. What I found shocked me: the demonstration was against the Obama administration for our lack of response to sexual assault on college campuses. But wait, I thought, don't they know that several years ago, we sent schools guidance about their responsibilities under federal civil rights law to respond to and prevent sexual assault? They didn't. They didn't know about all the work we were doing behind the scenes to make things better, so much of it subject to slow processes and legal review. Most of all, they couldn't have known how personally I would take this demonstration.

I've always been an activist. Demonstrating and marching is in my blood. My mother took me out marching for Eugene McCarthy when I was ten, because he was the antiwar candidate. In my twenties, I was often on the protest line, demonstrating against the nuclear weapons buildup at Cape Canaveral and marching for abortion rights and against U.S. involvement in Central America. I'd been to big rallies and national marches for LGBTQ rights, for women's rights, for peace. I'd put in my time on the barricades, and I never envisioned being on the other side as a government official. As I thought about the upcoming demonstration, I felt a sense of personal failure, like the work we were steadily engaged in was not real. I was embarrassed. When I conferred with Valerie Jarrett and Tina Tchen, who were leading the White House Council on Women and Girls, Valerie said, "Let's invite them in to talk."

The demonstration took place on a blistering hot day in July. The students delivered boxes of petitions to the officials at the Department of Education, and with a bullhorn told stories of sexual assaults they had experienced. Their courage was breathtaking and I watched the streaming video in awe. Tina and I reached out to the group and invited them to come see us in the White House later that day. As luck would have it, I had incorrectly entered several names in the security screening database, and the group's entry into the building was delayed. I knew these young activists were standing outside in the July heat, and I knew the delay must have felt like a personal insult. The meeting started nearly an hour late, and I wondered what else would go wrong.

As it turned out, it was one of the most important meetings I attended during my time in the White House. There were tense moments, with students commending us for our efforts, but calling for stronger enforcement and greater transparency about the status of school investigations. They told their own stories: of university administrators who questioned whether they had been sexually assaulted, of disclosing to school officials who refused to provide even basic help, of being told to leave campus themselves. They talked about how the guidance we had issued gave them a blueprint to file complaints, but also how slowly these investigations moved and how difficult it was to get information about complaints against their schools. As it turned out, they *were* aware of what we were doing; it just wasn't enough.

The students were articulate and compelling, and they linked their personal stories with the need for specific changes in federal policies. As I listened, my defensiveness faded away. I knew that we had the same goals, and that we needed this outside pressure to keep moving forward. I admired their strength and their passion. Some months later, I saw a picture of the group taken on that day in the White House, and it brought tears to my eyes. They looked so strong and so hopeful, and I wondered how they would remember that day years into the future.

Because of their efforts, our work accelerated, and the idea for the White House Task Force to Protect Students from Sexual Assault was born. Just a few months later, Vice President Biden and the White House Council on Women and Girls released a first-of-its-kind report called *Rape and Sexual Assault: A Renewed Call to Action*. I worked on this report for months, through all hours of the night, combing through data about the impact of sexual assault. I read about the effects of trauma on the brain and immune system. I read about low reporting rates and poor law enforcement response. I learned about the additional barriers women of color face in getting help, and the disproportionate rates of sexual assault experienced by LGBTQ people. I reflected on the meetings we held with sexual assault survivors, who felt their stories were not being heard.

In January 2014, I stood in the East Room listening as President Obama gave the first-ever speech on sexual violence by a sitting president. One of the young women who wrote for the President worked hard to get it exactly right and I knew what the President was going to say. I knew he would say to survivors, "You are not alone, I've got your back." I knew he would announce the White House Task Force to Protect Students from Sexual Assault. I knew he would issue a call to action for federal agencies to step up their work to prevent sexual violence. I knew that Vice President Biden would assure survivors—as he always does—that it's not their fault.

As much as I knew, I wasn't prepared for how I felt. As I listened to the President and Vice President, I took a deep breath and let myself remember.

I remember some details with startling clarity and others not at all. I remember my clothes: yellow shorts, green T-shirt one day; white shirt, blue pants the next. I was fifteen when I was sexually assaulted several times by a family friend, an older teenager. The attacks happened at neighborhood parties and in my home. I remember how, each time, he violently threw me down and tore at my clothes, forcefully shoving his hands down my pants and up my shirt, trying to rape me. I don't remember his face during the attacks or what he said.

The first time, with friends and family nearby, I was too stunned to yell for help, thinking I must have done something to bring it on. I felt what every survivor feels: the sudden shock, the pounding heart, the sense of unreality. After that, I did everything possible to stay away from him, but because he was a close family friend I was not successful. Each time, he escalated the violence. I physically fought to get away and to stop him from hurting me. Each attack seemed to happen in slow motion and ended only because he was distracted by a ringing phone, a door opening, people walking nearby.

Finally, I mustered up the courage to tell my parents what was happening, but I couldn't bring myself to say just how violent these attacks had been. Somehow, I was the one who felt ashamed. I said only that he had touched me inappropriately. When confronted by a family member, this young man said that I had an overactive imagination. The violence stopped after that, but his attempts to corner me alone did not, and my fear and anxiety never have.

Far from remarkable, my story is all too common. And while it happened a long time ago, it was this experience as a teenager that most affected my sense of bodily autonomy and safety in the world. Four decades later, it was my fifteen-year-old self who heard the words of President Obama and Vice President Biden. You are not alone. It's not your fault. This is a call to action.

It's my great hope that, because of these words, fewer girls and women will suffer as I did.

Over nearly six years, I worked on many initiatives to improve the national response to violence against women. Most of this work happened without fanfare or public attention, but that didn't make it any less important. Like thousands of other actions big and small in the Obama administration, we hoped that this behind-the-scenes policy work would help improve people's lives and make communities safer.

When I started at the White House, I often dealt with my anxieties by imagining all the courageous survivors and tough advocates walking through the gates with me each day. Even as I got stronger and braver myself, I never stopped thinking about them. But this wasn't just personal. President Obama and Vice President Biden always challenged us to remember the stories that shaped our policies. The stories I heard—the countless letters and emails from survivors, Lisa Marie Iyotte, the student protesters, and so many more—helped change our national conversation around sexual violence. Under the bright lights of the East Room of the White House, I felt the power of all our stories, together.

In 2017, in an unprecedented act of national storytelling, thousands of women shared their own experiences of sexual harassment and assault, including some by the current occupant of the White House. For every woman who has come forward as part of #MeToo, and for all those who are not safe to tell their stories, I repeat the words of President Obama and Vice President Biden. You are not alone. It's not your fault. This is a call to action.

BEHIND THE MAHOGANY DOORS

Bill Yosses

I n 2006, I was asked to present a sampling of my desserts in a small room on the first floor of the White House known as the Old Family Dining Room. Here, the First Families, dating back to John Quincy Adams, took their meals until Mrs. Kennedy moved family dining upstairs in 1961. I was there interviewing for the job of White House pastry chef, one of the many behind-the-scenes roles that help keep the White House running, regardless of its current resident.

It was four o'clock on a Friday and First Lady Laura Bush's staff was invited. Knowing my guests would be ravenous at the end of the workweek, I served some desserts I knew would be crowd-pleasers: small canapés and petits fours, a double chocolate cookie, and several fruit panna cottas. The young and eager staff devoured everything in seconds. Luckily, both Bush daughters attended as well, bringing their energy and enthusiasm to the event. After both of them snuck me an encouraging thumbs-up, I felt even more awed by the experience. I owe all those hungry young people a debt of gratitude: the next day I was hired.

That day, I walked through those double doors leading into the Old Family Dining Room for the first of so many times. I couldn't help but marvel at the luster of their magnificent mahogany, polished to such a gloss you can faintly pick up your own reflection. I felt intuitively that walking through those grand doors every day into the beauty and glamour of the residence would bring me a sense of delight and gratification that time couldn't dull any more than it had the shine of those doors.

However, I quickly realized that my day-to-day experience would be far less glamorous. The White House pastry kitchen is *tiny*, a former dishwashing room that was converted in the 1990s into a kitchen. It was a good thing I started my culinary career in New York, where kitchens were so small that the pastry "kitchen" was often an aluminum sheet pan placed over a trash bin. Nonetheless, I grew to love my presidential kitchen, small as it was, and as a lover of history, I relished the opportunity to work in a place where so much history is made. Despite having worked my way up through some of the country's most storied eating establishments—like Michelin-starred Bouley and Central Park's Tavern on the Green—Pennsylvania Avenue was so far from where I expected to end up practicing my craft. But that only made it all the more extraordinary.

I also thoroughly enjoyed my new clients. I found President Bush to be a genuine, natural, easygoing man with a keen sense of humor. Once, while snacking backstage after a White House performance, B. B. King remarked to me, "Everyone who sits and has a conversation with that guy comes away liking him." He and Mrs. Bush are the kind of southerners who give the phrase "southern hospitality" its true meaning.

It helped solidify my relationship with President Bush that he never met a dessert he didn't like. My seven-layer chocolate cake was one of his perennial favorites. "Do I get ice cream with that?" he asked every time. I did make one misstep in those early weeks, though. After hearing that the President was making an effort to lose weight, I made an apple salad for dessert with minimal sugar: Seasonal Apples with Crushed Almonds and Honeyed Yogurt. It was later reported to me that on hearing what was for dessert that evening he quipped, "Apple salad is *not* a dessert. It's a salad!" After that, I stuck to the classics, like the peach pie he loved. Most of the desserts I made—whether folksy cobblers or grand sweet monuments—were well received, and my time working with them was a very happy one.

Part of the duty of a White House chef is to try to make the hardest job in the world a little more comfortable. The right slice of pie or piece of cake, served with a scoop of homemade ice cream, can sometimes do that. There are no words to explain the satisfaction I felt to see the leader of the free world find some pleasure and relief—even if just one little moment—as he tucked into a homemade dessert of my creation.

But there is an essential distinction between the White House residence staff and the rest of the President's staff: the residence staff always remains apolitical. It is an essential part of our culture, a point of pride to the extent of occasionally feeling like a religion. I worked with over one hundred employees there, and I honestly still don't know the party affiliation of most of them. In the military, you respect the chain of command whether you agree with the decision or not; it was the same for us at the White House. We took pride in giving our professional very best at every moment, no matter who we voted for. After all, you wouldn't disrespect someone in their own home, and when you serve food to the President, you are in the man's house!

* * *

Our apolitical presence also means that unlike most staff, we don't leave with the outgoing president. That means we're there to witness firsthand one of the hallmarks of our democracy: the peaceful change-over from one president to the next, and sometimes from one party to the other. On January 19, we worked with buildings full of people whose every waking moment was devoted to President Bush. On January 20, 2009, those buildings emptied out and new people were walking in, many looking for their desks for the first time.

As the residence staff, our job was to make the "principals"—the First Family—comfortable, and do the best for their team, friends, and family. But in order to do so, we had to build trust—and get over the initial awkwardness of having dutifully and proudly served the opposition party's leader. Never was that apolitical approach to the job more crucial; it had to be conveyed in every deed. We wanted to make our experience and expertise useful to the incoming Obama staffers in whatever way we could, even if just in gestures as small as helping lost newcomers find the bathrooms. There was certainly some distance in the first few weeks between the Obama appointees and the residence staff. Though we liked to keep the White House running like a well-oiled machine, we knew flexibility was key—we could never say, "We used to do it like this!" But over time, as we worked together on complex events like state dinners and the Easter Egg Roll, any lingering mistrust evaporated. We had a lot of work to do and no time to waste on needless drama.

My first meeting with President Obama and the First Lady took place in the East Room of the White House during a meet and greet for the residence staff. The Obamas had moved in several days earlier, but the first few days were so busy there was no time to pause for a formal greeting. So once the furniture, dishes, and clothes had been put away, the First Lady came around to say hello and speak with each of the ninety-six residence staff members one by one. I recall her saying how much the President loved the apple, pecan, and huckleberry pies the pastry team had sent to their quarters on the second floor. I had a terrific sous-chef, Susie Morrison, and we were so excited to impress our new bosses that we went overboard trying to make sure each pie was perfect—freshly baked and served just cooled enough to stand on its own. We aimed for a balance of natural fruit flavor with minimum sweetness, often adding orange or lemon zest to give the pie a little more layered flavor. As the President and First Lady moved separately around the room talking to everyone, I was brimming with pride and couldn't wait to hear the compliments I was sure were coming our way.

But when he got to me and Susie, President Obama wasted no time on empty praise. Instead he instructed us, "Stop making so many pies! If I keep eating pies I'll start to look like Taft." I'd been yelled at by plenty of bosses, but now I was getting scolded by the President; we all laughed, but it was also a no-nonsense moment. It was clear from the start that this was a man who wasted no time on stilted greetings and who, we soon learned, abhors flattery. The quickest way to be ignored by Barack Obama is to give an offhand compliment.

This was also our first hint that this First Family was focused on healthy eating. One day, Mrs. Obama called a meeting of the chefs and spoke about the difficulty of ensuring that her daughters ate healthy meals during the campaign and now in the White House. She asked for our help as chefs in making healthier food a priority not just in her home, but throughout the country—to help her implement a program that advanced the cause of eating better on a national scale. That program was to be called "Let's Move!"

You may think a conversation about healthy food would have a pastry chef worried about job security. On the contrary. I was thrilled to hear that this would be the national agenda of the First Lady's Office. For years, I had been involved with advocates for sustainability and healthful eating such as Dan Barber and Michel Nischan. In fact, most chefs try to cook responsibly, knowing that many ingredients such as fats, salt, and sugar can be harmful in excess. And no good chef uses processed ingredients or preservatives if it can be avoided. There's no reason healthy eating can't also be delicious eating.

Michelle Obama had a rational approach to dessert based on these two principles: eat healthy, and if you're going to have a sweet, make sure it's a good one and a reasonable portion. Thus, it became our mission to continue serving mouthwatering desserts at the White House, but serve smaller portions made from the best ingredients.

Although the First Family's emphasis on healthy diet meant eating dessert only once or twice a week, we were far from wanting for work. The President and First Lady do a lot of entertaining, some of it political, some for civic groups, churches, foundations. These events, whether for personal friends or official guests, gave the pastry team a chance to flex our culinary muscles and showcase desserts that were delicious but still within the First Lady's guidelines. Thus began a culinary adventure creating recipes that provided great flavor in small portions and where possible used healthier grains and alternative flours. Susie and I introduced several new luscious desserts that worked well in small portions—sometimes maybe too well, judging by how many guests I saw take second helpings of our sticky toffee pudding! Our pavlova, small and sweetened with honey, morphed into a crackling meringue loaded up with mangoes and pineapples; our greengage plum cake used a light maple syrup instead of sugar. We kept a rotating repertoire of small, healthy cookies on hand in the

kitchen for events on short notice: oatmeal golden raisin, salted cara-
mel butterscotch squares, and milk chocolate malted rounds.

None of this was as important as Mrs. Obama's next idea: a garden
on the South Lawn. Certainly there had been vegetable gardens at the
White House before. Of course, our first presidents were all adept
farmers. John and Abigail Adams, the first president and first lady
to reside in the White House, planted a garden in 1800 to grow produce to feed their family. Thomas Jefferson expanded this garden to
include fruit trees. Andrew Jackson built an orangery to grow tropical
fruit, replaced by a greenhouse in 1857, and then replaced in 1902 by
the West Wing. The food rationing of World War II inspired the
Roosevelts to plant a victory garden on the White House grounds.

But in modern times, there were obstacles to planting and maintaining a garden. The Clintons' attempt to create a garden on the
grounds was denied because it was thought it would not fit in with
the formal landscaping of the White House. They had to settle for
planting a small garden on the White House roof instead.

Even though it was a directive of the First Lady herself, there was
still considerable resistance to Mrs. Obama's garden. Having been on
the residence staff for several years by this point, I knew there was
considerable red tape at the White House along with lots of old habits
and a tendency to reject anything new. Some of this is unavoidable.
With such high stakes, every decision is subject to public scrutiny and
security is always a concern. The South Lawn is no different, and any
changes made there needed to be vetted by the National Park Service,
an outstanding team that keeps the eighteen acres of grounds surrounding the Executive Mansion beautiful at all times of the year (no
small feat).

But, Mrs. Obama? Iron hand in a velvet glove. Or rather—when
she launches a charm offensive—a Sherman tank covered in velvet.

It worked, and on March 25, 2009, just a few months after the Obamas moved in, we celebrated the planting of the kitchen garden on the South Lawn. The point person was Dale Haney, the long-serving and devoted head of the grounds (and caretaker of presidential dogs), who knew every square inch of the eighteen acres. He found a spot that was suitable, ideal even, with good drainage, good sun, and in view of the public from the south fence. It was such a perfect spot that it seemed inconceivable that a garden hadn't been planted there before. Students from local elementary schools joined Mrs. Obama in planting the 1,200 square feet of soil that had been prepared by the Park Service for maximum fertility. There was also a compost bin and a beehive managed by White House carpenter Charlie Brandts. I have never seen a more beaming First Lady, and the President soon came down to see it and showed his approval with a hug for his wife.

Sam Kass, the White House chef who had accompanied the Obamas from Chicago, was a dynamo in caring for the garden, promoting it to anyone who would listen both inside and outside the government. I'm sure together we must have overwatered, overweeded, and overstared at those plants for the first three months it was there. And yet, the garden flourished.

When the plants bloomed, the First Family enjoyed the freshest vegetables on their family dinner table. The beehive was put to good use as well. As the hive produced a record amount of honey due to Charlie's careful stewardship, the First Lady's Office started to think of creative ways to use it. A one-of-a-kind glass jar created by glassblowers in Illinois was filled with White House honey and given as gifts to the spouses of heads of state at the G20 economic forum in Pittsburgh in 2009. It was, to me, a powerful reminder of the interconnectedness of everything: those little insect pollinators are the link in the chain that grows one-third of all our produce, and the honey they produce is a powerful symbol of our debt to the natural world and of its fragility.

However, the garden was a sensitive point to the managers of the residence, the White House ushers. Rarely were the lines between defending our apolitical values and entering the fray so blurred. In the end, though, it was the First Family's personal wish to eat better, carefully sourced food, and we were there to serve the needs of the President and his family. If I had been asked to make towering chocolate sculptures of Mount Rushmore, I would have done it, but that was not the mission given to us. It was healthier food. That was the job, clearly stated by the First Lady. When later the chefs began speaking to school groups and giving tours of the garden, it was always on our volunteer time, off duty.

* * *

It turns out, we were only just getting started. The garden was a symbolic action, a trial balloon for pushing healthy eating from the White House. But next, the First Lady asked us to help her ensure all children across America have the same opportunity for a healthy start in life. It was apparent to us chefs that this was a watershed moment: the first time we had been enlisted to help achieve a public policy goal, albeit at a distance and not in the same way as the political staff appointed by the President. At times, I felt a little discombobulated trying to remember not to cross those lines and to keep my distance from the politics, contributing according to my role but not overstepping it. All that said, we could not have been more proud to see the focus of better, healthier food get equal billing with the most important issues of the day.

In 2010, thanks to the help of the nonprofit organization Share Our Strength, the White House hosted "Chefs Move to Schools," a big party on the South Lawn intended to drum up enthusiasm around healthier cafeteria offerings. Even though Michelle Obama was beloved across the county we still needed extra help to inspire healthy eating in schools and among young children throughout America. Close to a thousand chefs from across the country came together to raise awareness that the quality of our meals has an exponential impact on our health. The habits we form early in life, good or bad, increase their effects as we grow older—so it's critical to develop good habits at a young age.

Mrs. Obama knew that children—who may not be so eager to hear about healthy eating from a parent—might listen to a chef. Chefs, after all, speak the language of kids: pleasure and deliciousness. As a result, people in the food world dropped whatever they were doing and high-tailed it to Washington, DC. Daniel Boulud, Lidia Bastianich, Rachael Ray, Michel Nischan, José Andrés, and other marquee names in food settled in folding chairs on the South Lawn on a sweltering June day, all because the First Lady asked them to serve their country. And because she led by example. Throughout her eight years at the White House, Mrs. Obama would do anything, it seemed—race across the East Room floor with Jimmy Fallon in a burlap bag race, jump around the Diplomatic Reception Room with a man in a huge balloon costume, hula hoop on the front lawn—if it got kids interested in healthier habits.

And she was willing to use the full weight and gravitas of the White House to achieve that goal. A few years later, the White House hosted the first-ever Kids' State Dinner, giving healthy eating the highest possible diplomatic treatment.

A true state dinner includes a South Lawn speech, a twenty-one-gun salute, and the Fife and Drum Corps. The Kids' State Dinner had none of these things; in fact, it was actually a lunch—bedtimes being a factor here—but it was as eagerly anticipated and planned with the same care as a dinner for any visiting head of state. The guests were children who had been selected based on original recipes they had submitted to the Healthy Lunchtime Challenge organized by Tanya Steel at Epicurious. The menu was selected from these recipes by the Let's Move! team and cooked in the White House kitchens, and the meal was served by the most seasoned butlers in the East Room with all the pomp and circumstance of a real state dinner. The President even swung by with a messages for the kids: "Look, let's face it, I don't cook that often these days. But I remember cooking and it's not always easy to make something that people like to eat. Then for you guys to actually come up with recipes that are healthy and tasty, and to do it in a way that helps to contribute to spreading the word about healthy eating among your peers—that's a really big deal."

And it was astonishingly good: Quinoa, Black Bean, and Corn Salad; Yummy Cabbage Sloppy Joes; Strawberyanna Smoothies. The looks of pride beaming on the children's faces lit up the room and we chefs could not have been happier if we had served three popes, a president, and a prime minister at once.

By this point, it was clear to me that my role at the White House had grown much bigger than just feeding the First Family. I had become a spokesperson for healthy eating, a liaison to the food community, and a partner to the First Lady. If we ever needed proof that our focus on healthy eating could have a global impact, we got it at the 2010 United Nations General Assembly spouses' luncheon. It was held at Blue Hill—a prestigious restaurant located on Stone Barns, a working farm in New York's Hudson Valley—in collaboration with host chef Dan Barber. Mrs. Obama invited all of the White House chefs to join Dan in preparing lunch for the First Ladies of over twenty different countries. The lunch started with a tour of the farm. As these distinguished guests stepped daintily around the grounds followed by geese and chickens—and the U.S. Secret Service—they learned about the latest experimental organic agricultural methods and ethically raised livestock. The ladies were delighted.

First Lady's Luncheon Menu for UN Spouses

First
Summer Fruit and Vegetables
White House Sun Golds, Homemade Yogurt, Purslane

Wine Pairing
Lieb Cellars Pinot Blanc (Long Island, NY) 2008

Second
This Morning's Farm Egg
5 Late Summer Beans from the White House & Our House

Wine Pairing
Red Hook Winery Chardonnay, Jamesport Vineyards
(North Fork, Long Island), 2008

Entrée
Stone Barns Pastured Chicken
White House Herbs, Eggplant, Ratatouille

Wine Pairing
Copain Pinot Noir, Wentzel Vineyard
(Anderson Valley, California), 2007

Dessert
Sacher Cake
Red Jacket Apricots, White House Sorbet

As the day's menu shows, we had vibrant ingredients available to us from the South Lawn garden: beans, sun gold tomatoes, all manner of eggplant, and zucchini, all right from our back door, which we combined with the gorgeous produce grown at Stone Barns. The menu was a shining example of the best American products and craft. The food was utterly delicious, but beyond that, the luncheon was a recognition of what we chefs were working toward with Mrs. Obama: a national awakening about the crucial nature of our food systems and its relation to our day-to-day health. Dessert was a small Sacher Torte and Roasted Red Jacket Apricots with White House Honey Sorbet, served with a mile-wide grin on my face.

This lunch validated everything I had been working for my entire career. If I had any remaining doubts, they were assuaged when I met the incredible Chantal Biya, the First Lady of Cameroon, whose hairstyle is so gravity-defyingly wonderful it enters the room a few seconds before she does. The very image of poise and elegance, she said it was the best diplomatic lunch she had ever attended. As chefs, we had been invited to do something highly unusual: participate in one of the policy priorities of the Obama administration. And it was a huge success. For years I had been preparing food for these events, but for the first time, my work was a crucial part of it, not just a side dish.

* * *

Everyone, including me, who works at the White House feels a special connection to the First Families for whom they work. For the residence staff, this means making the White House a home for the President and his family. Even though there are moments that evoke the "upstairs-downstairs" feeling of Downton Abbey, Mrs. Obama and the President went out of their way to make us feel welcome in their home, and I felt profoundly connected to the Obamas by the experience of sharing space with them and working toward shared goals.

I felt that connection especially keenly toward the end of my time at the White House. I had only a few days left in the job before returning to New York. My able assistant Susie was already handling the job like a pro, so even as I felt nostalgic about my impending departure, I was satisfied that my work was continuing in the hands of the next chef.

That's when I got a call from the Social Office asking me if I wanted to attend one last official function—as a guest, not as staff. It was especially meaningful since it was the White House reception celebrating LGBTQ Pride Month. Furthering the rights and status of LGBTQ people had been one of the signature achievements of the Obama administration. I was a beneficiary of that work, having recently married my partner of fourteen years.

The reception was extremely meaningful for me to begin with, but nothing prepared me for getting a shout-out from the President. As he recalled openly gay people who had been influential in his life—friends, teachers, neighbors—he ended with these words:

> Finally, I have to mention a man who's made life at the White House very sweet. This is one of Michelle and my favorite people—our executive pastry chef Bill Yosses—who's here tonight with his husband, Charlie.

We were floored. But if that weren't enough, the President then gave me the best compliment I have ever had:

> We call Bill the "Crustmaster" because his pies—I don't know what he does, whether he puts crack in them . . .

Of course, Mrs. Obama immediately corrected the record that, no, there is no crack in my pies.

That shook up the news cycle for a few days! But the humor of the moment aside, in that moment the Obamas put me on the pages of history for the two things I love most: my husband and my profession. And I was proud to serve in their White House.

In the great scheme of things, I think there are few things in my life that have been as important as giving those hardworking and overly scrutinized families in the White House a chance to enjoy their private time together. The honor and privilege of serving the First Family and their guests was thrilling as a job, yes, but it also instilled in me a pride in our democratic heritage, and traditions as Americans, that I was surprised to discover in myself—just behind those mahogany doors.

FULL CIRCLE

Darienne Page

Military service has always been the backbone of my family. It's in our blood. My family has served in the military since the Civil War. My grandparents served. My mom and dad served. And at the heart of this service is a simple belief, one that my mom instilled in me and all five of my brothers and sisters: that we have an obligation to give back to a country that has provided us with so much opportunity.

In the early 1990s, my mom deployed to the Gulf War shortly after giving birth to my youngest sister, Darlene, leaving my father to care for a newborn and five more kids under the age of eleven. Growing up, I attended high schools all over the world—in Tokyo, Okinawa, southern Arizona, and Maryland. And after I graduated high school, my mom swore my eldest sister, DeAnna, and me into the army.

DeAnna and I enlisted as members of the army's "buddy program." It meant that we would attend all of our initial military training together. It also meant that we would go to our first duty station together. Having been raised in a tight-knit family, the idea of having her by my side during this new adventure was tremendously comforting. We would eat our meals together, see each other throughout the day, and share the same barracks at night. At the end of the day, no matter how hard the training, I knew that she'd be there for me.

Unfortunately, that comfort was short-lived. Four weeks into basic training at Fort Jackson, South Carolina, we discovered that we are—like many women in our family—pretty allergic to fire ants. Go figure. However, DeAnna's allergy was significantly more severe than mine. She went into anaphylactic shock multiple times, and the doctors determined that she could no longer continue in military service. She was medically discharged and well on her way back to our family in Maryland before anyone even told me. I was devastated. I was still contractually obligated to four years of military service—only now I would go on my own.

But I persevered. I graduated as my company's distinguished honor graduate and platoon leader in March of 2001. On my nineteenth birthday I arrived at my first duty station with U.S. Army V "Victory" Corps, in Heidelberg, Germany.

V Corps, which was inactivated in 2013, was known for deploying the first American troops in Europe during World War II, leading the assault at Normandy, and fighting in the Battle of the Bulge. In peacetime, V Corps was charged with supporting the U.S. Army's European Command and NATO while maintaining security throughout Europe. It was headquartered in beautiful Heidelberg, home to one of the largest universities in the country and nestled along the Rhine River. Our base was near downtown, which meant we could walk to the Hauptstrasse, the main road in the business district, and the historic Heidelberg Castle.

I loved my job—serving as a military paralegal in the Judge Advocate General (JAG) Corps office—and living in Germany was incredible. I made new friends and together we explored all Heidelberg had to offer. We worked hard during the day and—as you do at that age—partied hard at night. It was similar to what I imagine a college freshman would experience, except we were charged with defending the Constitution of the United States, by force if required.

To make the deal even better, my brothers Garon and Gustin joined me in Germany. They served with V Corps's subordinate units, the First Infantry Division and the First Armored Division. Family dinners, an old tradition, became new again, even when we had to make a three-hour drive to be with each other. We toured Germany as a family and soaked in the culture. The military bases in Germany were relatively open to local citizens, and the relationship with the German community was friendly and collaborative. I was happy, and life was relatively easy—as easy as it could be in the army, at least.

September 11, 2001, changed all of that.

It was midafternoon in Heidelberg when the second plane hit the South Tower. Like so many other Americans, we huddled around a television, worried about friends and loved ones, unsure of how the world was about to change. My mom was a special agent at the National Security Agency. My entire family was in Hanover, Maryland, right outside of Fort Meade and the NSA headquarters. I didn't know where anyone was, and worse, I didn't know how to get in touch with them.

For those of us in uniform, we knew the change would be swift and serious.

Immediately, all of the military bases went on lockdown and we moved to Force Protection Condition Delta, the highest force protection condition available. This meant that our base was now only accessible to military personnel, and all regular work activities were essentially canceled. Our sole goal was the protection of our assets and personnel within our area of responsibility. All available service members reported to the armory to draw our weapons and—for my first time outside of a military shooting range—live ammunition. The responsibility of protecting and defending our nation's citizens abroad, and the potential ramifications of the attack, came crashing in. U.S. Army V Corps was in the unique position of being the largest corps-level tactical force near the Middle East. We stood ready to deploy in the "War on Terror."

Over the next few months, we watched as our fellow corps units from across the globe took part in the growing war in Afghanistan. I took shifts pulling security at our base's entry and exit points, checking incoming and outgoing vehicles for potential threats and verifying military identification. When I wasn't on duty, I was taking meals and coffee to my fellow soldiers, all the while continuing to work in our JAG office. Watching the political situation in America unfold, we knew a war with Iraq could not be far off. Our unit, as well as many others throughout Germany, began taking part in numerous training exercises in preparation for a potential deployment.

In December 2002, warning orders for deployment came down from our battalion's headquarters. A forward unit of troops was sent to Kuwait to take part in maneuvers with the U.S. Central Command. In Germany, we were instructed to make the necessary arrangements for our homes, vehicles, and families in the event we were away for an extended period of time. The invasion was happening and V Corps was going to lead the "long ride" (540 miles) into Baghdad.

How do you feel when you get news like that? I felt so many different emotions, but mostly extreme nervousness. The thought of leaving all I had grown accustomed to in Germany for an undetermined amount of time, with unknown danger awaiting, was staggering. To add to my anxiety, I would need to complete a leadership

training course, as part of my pathway to military promotion, prior
to leaving.

I joined our unit after the fall of Baghdad.

Flying into the Baghdad Airport on a C-130 Hercules was surreal.
The evasive maneuvers of the plane, intended to avoid detection and
potential missile attacks, made me sick to my stomach. The anticipation was worse: I was in full combat gear, prepared for whatever met
us upon arrival. Luckily, my JAG family awaited me. I quickly got up
to speed on our new reality. The way we traveled, where we lived, the
missions we were assigned, the way we utilized our weaponry—all of
it was much different from the stories my mom told me, and nothing
like what the media made it out to be.

V Corps helped form the Combined Task Force-7, a multinational
force that directed the U.S. military effort in Iraq, and occupied the
Al-Faw Palace compound in Baghdad, renaming it Camp Victory.
The palace—formerly used by Saddam Hussein for duck-hunting
expeditions—was grand, surrounded by a man-made moat and decorated ornately with enormous crystal chandeliers and marble floors.
Our JAG office was close-knit, and we slept next to one another outside on a balcony of the Al-Faw, overlooking the palace canal and the
Australian military barracks. Every night I'd come home and walk
around a massive hole in the floor where a bomb had blown out the
bottom two floors. It was a wonder the balcony was still standing.
There was no running water or functional plumbing. The marble
in the palace absorbed the heat, making it intolerable to be inside, but
the war made it too dangerous to venture outside the camp without
full protective armor. With nearly forty pounds of gear required in
one-hundred-plus-degree temperatures, it wasn't much better outside.
The only thing that brought me comfort was sleeping next to my

peers every night, knowing we'd have each other's backs no matter what.

The Baghdad JAG office's mission was focused around the judicial reconstruction of Baghdad's court system and military tribunals for high-value detainees (HVDs). My work was a little different. I was responsible for providing support for the criminal law division, processing American soldiers accused of wrongdoing within Iraq. There was a wealth of misconduct to examine—everything from drunken soldiers killing a tiger in the Baghdad Zoo to extreme sexual misconduct and violations of General Order Number 1, which prohibited alcohol, drugs, and pornography. We set up a courthouse and conducted hearings when necessary. After a court-martial, I was responsible for ensuring convicted personnel got to the Baghdad Airport for transfer to military prison. At five-eleven and a little over 130 pounds, I doubt that I was very intimidating, but it helped that I had ownership of several sets of wrist, belly, and leg shackles, an M16, and an M9.

We traveled in and out of the Green Zone numerous times a day, finding ourselves on "IED Alley" more times than I can count, frequently traveling to Abu Ghraib, the Baghdad Airport, and downtown Baghdad. As the war intensified, so did the sounds of nightly gunfights between our forces and the enemy and the use of unarmored vehicles for any travel between military posts. By the end of that year, things were very different than when we arrived.

After being deployed for nearly a year, I returned to Germany in early 2004. Ours was one of the earliest groups to arrive, but there was no precedent for greeting returning troops. As a result, there was no one to welcome us upon our return in the early morning hours at Ramstein Air Force Base. No banners, no balloons. I checked my weapons at the armory and went home to Heidelberg as if I'd simply been gone on a field exercise. The rest of the unit joined us weeks later.

Readjustment to "normal" life became a challenge for me. I'd seen a lot in Baghdad that I wish I hadn't. One of my mentors, Sergeant Major Cornell Gilmore, and our regimental chief, Chief Warrant Officer Sharon Swartworth, were killed when their helicopter was shot down in November 2003. So many friends were injured or killed. I'd come to fear so much about the night that I stopped sleeping. What I experienced in my dreams, the sounds and smells, started to manifest when I was awake. I could easily go forty-eight or more hours without any real sleep. I sought treatment and was prescribed antianxiety and sleep medicine. I met with support groups around postdeployment issues. Back then, the concept of PTSD was never addressed. I was just "having a hard time readjusting."

During one of my restless nights in Heidelberg, something interesting happened. While watching the news, I heard bits and pieces of a speech at the 2004 Democratic National Convention:

> When we send our young men and women into harm's way, we have a solemn obligation not to fudge the numbers or shade the truth about why they are going, to care for their families while they're gone, to tend to the soldiers upon their return, and to never ever go to war without enough troops to win the war, secure the peace, and earn the respect of the world. . . .
>
> There are patriots who opposed the war in Iraq and there are patriots who supported the war in Iraq. We are one people, all of us pledging allegiance to the stars and stripes, all of us defending the United States of America.

I had never felt an allegiance to any political party, but at that moment, I thought, *This makes sense.* My mother is white and my father

African American. We were never raised to see race or color. We were never raised to take a side politically, just to do what was best for our country and our family. We had seen the way military families across the country came together to take care of each other, and had grown accustomed to the responsibilities that came with military service—duty, honor, country. Country above all. I was used to hearing debate for and against the war in Iraq, but this politician sounded more in line with the unique vantage point of the families responsible for actually carrying out the war.

In the moment, I remember wondering what it would be like to meet Barack Obama. Nearly three years later, I'd have the opportunity.

I left the military, deciding ultimately that my health and future education required it, and moved to Chicago. It was a significant move for me because, at twenty-three, I had never chosen anywhere I'd lived—the army had always chosen for me. I majored in political science at the University of Illinois at Chicago and got my first lessons in how the political system—the one that sent me, my family, and my friends to war—worked. It was a great time to be a student of politics in Chicago, especially when a few years later, Barack Obama announced his intent to run for President of the United States. The city was abuzz with excitement and many of our studies focused on his rise to political office.

One night, I went out with my girlfriends and we ran into a group of people with Obama shirts on. My girlfriend Missy knew I was interested in the campaign and pushed me to talk to them. As we engaged in a discussion with the group, I learned that one of the guys had been in Baghdad at the same time as me. Bobby Wise was a former helicopter mechanic and passionate about working for Barack Obama. We talked at length that Friday night, and he said if I was serious, I should send him my resume.

I thought about the conversation all weekend. It was a rough time for me. I was once again away from my family, and recently divorced. I was looking for a place to focus my energy and this opportunity seemed like the right thing. I sent Bobby my resume on Monday and by Tuesday night I had an interview with the headquarters campaign manager, Pete Dagher. During my interview, Pete dazzled me with possibility—teamwork, inclusion, late hours, travel, and maybe even getting to wear a gown at an inaugural ball someday.

Hours later, I was sitting at a desk in the mailroom. Not the most glamorous start, but I'd had worse offices. I was just thrilled to be around young, energetic people who were so excited to be a part of this movement.

I started volunteering with the campaign fifteen hours a week, while still going to school full-time and working a full-time job. We were down in the polls in Iowa and some voters couldn't even spell "Barack Obama." I worked my way from the mailroom to the front desk and was thrilled to greet everyone (especially the candidate) every day. I found myself drawn to the infectious energy of the campaign staff. I loved knocking on doors, making phone calls, opening mail, and answering countless Myspace and Facebook messages.

And when we won the Iowa caucus, I quit my job and became a full-time staffer responsible for coordinating travel for our field staff across the United States. The more time I spent at headquarters, the more I felt like myself. I made incredible new friends. For the first time since military service, I felt like I was a part of something greater than me—something that could actually change the way people engaged with each other, how they viewed politics and citizenship. It was special. Coincidentally, the day Barack Obama secured the Democratic nomination was the final day of my military contract. I was happier than I'd ever been. I was also more exhausted than ever! The campaign drew every ounce of commitment and determination I had—but it was worth it. Barack Obama had to win the White House.

And win we did. Watching the election night returns come in, surrounded by friends and family, was like a dream. We rushed to Grant Park, just in time to celebrate with our Obama team from across the country. By the time the President-elect took the stage with his family, I was a blubbering mess.

The following morning, I was on a six a.m. flight with campaign manager David Plouffe, a handful of campaign staff, and U.S. Secret Service to Washington, DC. We arrived at presidential transition team headquarters and were met with our new reality: a lot of security and even more rules. After watching Secret Service K-9s tear our luggage apart, we finally got into our new offices and started the process of putting together an Obama-Biden administration staff. It was a long seventy-five days, filled with organizing and scheduling travel for the newly appointed and potential cabinet members, ensuring all of our processes were in line with government regulations and helping our entire traveling staff understand how to get where they needed to be.

A week before the inauguration, the newly appointed director of management and administration, Brad Kiley, called me into his office. He laid out the blueprints of the West Wing and pointed out the Oval Office, the Vice President's Office, the Chief of Staff's and the National Security Advisor's Office. And then he asked me: "Can you sit in the West Wing lobby and run the place?" Without hesitation, I answered yes. The role of West Wing receptionist, or ROTUS— Receptionist of the United States—was mine!

I walked into the White House complex bright and early on January 21, 2009. I stood in the Indian Treaty Room, a ceremonial space in the Eisenhower Executive Office Building, with a dozen former campaign staff and, for the second time in my life, took an oath of office. While it was a much different setting than the first time, one thing remained the same: I had no idea what I was getting myself into.

My first few days at the White House were spent just trying to figure out what my role entailed. I had no idea where to sit, who to talk to, what gate to walk in, and what privileges came with being a West Wing staffer. There was no instruction manual and I actually sent a Facebook message to the previous receptionist for guidance. She, along with the Marine Corps sentries that stood ceremonial guard outside of the West Wing entrance, helped me eventually get my bearings.

I was fascinated with the building and all of the people who came in and out. It quickly became apparent to me that everyone who came to visit had one thing in common: they had to wait. And it was my job to keep them entertained, especially if the President was running late. I learned to manage relationships, conversations, and conference rooms. Did the President need to call the space station on Monday? Sure, I could get that set up. Was Beyoncé coming in to tour the West Wing? I could handle that, too. Did the cabinet need the Presidential Box at the Kennedy Center to see *The Color Purple*? Of course they did. I met with everyone from celebrities to world leaders. I had the honor of being present for momentous occasions, from our first bill signing to greeting every former president as they visited the Oval Office. I learned to give interviews, manage press, and handle challenging guests. I met our nation's best and brightest and learned a tremendous amount about respect, politics, and people in the process.

Despite the excitement of the West Wing, I found myself constantly drawn to the work taking place around veterans and the military. While on the campaign, I'd met Matt Flavin, a decorated naval intelligence officer who had been embedded with Navy SEALs. Like me, he wanted to help Barack Obama address important military policy issues. After the election, he was appointed to the National Security Council, focusing on veterans, wounded warriors, and military policy. Matt let me shadow him on occasion to meet with veterans' advocates from across the country. I was intrigued by the idea of continuing to serve a community that meant so much to me and my family.

Then in the spring of 2010, my family was met with a life-altering tragedy. My brother Gustin had been recalled to active duty, then discharged due to PTSD before serving a second tour in Iraq. Shortly after, he was killed in a motorcycle accident. One of the first calls I received that day was from the President and First Lady. The Vice President and Dr. Biden sent handwritten notes and flowers to my family. Our veteran partners ensured the logistics for my brother's military burial were taken care of. And on the day of his funeral, the West Wing essentially emptied and staff made the trek up to Baltimore National Cemetery, where we laid Gus to rest. I was allowed all the space and time I needed to grieve. And when I returned to work, the President and First Lady greeted me in the Blue Room of the White House with hugs. My entire family was extended an invitation to meet with the President in the Oval Office and Gus's son, Jordan, became a common fixture on the White House grounds.

As I settled back into life in the West Wing, the outpouring of support offered by our administration staff was tremendous. We looked out for each other. We were a family. The faith I'd placed in our whole team from the beginning had been rewarded. And I threw myself back into the work of doing whatever small part I could to make sure all our veterans had the same type of support system I had.

I assumed the role of assistant director of the Office of Public Engagement with a veterans, wounded warriors, and military families portfolio. I worked diligently with the Domestic Policy and National Security Councils to bring veterans advocates from across the country to the White House to discuss issues that directly affected them. I staffed the President, Vice President, First Lady, and Dr. Biden for events with wounded warriors and military families. I created meeting schedules that would not only help drive the administration's message, but also help the President and Vice President better understand the unique needs of the military community and the organizations that support them. We attended military memorials, visited injured service members and their families, laid wreaths across the country, and in one instance attended a college basketball game held on the same aircraft carrier that dropped the remains of Osama bin Laden into the ocean. I developed a program that allowed injured service members a special opportunity to privately tour the White House and visit with the President. The day I was able to introduce Sergeant Major Gilmore's widow to the President in the Oval Office was one of the highlights of my life.

I took part in nearly every military hospital visit from Walter Reed to Landstuhl. We prayed with families, listened to their concerns for the future. We visited with Gold Star families, those who had lost loved ones to war, whenever possible. Little is ever disclosed of these private visits. They are some of the most intimate moments a commander in chief gets to spend with service members. And our leadership never took that solemn oath—to care for those who have borne the battle—for granted.

As we worked through specific policy issues, I met advocates from across the country who were adamant that the President hold true to his pledge to end the war in Iraq. After all, he campaigned on bringing our nation's war fighters home. As we launched the First Lady and Dr. Biden's Joining Forces initiative in the spring of 2011, bringing together public and private sectors to support veterans, service members, and their families, I heard from people across the country who wondered when they wouldn't have to worry about another deployment, another separation. It was eight years after President Bush's "Mission Accomplished" proclamation, and combat operations were still ongoing. I met service members who had four and five deployments under their belts. I met children who were born during a parent's time away, spouses who had essentially learned to operate as single parents. The questions of "when" and "how" were constant topics of conversation as we met with veterans' advocates and military groups throughout the country.

Early in the fall of 2011, I was invited to a strategy meeting. Stephanie Cutter, one of the senior advisors to the President, told us, "The President is going to announce the end of combat operations in Iraq and will bring our troops home." I was floored. And personally thrilled. Garon, Gustin, and I served in Iraq on consecutive deployments. Another brother, Peter, was just returning from a combat deployment to the Middle East. At that point, I had sat with more wounded warriors and Gold Star families than my heart could handle. I had stood with the President as he held the hands of military spouses, acting in his role of comforter in chief to help them say good-bye to their loved ones. I'd been to memorial service after memorial service, and every Memorial Day and Veterans Day event at Arlington National Cemetery. I cried every time "Taps" was played. After hospital visits, I would often take the remainder of the day off just to process the raw emotion. Operation Iraqi Freedom was deeply personal for me and now to be in the room, hearing that we would fulfill our campaign promise to bring our troops home—it was an emotional moment.

On October 12, 2011, President Obama addressed our country and spoke the words I'd longed to hear.

Today, I can report that, as promised, the rest of our troops in Iraq will come home by the end of the year. After nearly nine years, America's war in Iraq will be over. . . .

Here at home, the coming months will be another season of homecomings. Across America, our servicemen and women will be reunited with their families. Today, I can say that our troops in Iraq will definitely be home for the holidays.

A few weeks later, I received an incredible offer from the Vice President's Office: *The Vice President is going to Baghdad for the change of responsibility from U.S. forces to the Iraqis. Would you like to go with him?*

I said yes, of course. For security reasons, I couldn't tell anyone I was going, which meant that I'd have to lie to my family about missing our annual Thanksgiving feast. I told them I was going to Turkey. Everyone believed me but my mom. As a former polygraph analyst for the NSA, she wasn't buying it.

I arrived in Baghdad three days before Thanksgiving. We landed at the Baghdad International Airport and were quickly escorted into the Green Zone to stay at the embassy headquarters. There were no evasive maneuvers, but the feel of the combat gear brought back many memories. So much had changed and yet the smells, the sights of the concrete barriers pockmarked from mortar attacks, the food in the dining facilities all remained the same. Sirens still went off nearly every night, alerting us to a potential mortar attack. Soon after our arrival, there was an attack within the Green Zone which killed two people. In truth, this triggered some of my PTSD symptoms, but after years of managing them, I was in a much better place to cope.

The arrival of the Vice President was met with great excitement. It was his eighth visit as vice president and the embassy and Green Zone staff loved him. I'd spent the days before his arrival planning complicated transportation logistics that included Humvees, helicopters, a C-130 gunship, and a heavily fortified motorcade. As I watched his plane land, I felt the excitement building. This was a moment I had been planning for days—but a moment for which I'd been waiting almost a decade.

Upon the Vice President's arrival in the Green Zone, we held a meet and greet with the embassy staff. Like a proud parent, he took the time to shake nearly every hand in the building. He doled out hugs and expressed his gratitude to every person he interacted with. When he saw me, he asked if my mother knew where I was.

Throughout our visit, we met with local officials, military leadership, and embassy staff as we prepared for game day. The Vice President asked the military leadership about potential risks, never wanting to unnecessarily put military personnel or the advance staff at risk. Everyone understood the ramifications of the task ahead of us. We left the Green Zone on helicopters, headed to Camp Victory, and as we flew over the base, the view took my breath away. I couldn't believe I was back after nearly ten years.

I walked into the Al-Faw Palace and was blown away by how much had changed. It was no longer the depleted, war-ravaged temporary barracks that it was when I first entered in 2003. It was a renovated, fully functional command headquarters. I climbed the stairs to the third floor and walked out on the balcony where I had slept years before. I sat in silence for a long time, reflecting on the changes that had taken place within my life over the previous decade. As a twenty-one-year-old junior enlisted service member, I could've never imagined that I would be afforded the opportunities that were now available to me.

I stood with our staff behind the scenes as the Vice President participated in a ceremony that would leave Camp Victory, and all of Iraq, in the hands of their people. The base that was once home to nearly forty thousand troops was being turned over in what the Vice President called a "solemn but glorious hour." The national anthem was played in the great room of the palace, filled with over two hundred service members standing in salute. Tears streamed down my face. I watched the Vice President shake hands with nearly every military service member in the palace. He asked them where they were from and who they were going home to. In that moment, it occurred to me that those service members would hopefully never see another deployment to Iraq. They'd never go home wondering—like so many others did—if they'd return to this camp.

After the ceremony, I spoke with the Vice President and General Lloyd Austin, the commander of military forces in Iraq, about my family's service and what the event meant to me. We talked about my brother and about the Joining Forces initiative, and strategized on how to better utilize the skills of our military veterans to better the business community. General Austin gave me one of his challenge coins—part of a long-standing military tradition, medallions symbolizing unit identity and esprit de corps given to service members as an award of sorts—to give to my mother, a way to thank her for our family's military service.

The military community has always been a source of comfort for me. It raised me, protected me, and provided me with a support system in the most trying of times. In the army, I learned to be resilient, resourceful, and tough. I earned my stripes. And without the experience of serving in our nation's military, I might not have had the opportunity to serve in a different capacity at the White House. Through both types of service, I was afforded leadership and direction at the highest levels, and have been able to pay it forward.

I am forever grateful, forever humbled by the opportunity.

IMPOSTER

Deesha Dyer

n my final interview to be White House social secretary, Mrs. Obama said something to me that sums up my entire life: "I'm not worried about you doing the job. I think you can do it. I want to make sure you have the confidence in believing that you can do it.

"Do you think you can?"

I've spent my whole life trying to answer that question. And as I sat there in the East Wing of the White House, gazing back at the glamorous and accomplished black woman who was the First Lady of the United States, I just felt like a girl from Philly who got lucky. I felt like an imposter.

Growing up, I never could have imagined flying on Air Force One, meeting the pope, or even stepping foot in the White House. My world was smaller. Things were simpler. I think back to the time when we'd have hot dogs for dinner, days in a row. I don't mean fancy hot dogs with infused herbs and spices; these were straight-up, eight-to-a-pack, no-frills hot dogs. We were kids and I just assumed that since we loved hot dogs, we ate hot dogs.

Although I had no clue what a social secretary was back then, I shouldn't be surprised that I ended up in a job that was focused on entertaining others and, well, socializing. I've always been a social person, and for me, school wasn't much more than another social opportunity. I think that is pretty normal for most kids, but it's especially true for kids like me who were surrounded by family members who didn't have an education beyond high school. I never asked my parents why they didn't go to college right away, but I suspect it's because they started a family young—and as long as they could pay the bills, they were doing okay.

I distinctly remember having to write in a journal in biology class, one of the few classes I was actually interested in. We were supposed to write about what we wanted our futures to look like. At the time, *Murphy Brown* was my favorite show on television, about a tough-as-nails, successful, working single mother. I wrote about how I wanted to be a black Murphy Brown. I didn't want to get married, nor did I care if any future children I birthed had a father. I just wanted to be Murphy Brown. Independent, doing my own thing, not leaning on anyone else. You better believe when I turned in the journal, it caused quite the uproar at my Christian school, where they were probably concerned that I was a lesbian. But when I think back to it, I realize it was an early sign of my natural inclination to stand apart and be different.

As I entered my senior year of high school, the only college I was interested in was Howard University—and if I am being completely honest it was because it seemed a lot like Hillman, the fictitious black university that Denise Huxtable attended in *The Cosby Show* spin-off, *A Different World*. I had been attending Milton Hershey, a private residential boarding school for low-income kids, for eight years. While the student body was very diverse, it lacked black teachers and general staff. The town of Hershey was also very white. I missed being around my black family with our traditions, food, and culture. I couldn't wait to be surrounded by black people again. I was intrigued to know what it would be like to be taught by black professors, and wondered if I'd be more interested in school if I felt it was relatable to me.

There was only one problem with my Howard scenario: I didn't get in. I was devastated—I mean, crushed. I cried because I felt terrible about myself, but this reaffirmed that, for better or worse, I should take another route in life. So I found myself at the University of Cincinnati, in the city where my mother lived at the time. I started out as a psychology major for reasons that I can't even remember. After getting a D in my first psychology class, I changed my major to elementary education, only to go on a classroom visit to an elementary school on the same day of a lice outbreak. There went elementary education.

By my second semester, I had changed my major twice, and I was already on academic probation. I also had a financial warning because I couldn't pay my room and board, which led to me simultaneously dropping out and getting kicked out of school. That was 1996. The next five years went by in a blur, but essentially, I was a hot mess. A *fun* hot mess, but a mess nonetheless. Around 2001, I became a little irresponsible with bills and got evicted from my apartment. I decided it was time to go back home to Philadelphia. I figured I would hit the reset button and start a new life.

When I returned to Philadelphia, a temp agency placed me as a secretary at a commercial real estate firm. I was proud of my newfound stability—a job with actual benefits!—and went looking for the city's hip-hop scene. This was the early 2000s and Philadelphia was exploding with neo-soul and hip-hop. DJ Jazzy Jeff had his A Touch of Jazz studio and acts like Floetry, the Roots, Erykah Badu, and Jill Scott would regularly do jam sessions around the way. I had always been a hip-hop enthusiast, but observing and absorbing the hip-hop scene the way I did at that time made me particularly interested in telling the stories of the people and culture of the colorful underground. There were some dope characters furthering the culture and some of them were women who were respected but not well known. I started writing for a friend's hip-hop website to give love and exposure to the nonrap elements of hip-hop like breakdancing, DJing, and graffiti. I didn't get paid much for my writing—definitely not enough to quit my job. But that didn't matter because I loved it.

I also started volunteering at the local AIDS organization Action-AIDS. I had been an HIV/AIDS activist since I was a teenager when I learned of Ryan White, the young man who contracted HIV from a blood transfusion. I was saddened that his friends abandoned him and people treated him as if he was contagious. This prompted me to start learning more about HIV/AIDS and meeting people who were infected with it. I also started mentoring and working with young girls who were at risk or in juvenile facilities. I remember being the black girl in high school who was too loud, too aggressive, too vocal, too everything. Often this got me labeled a "bad kid" and I wasn't—so I knew I had something to offer in being nonjudgmental. I didn't want girls like me to feel like they were less valuable, or had any less potential, than anyone else because of their gender, race, or personality.

As I got more passionate and serious about social work, I realized if I wanted to make a career out of it, I would need a college degree. That meant I would have to swallow my pride and find a way back to school. At twenty-eight years old with a spotty academic record and finances, my only option was community college, so I enrolled at the Community College of Philadelphia. Part of my admission requirement was to take a basic high school math course because I had been out of school so long. Not ideal, but I did it, and I started school as a part-time student while working full-time and volunteering on the side.

In the middle of all this, two miracles happened: the Philadelphia

Phillies won the World Series and Barack Obama became the Democratic nominee for President of the United States.

If you are from or know anything about Philadelphia—and no, please don't start singing the *Fresh Prince* theme—you know that we don't win sports championships every day. On that summer night in 2008 as we were celebrating the Phillies, I just kept thinking to myself, *Okay, God, we are on a roll here . . . now we just need Barack Obama to win this election.*

I have to admit that the first time I learned about Barack Obama I wasn't optimistic about a black man becoming president. I would hear his speeches and feel how passionate he was about being president, but think to myself, *Who is he fooling?* But once he won the primary election, that turned into *Damn, this guy may have a chance.* I got a magazine with his face on it and hung it up by my desk, thinking that *if* he won, I would work for him someday. Really, it was nothing more than a passing thought, though. I didn't know anyone in the Obama world and I certainly wasn't connected.

Then it happened. Barack Hussein Obama was elected the 44th President of the United States of America. There are no words to describe the emotion that night. I still get chills thinking about watching the results in my West Philly apartment. It was like the whole country had won the World Series. Everyone in our neighborhood started flooding the streets, cars were honking, music was blasting from stereos and houses. Even the rain couldn't stop the festivities. It was magical. I vowed that night to bottle up that feeling and take it with me wherever I would go. Immediately things felt different. I went to work and smiled at the photo on my desk every day after the election. *We did it.*

That following April, just months after President Obama took office, I got an email through a mentoring listserv. It was an application for the White House internship program. I assumed it was meant for young people attending prestigious universities, not an older, nontraditional community college student. But when I read the application, I didn't see any age or college requirement, so I applied. I tried not to think too much about it. I didn't think it would actually ever happen and I didn't want to be disappointed.

Life went on and I didn't hear anything for weeks. Then late one night I got a phone call from the White House! They conducted a quick interview . . . and then it was back to radio silence. I accepted that I didn't get the internship and told myself that was fine. After many silent weeks, I got an email from the White House but ignored it because I was certain it was a rejection email. A few days later, another email arrived with "following up" in the header, so I opened it—and there it was: my acceptance to be a fall 2009 White House intern. I read that email four or five times in total disbelief. And then I immediately went into panic mode. How was I going to afford an unpaid internship in a new city? Where was I going to live? I started to get to work on finding a part-time job and an affordable place to live. And then I emailed the good news to all my friends, family, and of course, my ex-boyfriends.

I can sum up my first day in one word: intimidating. Starting a new job is scary anywhere, but this was the White House. I put on my best clothes: a black blazer, black slacks, and a red turtleneck. I also had fake glasses on in order to look a little smarter. I felt self-conscious about not having a college degree and being in my thirties. As someone usually so confident in myself, I wasn't used to feeling like an imposter, but I tried to reassure myself that though I was a bit older and had an unconventional story, we all were nervous and there to do our best.

As an intern in the Office of Scheduling and Advance, I was

tasked with responsibilities related to organizing the logistics of the President's schedule. This included responding on behalf of the President that no, he can't attend your wedding, your kid's bar or bat mitzvah, christening, come over for dinner, be a guest at your family reunion—any of the ordinary requests the President receives every day. I also supported the staff who organized his domestic and international travel, working with other White House entities like the Secret Service and White House Military Office to make sure the President and First Lady were supported and safe at every moment of their personal or professional trip.

That meant I got to travel. My first trip with the Obamas was to Fort Hood, Texas, after the devastating shooting in 2009. We had forty-eight hours to assist the military base with the memorial event that the President and First Lady were attending. Throughout the somber and sad visit, I witnessed grace in its highest form from the grieving families, the troops, and the Obamas.

As we were on our way home on Air Force One, the President turned the corner to where I was sitting just as I was sneaking a paper napkin with the presidential seal into my purse. I didn't think I would ever be back on this historic plane so yes, I stole a napkin! This was a whole 'nother world for me. Imagine that. Just two years earlier I was trying to figure out high school algebra again, and now I am on the President's plane. It felt like my world was spinning. I kept thinking, *I am just an intern . . . what am I doing here?*

And then the internship ended as quickly as it started. In December 2009, I went back to Philadelphia. I figured getting that opportunity was my big blessing; I wanted to work for President Barack Obama and I did. Now I needed to return home, finish community college, go on to a four-year college, and start my social work career.

But something didn't feel right about going back to my former life after the White House. For the first time ever, I realized that I had the potential to do more. I didn't know what that "more" was, but I needed to find out. So I took a risk and gave notice at my full-time job. My plan was to get a part-time job and start going to school full-time to speed up the degree process. I figured I would do this until something came up. And it did.

A week after putting in my resignation, just five months after my internship ended, the White House reached out to me about a full-time job. Again, I didn't think it was real. But they must have seen something in me because I got the job offer—with the caveat that I could finish school remotely.

This was scarier than the internship. That was just a temporary move to Washington, DC, knowing in three months I'd be home to everything and everyone I knew in Philadelphia. Regardless if I succeeded, failed, or barely got by in my internship, my life would go on. But this was different. I was uprooting my entire life. I was terrified, but I packed a suitcase and started a journey with no idea how long it would last.

I knew working at the White House would mean long hours, being ready for anything, adjusting to new bosses (who were younger than me), snazzying up my wardrobe, and giving up a little bit of my former on-the-go life. What I didn't realize was that my biggest challenge would be overcoming my own insecurities.

One of my first jobs was handling the President and First Lady's hotel stays on their international and domestic trips. That didn't just mean booking hotels; it also meant covering details as small as scouting out the gym for the President's morning workout. One time, we were in Cambodia for the Asia-Pacific Economic Cooperation summit. I had camped out on a treadmill, holding the spot for the President while studying for one of my college classes. But when the President walked up and asked what I was reading, I hid my book and replied, "Oh, nothing."

Frankly, I was embarrassed. I didn't want him to know I was a thirty-four-year-old with biology homework. Even as I continued to rise up through the White House ranks, that feeling persisted. In 2012, I graduated with an associate's degree in women's and feminist studies. It should have been a proud moment for me, but I couldn't see it that way. It was a reelection year, so I used that as an excuse to not make a big deal about my community college graduation—and to hide my shame and embarrassment that I didn't have a higher degree.

Being promoted helped fuel my confidence a bit. The staff at the White House saw my hard work and dedication from my very first day. My work was never insular; all of my jobs there required interacting with people and building relationships. I have always been a people person and loved being a team leader. And anyone I worked with knew that it was never about me or what I could gain from having a job at the White House. That's the up- *and* downside of insecurity: you make yourself as small as possible not to be noticed but big enough to get your job done well.

After two years as deputy social secretary, the job of social secretary opened up. This is a highly esteemed and coveted position whose main responsibility is to assist the President and First Lady in making the White House "the People's House." The Social Office, led by the social secretary, is responsible for the planning, coordination, and execution of all the social events at the White House. From musical events with Usher, Aretha Franklin, and Sting to visits with foreign leaders like Canadian prime minister Justin Trudeau and the pope to the July Fourth celebration and holiday parties, we handled it all.

If being a White House intern was a stretch, then being the social secretary was definitely out of my league. But fellow colleagues and friends suggested I express interest in the position, so I went for it any-way. In many ways, I felt like I did when I applied for the internship: hopeful, but not *too* hopeful. The job involves becoming part of Wash-ington's social scene and socialite circle. I didn't know too much about that. But what I did know was how to welcome, entertain, host, and be creative. I had also gotten to know the talented staff in the East and West Wing and had a great rapport with the U.S. Secret Service and other offices with which the Social Office worked hand in hand.

So when the First Lady asked me in my final interview, "Do you think you can?" of course I answered, "Yes, ma'am." There was no way I was going to admit otherwise to the First Lady, especially one as confident and accomplished as Michelle Obama. When I got the job, I cried and called my best friend—but then I snapped back into work mode, as we had a big White House gospel concert with Tamela Mann, Aretha Franklin, and Robin Roberts that very night.

While waiting in the Green Room—where we held the President and First Lady before they went onstage—President Obama came over and congratulated me on getting the job and asked if I was ready for the next two years. I smiled, thanked him, and said, "Yes, sir—I'm ready." But at the same time I was asking myself: *How exactly do you get ready for an adventure like this?*

My first big test came early. A few months later, the White House hosted a state dinner for President Xi and Madam Peng of the Peo-ple's Republic of China. I felt like all eyes were on me during the week the media called my "Social Super Bowl." Though I was absolutely exhausted from Pope Francis's recent visit—which welcomed over ten thousand people on the White House lawn—I had my makeup done, hair done, and was ready to conquer the most prestigious event in Washington. But the night didn't go exactly as planned. Just hours before the dinner was scheduled to start, some of my colleagues gently suggested that I reevaluate my choice of dress. This knocked me off my game just as I was getting comfortable with being who I was in this high-profile role. Through my clothes, I express myself and my individuality—something I felt was especially important in a position that tends to focus on history and traditions.

But all I could do was focus on not messing up anything, especially given the value of protocol and tradition in Chinese culture. So an hour before the gates to the White House opened to let dinner guests in, I ran to Macy's and tried on two new dresses; luckily one fit okay enough to wear. The lovely saleswoman cut the tags while I was in the dress, then I ran the two blocks back to the White House. By this point, my hair and makeup were totally ruined—but it didn't matter. Despite the last-minute personal drama, the dinner went over extremely well, ending with all the leaders and guests on their feet dancing to Ne-Yo . . . and compliments on my dress.

Over the next few years, I never stopped asking myself what they saw in me that I couldn't see for myself. But I was determined to project confidence even if I didn't really feel it. I always felt like expectations were personally high for me, not just as an ambassador, but also as a community advocate. I struggled at times. At my first LGBTQ Pride reception, one of the guests heckled the President on the treatment of transgender people facing deportation. Working with my colleagues in the Office of Public Engagement, we were determined to make this Pride reception the most inclusive one yet, and purposefully included a significant number of trans women of color. Although she was a guest of a guest and so we had no way of predicting what she would do, my sheer horror at having someone yell at the President in his house turned to sadness once people began criticizing our handling of the incident. My activist friends in the LGBTQ community blamed me for silencing her and not letting her talk—although she was yelling, not talking. I truly felt I let the LGBTQ community down, but even today I know there was nothing we could have done differently. And that haunts me.

I was also very aware that I was only the second black person in the role. For me, that stressed the importance of always staying connected to the black community by always being a representative of the black community. Like making sure that we had diversity throughout all our events in entertainment, participants, and even volunteers for the holiday decorations.

And as a black woman, I recognized that being myself came with certain risks. You can blink too fast and people will think you are being aggressive—and I wasn't willing to be someone's angry black girl stereotype. As a result, I would internalize my emotions or water down my personality to make others comfortable. I also had to check my Philadelphia approach to conflict. We are a pretty defensive city, which came in handy sometimes, like when I was dealing with the foreign press corps or pushy guests. But when you are part of a team that you need in order to execute your job flawlessly, you have to learn to curb your impulse to defend yourself and your decisions all of the time. Even though it sounds noble, it's not always good.

For years I watched the First Lady exude calm and grace, not only under pressure but also when there were attacks on her and her family. She used to tell us how important it was to use our voice and passion in an appropriate manner to ensure that we were heard. She encouraged us to step back from a difficult situation, discuss it in a respectful manner, and play out all the possible solutions before deciding to take action. These lessons shaped me as social secretary—and helped me mature as a woman—and I continue to learn from them even to this day.

Over time, working through my doubts and anxiety became an

affirmation of my success. I know that I brought something fresh and unique to the White House. During my first year as social secretary, we worked with PBS to host a concert series focused on celebrating American music. I knew I would have been laughed out of Philadelphia if hip-hop wasn't included. In the Obamas' first year at the White House, rapper Common had graced the stage, but it became a huge media controversy because of his lyrics. I was conscious of this but also didn't want it to dictate how we ran this event. I suggested inviting MC Lyte. She was the first female emcee that I could remember being hooked to. As a teen, I knew all her lyrics. Bringing her to the White House was an incredible moment. When I met her, I could barely get any words out. I wasn't someone who got starstruck in that job, but seeing hip-hop performed live with turntables in the White House was a big deal to me. And she was amazing!

Even with so many good moments, I felt like an imposter up to the very end. The very last state dinner I planned was for the prime minister of Italy with entertainment by Gwen Stefani. It took place on the White House lawn, where a team of designers constructed a beautiful, classic look with large hanging chandeliers. I glided from table to table checking if everyone was okay, making sure that Mrs. Obama could see me in case she needed anything. Weaving in and around the tent, I congratulated myself for making it through the last dinner—even if I still felt out of place among all the accomplished people in the room.

A few days later, we reused the tent for a BET tribute to the Obamas called *Love and Happiness*. It was our last official concert at the White House and featured an incredible lineup: Janelle Monáe, Yolanda Adams, Jill Scott, De La Soul, the Roots, and more. It was televised and later won an NAACP award. On the trolley ride back up to the Executive Mansion from the tent, the President gave me a hug and told me he had fun and I had done a great job. The First Lady smiled and nodded her head in agreement.

On January 20, 2017, my seven-year career with the Obamas and the White House ended. I was one of several employees still working on the last day to organize a welcome tea between the Obamas and the Trumps. President Obama even joked a few times that inauguration morning about not messing up my last official event. Once the Obamas and the Trumps were loaded up in their vehicles and on the way to the Capitol Building for the swearing in, I went back to my office to grab my stuff. From the East Wing stairwell, I watched the new military staff start switching things over. I nodded, said hello, and gathered my things.

A few of us had spent the previous night at the White House to ensure we wouldn't have to commute to work in the middle of the inauguration madness. I walked around that last night while the house was quiet and still, going from room to room reflecting on all the joy and memories. I could hear the laughing children at the Turn-around Arts Student Talent Show, the military band playing the ruffles and flourishes when the President entered the state floor, the clacking of heels from employees searching the foyer for wandering guests needed back at an event, the familiar voices of the President and First Lady giving monumental speeches, the clinking of silverware, and all the life-changing moments we had created not just for ourselves but for the nation.

This president and first lady proved what is possible. They allowed me to live in their realm of infinite possibility. When the President gave his farewell speech in Chicago he said these words to his staff: "And the only thing that makes me prouder than all the good that we've done is the thought of all the amazing things that you're going to achieve from here."

Living and making history in a rare universe that not everyone gets to see or experience is *something special*. In those years, I learned to believe in myself and believe in my ability to do hard things. I learned that I did not have to earn my worth; I was born worthy of the opportunities that stood before me—I only had to seize them to succeed with grace and tenacity. And because I did, I got to help make the White House "the People's House," throwing open its doors for three years of amazing parties, elegant receptions, memorable ceremonies—and a little Philadelphia flavor.

Today, I have confidence that I didn't own when I walked down those historic White House halls in 2009. And today, I know I was not and will never be an imposter—because I deserved to be there.

SEPTEMBER 12

Ned Price

Tuesday, September 11, 2001, dawned temperate and nearly cloudless in Washington, DC—or so says the official account published years later. I don't quite recall the weather conditions that day. It's not that my memory has faded. It hasn't. Those details just never quite registered in the first place. In their place are indelible and vivid memories of phone calls, fire alarms, smoke in the distance, uncertainty, and—most of all—fear. My memories may be unique, but the collective experience for millions of Americans isn't.

I was a few weeks into my freshman year at Georgetown University when a phone call just before nine a.m. roused me from my sleep. It wasn't entirely a surprise. My sister was nearly nine months pregnant at the time, and each night I went to bed half expecting to be stirred awake with good news. But it was clear from my father's tone on the other end of the line that morning that he wasn't calling about my sister—and that the news wasn't good.

Like so many in Washington, DC, that day, I spent the subsequent hours wandering, sometimes in herds, sometimes alone, never quite sure where to go. Once the immediate threat of weaponized aircraft seemed to have subsided, I climbed the stairs to one of the highest points on campus, where I watched the Pentagon burn, then smoke and smolder. I was joined by several classmates, but I never felt more alone that day.

For many, a newfound commitment to public service was born out of the ashes of that day. Several of my classmates enlisted in ROTC, ultimately serving time in Afghanistan and Iraq, the wars of necessity and choice, respectively, whose origins are also found in that day. Others pursued careers in diplomacy, opting to represent the United States to a world that—on that bright, late summer day—seemed so dark.

I, too, felt moved to serve. As I set out on a path that would eventually lead to the CIA, my story was that patriotism and devotion to public service in the aftermath of 9/11 had steered me toward a career in public service. And that was true, at least in part.

If I were to be completely honest, however, another emotion also spurred me down that path: fear. It was residual fear from 9/11, compounded regularly by new warnings and pronouncements—most from my own government. We heard admonitions to stock up on duct tape and plastic sheeting. The specter of a "mushroom cloud" regularly featured in the Bush administration's stump speeches. Color-coded threat warnings became a part of life, almost as routine as the weather forecast. Fear became a key part of the national consciousness for some time.

But I never quite articulated that emotion during my application process to join the CIA. That's not to say I wasn't asked what had motivated me to seek this path. To the contrary, in every cover letter, interview, and polygraph session, I spoke, sometimes at length, of my desire to serve my country and fight against the constantly looming terrorist threats. I articulated my patriotic convictions, my skills for the job, and the character traits so prized in the intelligence business—honesty, integrity, and judgment. But by omitting that pervasive and ever-present feeling of fear, I never told the full story.

* * *

I reported for duty in Langley, Virginia, in early 2006, some four and a half years after my classmates and I watched smoke billow from the Pentagon. But it certainly didn't feel that long to me or, I soon realized, to my new colleagues. There was a sign in the Counterterrorism Center, my new office, that captured the CIA's reigning psychological and temporal ethos: "Today Is September 12th."

And that was precisely how it felt. There was an enduring sense of urgency to the work, which we referred to as "the mission." Some of my more senior colleagues had trained their sights on al-Qaʻida long before Osama bin Laden was a household name; for them, this assignment was personal. Others like myself, who were too young to do anything but observe his group's horrific attack on the United States, had held those memories and feelings in reserve.

But it wasn't just 9/11 that fueled the passion and intensity of the workforce. It was a feeling that was born on 9/11 but reinforced by successive attacks in places like Bali, Madrid, and London as well as by the constant influx of threat reporting. Certainly not all threats were credible, but this constant din was the mood music that fueled the relentless drive of the perennial September 12th, our version of Groundhog Day.

On one of my first days in the new office, a senior officer offered advice that I would take to heart. "Whatever opportunities come your way, take them," he counseled, even if they were out of my areas of expertise. It was a tried-and-true way throughout the agency to signal dedication to the mission. And that's exactly what I did. I held up my hand for tasks small and big, most of which I've long since forgotten. But there's one that has stuck with me.

It was early in my CIA tenure when I was offered the opportunity to take part in a program that would later come under intense scrutiny. I jumped at the invitation. The details remain classified, but I spent several weeks immersed in this program at a remote location far from the sterile setting of Langley. I was fascinated by the day-to-day work, coming to know, for the first time, the granular details of an effort I had previously only read about in highly classified cables back to headquarters. And the sense of mission—the ability to heed that call to September 12th service—was front and center.

What now strikes me most about my recollections of that period aren't my memories but rather what I distinctly don't recall: any sense of doubt or even moral ambivalence about what the Bush administration had asked of the CIA in the name of counterterrorism. In fact, the only tinge of doubt or regret I recall experiencing came at the end of that stint. I wanted to remain not because I enjoyed the experience but because I felt the work was important, even indispensable, given the continuing threat. The drive—fueled by passion and, yes, fear—crowded out just about every other emotion. Looking back, nothing better captures the ethos of that period.

* * *

Though I returned from this experience just as the 2008 presidential election was moving into high gear, it wasn't readily apparent at CIA headquarters. Even though it is located just ten miles from the center of the political universe, Langley traditionally has been an apolitical oasis. The Potomac River, which separates Virginia from Washington, DC, might as well be a political moat. Politics were rarely discussed at the CIA, even as America's role in the world and approach to terrorism remained a constant topic of debate among the presidential contenders.

As the election proceeded, two distinct visions emerged. John McCain hewed closely to the Bush administration's foreign policy. His campaign frequently pointed to the threat of terrorism, signaling to American voters—both implicitly and explicitly—the danger of changing horses midstream. Barack Obama, on the other hand, made no bones about the fact that his election would usher in a new strategy, one that rejected the politics of fear. He most cogently put forward his vision in a July 2008 address at the Ronald Reagan Building, named for one of America's clearest-eyed Cold Warriors, where he told the crowd: "For eight years, we have paid the price for a foreign policy that lectures without listening; that divides us from one another—and from the world—instead of calling us to a common purpose."

Those who know the agency and its employees tend to say that the workforce's politics largely mirror those of the country it protects. Analysts, some forged in the ivory tower, tend to be more progressive, while operations officers, including a large contingent with military backgrounds, skew more politically conservative. It was unsurprising, then, to hear from my superiors within the Counterterrorism Center reservations about what they had heard from Obama. Not only would his election augur a change in approach, they noted, but Obama had taken direct aim at some of the Bush administration's tactics, including the CIA program to capture, detain, and coercively interrogate high-value terrorism suspects. To some of the senior officers I most respected, the Obama approach was tantamount to reverting to a pre-9/11 strategy, one they believed was ill suited to take down America's most dangerous and committed terrorist enemies. There was a sense that an Obama victory would see the agency taken out of the counterterrorism mission. To the dedicated professionals who had made this mission their life's purpose, there were few specters more concerning. They spoke of their misgivings quietly, but there was no mistaking the concern. As a junior officer in the habit of deferring to the judgment of my superiors, it was difficult not to share their skepticism.

Some of my colleagues had hoped that Obama's campaign trail rhetoric was little more than that, but his first acts in office suggested otherwise. On his second full day in office, he signed an executive order putting an end to the CIA's detention and interrogation program, limiting U.S. personnel to only those techniques approved in the U.S. Army Field Manual. The general skepticism toward the new commander in chief was still fresh in our minds when President Obama traveled to CIA headquarters for the first time in April 2009. In an effort to reassure the workforce and affirm that he had its back, he told the assembled CIA crowd that the United States is special in our willingness "to uphold our values and ideals even when it's hard— not just when it's easy; even when we are afraid and under threat— not just when it's expedient to do so." It wasn't the first time President Obama had made that case, but it was the first time he had done so before this unique audience, some of whom viewed it with more than a bit of skepticism.

He continued to develop these themes in an address at the National Archives the next month, underscoring that fear must never separate us from our values, as they did during the previous administration. But this wasn't about a single president or administration; ours was a national failing. He told the crowd: "And during this season of fear, too many of us—Democrats and Republicans, politicians, journalists, and citizens—fell silent."

In the midst of these public remarks, what was most important to my CIA colleagues and me was the behind-the-scenes, private direction and guidance emanating from the White House. And the message was unequivocal: the CIA will retain the core resources, authorities, and tools necessary to bring al-Qa'ida and its terrorist ilk to their knees. Fears that the young administration would seek to handicap the CIA's counterterrorist mission subsided with each operational success—and there were many around the world during the first months of the Obama presidency.

Just as significant, there never was a need for the limited tools no longer on the table, including coercive interrogations, indefinite detention, and trial by military commission for detained terrorism suspects at Guantanamo Bay. Instead, the new president made it a point to seek justice in America's civilian court system. And, in all cases, that justice was delivered, fairly and swiftly, by a judge and jury. Not only was this route more efficient and effective than military commissions, but it underscored a key tenet of President Obama's approach. These terrorists were not ten-foot-tall giants; they were killers and criminals. And the President was not willing to allow them to change our way of life or, in this case, our system of justice.

* * *

The successful track record of terrorist captures and convictions bolstered the President's case within the CIA workforce, but what sealed it in my mind was taking part in the process. As I was preparing to leave the office for the day relatively early in the administration, I learned that a close U.S. ally thousands of miles away had arrested a key suspect, whom I'll call "Ibrahim," responsible for a deadly attack that had claimed American victims. I had closely tracked Ibrahim for some time and, by the time of his capture, was well acquainted with him—his travel, motivations, associates, even his upbringing. I had read hundreds, if not thousands, of pages of material on him derived from virtually every source available to the U.S. government. Within a day or two, I left a bitter cold Washington, DC, en route to a much warmer capital, where I would come face-to-face with Ibrahim, who remained in the custody of the close U.S. partner.

The Ibrahim I expected to find was a terrorist mastermind, a beguilingly evil, battle-hardened foe who had commanded a sophisticated and deadly operation. The Ibrahim whom our partners ultimately sat in front of me was diminutive and spoke with a soft voice, sometimes wearing an uneasy smile. I spent days posing questions to him, in the end developing something of a strategic rapport that was aided by the candy bars and fresh fruit I brought to him every morning. We exhausted every topic imaginable, from the most pressing—his potential knowledge of any additional attacks in the works—to the mundane, including his upbringing in a war-torn region and his curiosity about countries and peoples beyond his narrow experience.

Ibrahim told me a lot, and I learned more from his wife, with whom I met in a public park toward the end of my trip. She didn't know precisely who I was, and I offered no indication that I had spent the past several days speaking with her detained husband. Neither did she volunteer much about him. In fact, he came up only once and rather indirectly. As she spoke to me, she held in her arms a baby, who cooed throughout and never once cried. The boy couldn't have been more than six months old, and he became the topic of conversation as I was preparing to leave. "What's his name?" I asked. "Ibrahim," she replied. "He's named after his father." I didn't want to tip my hand as to how much I knew about her husband, so I ended the conversation there. But as I walked back to my hotel, I couldn't stop thinking about these two Ibrahims—one a hardened terrorist, and the other an adorable child who would probably never meet his father.

Indeed, it's not as though I came away from this experience

believing the elder Ibrahim to be any less capable of evil or with any less blood on his hands. What I learned from him only reinforced what I had garnered from painstaking research into his background. But it wasn't the details of attack planning or nefarious connections that stuck with me over the months and years that followed. What proved indelible was the experience of coming face-to-face with a man emblematic of a force—international terrorism—that had caused so much anxiety and fear in the United States and around the world. He was physically diminutive, uneducated, and—like most of his terrorist brethren—fell into extremist circles largely by happenstance. As I later sought to describe Ibrahim, one word consistently came to mind: pitiful. And in months and years since, one question came to mind: *"This is what we're so afraid of?"*

There's no denying that Ibrahim and his ilk could cause pain and destruction—massive amounts of it, in some cases. But, more than ever, that experience brought into stark relief President Obama's contention that we cannot allow a ragtag band of terrorists, even capable ones, to change who we are as a people, the values that have undergirded America's actions at home and abroad, or the institutions that have served us so well.

* * *

In early 2014, I began to think about my next steps. CIA officers' careers are often punctuated by multiyear rotations—whether to other offices within Langley, to overseas posts, or to positions within the policy community in Washington, DC. It was the latter opportunity that held the most appeal for me, as the policy process—which is, by design, kept at a distance from intelligence analysts to prevent politicization—was an element I had yet to see up close. But there was an additional catalyst: I had come to believe in President Obama's foreign policy vision, approach to national security, and broad conception of American strength in a way that had nothing to do with partisanship or even politics. Part of it was witnessing how he reinfused values and core American ideals into our conduct on the world stage. I later saw this in the President's interactions with his foreign counterparts, but it was even more pronounced when meeting with civil society leaders and—in the case of more authoritarian regimes—dissidents, who so obviously looked to our president to stand up for them and the universal values they, too, championed.

But it was also empirical: I saw that his approach was effective. This initial skeptic had been won over, which is, in part, why a new vacancy on the White House's National Security Council (NSC) staff was such an appealing opportunity. Over the course of several informal conversations and formal interviews, I came to know the individuals who, in the span of a few weeks, would become colleagues. As with everyone on the NSC, they had a reputation for working nonstop. Nights. Weekends. Holidays. Without fail, my emails to them would be returned within a matter of minutes—if not sooner—regardless of the time of day or night.

It was clear they were workaholics, but what also became apparent during the interview process was that—just like my CIA colleagues—they were talented and dedicated public servants. And, as you might hope for a team that spent days, nights, and weekends together, they seemed to genuinely enjoy each other. After all, why else conclude a long and grueling day with beers at the grungy watering hole two blocks from the White House, as they often did? But it wasn't until I'd served with them in the trenches, however, that I came to realize the true character of the cast I'd joined.

I'd been in my new position for just a couple months. Everything still had a veneer of newness—the people, the issues, the technology.

Any professional transition presents its own challenges, but those obstacles seemed all the more daunting given the ferocious pace of work and monumental stakes. On top of that, I'd gone from an institution that, quite literally, forbade employees from taking their classified work home with them to an office that, almost quite literally, required all of us to be on call twenty-four hours a day. And if you had the temerity to be unresponsive, it was a safe bet that a call from the Situation Room would change that soon enough. Working long hours at a breakneck tempo quickly caught up with me with a sloppy mistake.

After composing an unclassified but still sensitive email on an intelligence-related matter, I addressed it to a handful of colleagues dealing with the legal, policy, and legislative components of the issue. I hit send unaware that anything was wrong until my phone rang about ten minutes later.

"Hey, did you mean to send this to a reporter?" I thought she was joking. "Very funny," I responded before I'd pulled up the sent email. That's when my heart sank.

I bolted from my desk, ran down three flights of stairs, and into my boss's West Wing office, where I explained for the first of several times what had happened. Not quite knowing what to expect from my still-new superior, I braced for impact in the form of an expletive-laden tirade. I figured that'd be the most likely recourse in an office where the stakes couldn't be higher. But that's not what happened. Instead, he calmly picked up the phone, called a reporter from the outlet now in possession of my email, and explained the honest mistake. We were hopeful the organization would, given the circumstances, opt not to publish. It wasn't long after that I received an email from a different colleague of the reporter included on the misfired email asking me to call him. If my heart had been in my chest when I first recognized my mistake, it fell to my gut when I heard what the reporter had to say.

"We've come into possession of a pretty interesting document . . . We're planning to write on it shortly . . . Do you care to comment?" The press story, which triggered a wave of coverage of my unfortunate error, came later that evening. But even before the story hit, I found myself fielding calls from a host of White House colleagues.

The first came from a senior West Wing official; when I saw her name on the caller ID, my first reaction was that she would ask me— still the new guy—to pack my boxes. "We gave this a shot," I envisioned her saying, "and it just didn't work out."

Instead her message was one of encouragement. "We all make mistakes . . . Don't let this discourage you . . . You're doing great work . . ." The subsequent calls from other senior colleagues echoed the same message, and, even more surprising to me at the time, they kept coming.

Even once the story was contained and faded into the news cycle, I didn't forget the kindness of my colleagues. They didn't have to respond the way they did. After all, I wasn't a longtime campaign aide– turned–White House official. I was the new guy on temporary loan from the CIA. In some ways, it would have been more convenient for them to explain away the story by describing it as a "sloppy mistake" by "someone who no longer works here." But I came to understand that was not who they were; that was not what the Obama White House was all about. It struck me that this was a group of people who refused to let the pace, the stakes, or the setting detract from what presumably brought them into public service in the first place, including their caring and humanity.

It turned out my mistake didn't change my colleagues' perception of me, but it did seem to augur change within the media industry. A couple weeks after the incident, an email to me from the outlet in question carried a disclaimer below the signature line: "If the reader of this communication is not the intended recipient, you are hereby notified that you have received this communication in error, and that any review, dissemination, distribution or copying of this communication is strictly prohibited." I couldn't help but laugh, and, most importantly, I was doing so alongside a group of beloved colleagues.

* * *

By the time I took on my NSC assignment, President Obama's counterterrorism credentials were, except to his most ardent and obdurate critics, unimpeachable. But despite the President's many counterterrorism successes, my most instructive insights into Obama the wartime president came from working alongside him and his team during times of failure, some of which were especially grueling.

In early 2015, we encountered the most gut-wrenching situation of all. Late one morning, a senior official sent me a cryptic unclassified email, asking me to drop by his office as soon as I could. The issues that came before the NSC were never light and were often tragic. This one fit the mold.

The official briefed me on what the President's national security team had just informed him of during his morning intelligence briefing in the Oval Office: a U.S. counterterrorism operation in the Afghanistan-Pakistan border region targeting a senior al-Qa'ida leader in January had inadvertently killed two Western hostages, American Warren Weinstein and Italian Giovanni Lo Porto. Both men had been abducted in Pakistan in separate incidents several years earlier by militants, who'd moved them from the country's urban areas to the lawless border region. Despite extensive American efforts to locate both men—as well as other civilian hostages—we lacked precise and credible intelligence on their whereabouts. It was only after the operation that U.S. analysts concluded the two men were at the targeted compound and perished in the operation. Neither hundreds of hours of surveillance of the compound nor any other information source had suggested their presence—which we later learned al-Qa'ida had gone to great lengths to conceal—but the analysts were now confident in their tragic conclusion.

Working in national security—especially in the counterterrorism realm—requires a certain stoicism; it's not that we became numb or inured to threat, setbacks, and, occasionally, tragedy, but we couldn't let emotion stand in the way of the mission. But this news hit me like few other developments had. Perhaps I had deluded myself in thinking something like this was inconceivable. Over the past six years, I had seen up close the care and caution with which the United States conducted its operations overseas, including those involving lethal force. But the unthinkable had just become reality, and the question became—what now?

My CIA experience had taught me that, in America's shadowy war against terrorists, there were some elements that could and would remain secret. In this case, there was nothing to force the President's hand in the direction of transparency. He could have directed his team to quietly inform the families of their loved one's passing, providing few, if any, answers about the especially tragic circumstances. But that was not the course President Obama chose. His directive, offered on the spot, was quick and decisive: his administration would take full and public accountability for their deaths and do everything to see to it that nothing of the sort would be repeated.

I knew going into this job that there would be a physical toll to the long hours, lack of sleep, and intense situations. It's precisely why NSC staffers typically spend no more than a year to eighteen months in the job. But the task of setting into motion the President's guidance had an emotional toll unlike other tasks I encountered. We had a short window to ascertain the full set of facts and determine what the administration could say publicly about the deaths of these two innocent hostages. And although the NSC is no stranger to classified matters—much of our work was classified "Secret" or "Top Secret"—we kept this matter especially closely guarded even within the NSC. We were determined there not be a leak of any sort. In this case, it wasn't as much about ongoing operational security; it was a realization that the families shouldn't have to endure the added pain of learning of their loved one's fate from a press story.

I spent much of the next few days in the Situation Room, a windowless, underground setting with two redeeming qualities: the history seeped into every cranny and the bowl of M&M's placed just outside the entrance every weekday at lunchtime. I typically measured the intensity of my week based on the number of M&M lunches I consumed, and that week saw nothing but. Following countless Situation Room meetings and a few sleepless nights, we finished preparing the materials for the announcement. We decided the President and Commander in Chief should deliver it himself, as it wouldn't be appropriate any other way.

For the first time in my White House tenure, I was one of the aides to follow the President from the Oval Office to the White House Press Briefing Room, where he informed the American people of the tragic mistake. I could barely hear the President over the clicking of the camera shutters, but it mattered little, as I had essentially memorized his remarks by then. As the scope of the tragedy was setting in for most everyone else, I had a different thought. How extraordinary to live in a country and, in my case, work for a leader strong and confident enough to acknowledge and own up to our mistakes. In what other country could a scene like this be unfolding? Later in my White House tenure, I would be a witness to history, much of it uplifting and triumphant: being part of the small team that oversaw the successful effort to stamp out Ebola, watching the President declare marriage equality the law of the land from the Rose Garden, and traveling with him around the world, seeing up close the inspiration he engendered, especially among young emerging leaders. But it was in some ways fitting that my first public foray with the President was in the context of that day's tragic news. It seared into my mind the stakes of our work and our solemn obligation to the truth, as painful as it could sometimes be.

* * *

I spent nearly two more years on the NSC staff, where I came to understand that time had a funny way of behaving. The days, sometimes eighteen or twenty hours long, would drag on, but the weeks and months would seem to fly by. If you let it, and I too often did, life outside the office could become an afterthought. I saw untended friendships take on distance, relationships end, and—I told myself, at least—my dog become more attached to his walker than me. I didn't realize until after the administration had ended the extent to which we all put our outside lives on hold, confident there would be light at the end of the tunnel in January 2017.

As that day approached—and especially as the spotlight shifted from the Obama administration to the incoming team—I finally found time and space for introspection. Three days a week, the deputy national security advisor hosted about a half dozen senior staffers for a morning meeting to discuss the day's agenda. And for the final hundred days or so, the meeting would start with a countdown. "Only ninety-nine more days until we're drinking margaritas on a beach."

"Ninety-four more days until we can get rid of the alarm clock." At first, it was offered with not an insignificant degree of humor; at the outset, a hundred days—long days at that—seemed almost like an eternity. But as the clock ticked down, the humor began to evaporate, eventually overtaken by the laundry list of remaining action items and, ultimately, the solemnity of the moment. Before long, we started to encounter the lasts: the last overseas trip, the last ride on Air Force One, the last meeting of the full National Security Council. There was another "last" that had special resonance for me: President Obama's final national security speech.

This speech was one of my final projects at the White House, but what made it so extraordinary for me is that it took me back to an earlier time—a period well before the privilege of working in the White House was something I could even fathom. As we thought about the frame, we decided it would need to discuss President Obama's counterterrorism track record, but these final remarks would have to do more than list tactical victories and offer platitudes about how much safer the administration had made the American people. We drafted the speech to remind the American people—who by late 2016 had endured more than fifteen years of war—of where we had been in this effort and where President Obama would leave it in just a few short weeks. In doing so, it reminded me of where I had been—and where I had the opportunity to go along this unexpected journey. As I stared out at the Pentagon on that Tuesday morning some fifteen years ago, never could I have imagined I'd have the opportunity to help write and plan what would become the definitive presidential account of America's counterterrorist campaign.

I traveled with the President to MacDill Air Force Base in Tampa Bay, where the speech capped a day of briefings from his military commanders and meetings with members of the special forces community.

As we gathered backstage in the hangar where the President would deliver the remarks, an aide reminded him—and all of us—that it would be the last time the President would hear "Hail to the Chief" while on the road. Even the President, renowned for his ever-present even keel, admitted to being sentimental.

We all knew, however, these remarks would be bigger than a single issue or even a single presidency. At its core, this speech was about American strength. About midway through the address, President Obama reminded the assembled military audience: "The whole objective of these terrorists is to scare us into changing the nature of who we are and our democracy. And the fact is, people and nations do not make good decisions when they are driven by fear. These terrorists can never directly destroy our way of life, but we can do it for them if we lose track of who we are and the values that this nation was founded upon."

I took away from my White House tenure that history tends not to register and permeate in the moment. The life of a White House staffer is a constant grind. You're consistently overworked, exhausted, and, consequently, all too often under the weather or on the verge of being so. And that was especially so during the final weeks of the administration, when the weather was cold and damp, and the pace of work only increased as the days of the 44th presidency waned. That's why meaning and import—from the personally special to the truly historical—tended to escape many of us in the moment, only to be recognized after the fact when the dust had settled.

And so I wasn't especially surprised to realize later that the lines hadn't struck me as particularly exceptional as I was reviewing and contributing to drafts of the speech. But there was no escaping their personal resonance in the moment of delivery, especially as they were punctuated by applause from hundreds of service members inside the packed hangar. The core idea was one that had eluded me for years. It had eluded me as I took part, without moral ambivalence or discernible doubt, in the CIA program; it had eluded me as I looked on with skepticism as the first-term junior senator from Illinois claimed that America had lost its way in the aftermath of 9/11; and it had eluded me as I, along with some of my colleagues at the time, feared that his new administration would render us less capable of taking on America's terrorist enemies.

It took more than fifteen years to understand the key point. There are times when I'm doubtful I would've done so had it not been for a president—and, later, a boss—who turned it into a core premise of his foreign policy. And just as importantly, the applause the lines elicited from the military audience signaled that I was far from alone in this realization. Others surely reached that conclusion sooner and through a different path. But there I was, surrounded by professionals, some of whom were schoolchildren on that dark September day, who had devoted themselves to defending America and her ideals, listening to a president who voiced them unequivocally—for us, for all Americans, and for the world.

* * *

My story came full circle that day, but it had also come around in a different, but equally meaningful, manner a couple weeks prior. As the final weeks of the administration were upon us, President Obama made it a point to pose for photographs in the Oval Office with members of his team. With just a few days' advance notice, I called my family to let them know of the opportunity to join me for the experience. The last-minute airfare was steep, and I had expected them to decline the invitation, as we would be convening days later for Thanksgiving in Nashville. Within hours, however, I found myself with five relatives, plane tickets in hand.

Introducing family to the President of the United States isn't a light endeavor even under the best of circumstances. In this case, my father— a lifelong Democrat and ardent admirer of President Obama—had passed away just a few months before.

This was the first time we had been together since his memorial.

But just as striking as his absence was the presence of another family member: my eldest nephew, a fifteen-year-old named Nicolas. When the phone rang in my dorm room at that seemingly ungodly early hour on that bright Tuesday morning fifteen years earlier, I had assumed the news on the other end would be his arrival. I ended up having to wait another two weeks for that message. The twenty-four/ seven network news coverage had barely subsided when he was born in late September.

In the Oval Office that day, however, Nicolas and President Obama shook hands, neither understanding the connection between them that had distilled in my mind. But, to me, it was as clear as the cloudless blue sky that September morning.

Nicolas need not live in a world of corrupting and corrosive fear, and President Obama had shown him—and all Americans—how it could be done.

SÍ SE PUEDE

Julie Chávez Rodriguez

n my family, *sí se puede*—"yes we can"—is more than a campaign
slogan. It is a way of life.

Most Americans know César Estrada Chávez as one of the
founders of the United Farm Workers movement, the organizing effort to improve wages, working conditions, and state and federal
laws protecting farm workers. But I knew him as my grandfather,
Tata César.

My grandfather was my entire world growing up. He represented
the powerful, often hidden, human potential that exists throughout
our communities. He was a small, brown, soft-spoken farm worker
with an eighth grade education who organized his fellow workers and
eventually brought down one of the richest, most powerful industries
in the United States. He was like a real-life superhero to me because
he fought for and with his values.

When I was in third grade, he came to speak to my class in Ken-
ilworth, New Jersey. Afterward in the bathroom one of my classmates asked me what it was like to have a "famous" grandfather. I
didn't think of my grandfather as famous; I just thought of him as

Tata, someone who worked hard, traveled a lot, and fought for the most vulnerable.

Growing up alongside my grandfather, I experienced hard work firsthand. Eighteen-hour days, early mornings and late nights, spending most of our time in the car traveling from house meetings to college campuses to farms to marches. The life of an organizer was one I admired and sought out because organizing, as the fabled community organizer Fred Ross put it, "is providing people with the opportunity to become aware of their own capabilities and potential." And in organizing farm workers, who are often seen as the poorest and least educated workers in our country, my grandfather showed people— and most importantly the farm workers themselves—they had the power and ability to change their own conditions.

I never worked in the fields, but my mother and her siblings did. She didn't talk about it that much because it was a painful part of her childhood, but every now and then she would share stories about how much she "hated cotton, the devil's crop" because the thorns would tear up her fingers and she only got paid by the weight of the bag. She, her older siblings, and my grandmother worked in the fields to support their family when my grandfather decided to quit his job to start organizing. She saw it for what it was: modern-day indentured servitude.

These early experiences made my mother a fierce advocate for justice and equity, and she worked hard to raise us with the same values. One of my earliest memories from school is from the second grade when my teacher put me in the lowest reading level, telling me, "You're one of the farm worker kids." My mother—who had taught me to read early out of spite for the "grower families" who assumed "farm worker kids" were all illiterate and uneducated—confronted her and had me moved to the top reading level.

Far from being uneducated, I had an incredible education growing up in the movement. Every day was Organizing 101 from some of the best in the business. In 1987, my sister and I joined our grandfather during his speech at the Second National March on Washington for Lesbian and Gay Rights. It was my first real experience with solidarity and coalition building. Carried on my grandfather's shoulders, we chanted, "Two, four, six, eight—Being Gay Is Really Great! Eight, six, four, two—Being Gay Is Good for You!"

In 1986, my dad was asked to lead the East Coast grape boycott, so we moved to New Jersey. This was the third grape boycott, demanding the ban of five pesticides primarily used on table grapes that were causing cancer clusters and leukemia outbreaks in farm worker communities throughout California's Central Valley. My dad's job, and by extension the marching orders I heard loud and clear at eight years old, was to generate as much public support for the boycott as possible. This was my first real experience with public engagement, including selling buttons and T-shirts and marching in the major parades in New York City. Living in New Jersey and spending time in New York also helped me realize the diversity of the Latino community and experience in the United States. The experiences of Puerto Ricans and Cubans were different from the Mexican farm workers I grew up around, but that didn't seem to matter; they still experienced discrimination because of their place of origin, the color of their skin, and oftentimes where they lived.

While I had a ton of fun marching in the annual Labor and Puerto Rican Day parades, meeting celebrities and important people, there were a lot of not-so-great moments, too, like the countless times people told us to "go back to Mexico" or "get a real job." Or the time in Fresno when, during my grandfather's thirty-six-day water-only fast, an old woman looked me in the eye and said, "I hope he dies this time."

While these were painful experiences at the time, they allowed me to see and confront hate and bigotry head-on from an early age. Raised by a community of organizers, activists, and regular people who believed that they could, and did, change the world was the best experience a child could have. My grandfather once said, "We can choose to use our lives for others to bring about a better and more just world for our children. People who make that choice will know hardship and sacrifice . . . And in giving of yourself you will discover a whole new life full of meaning and love."

I knew that was the kind of life I wanted to lead, so I started volunteering at age five, throwing out the trash at the Farm Workers Credit Union where my grandmother, Helen Chávez, worked. From there, I got to work volunteering whenever I could—after school, on weekends, during Easter and summer breaks—and learned the lessons that shaped me as an activist. Educating the public about cancer-causing pesticides taught me that it's never about grapes, as my grandfather once said; it's always about people. Leading sit-ins in Sacramento when I was sixteen taught me that we need to stake out our rightful seat in the halls of power because as my grandfather prophesied in 1984, "The day will come when the politicians do the right thing by our people out of political necessity and not out of charity or idealism." Registering voters at seventeen to combat the anti-immigrant Proposition 187 in California taught me that voting matters and we need to exercise our right to vote for our immigrant brothers and sisters who aren't able to. Seeing the sacrifices my mom and dad made and shadowing them at meetings, rallies, and conventions taught me what it meant to be a part of something bigger than myself.

The farm worker movement will always be the roots of my conviction, but I finally found my own version of that "something bigger" when I found Barack Obama . . . or rather, Michelle Obama. I was speaking at a Campus Compact event at UNC Chapel Hill when I saw a video message from a woman who spoke of national service in the same vein as community organizing. I knew I had found a kindred spirit. A few months later, when her husband, Barack, announced his candidacy for president, I was an instant fan. I knew someone with a strong, powerful woman by his side would be a leader with character and conviction, just like my grandfather. My family was connected to the old-school Latino political circles at the time, who had been staunch supporters of the Clintons, so they endorsed and supported Hillary Clinton. But my cousin Christine and I were all Obama from day one. I knew I had to prove these skeptics wrong, but being stubborn like my grandfather sometimes pays off, so I took the challenge head-on and took a monthlong vacation to go out to Colorado and help get Obama elected.

After the election I went back to my nonprofit job with the César E. Chávez Foundation, which I loved, but I wasn't the same. I had just turned thirty-one, but with twenty years of political organizing and activism under my belt, I needed something new and different. I needed to get out of Los Angeles, where I had lived for the past nine years, and experience achievement and success apart from my family. Joining the Obama administration felt like a good way to address my early-onset midlife crisis.

The hardest part was telling my father and my uncle that I was quitting the family business to join the ranks of a federal government that had rarely been on our side. I spent many restless nights thinking about my grandfather's decision to turn down an appointment from President Kennedy because he believed that government was not the best way for him to help his people. I wondered if I was being too idealistic believing President Obama could lead the country with integrity and values in the same way my grandfather led the farm worker movement. I worried that my father and uncle might think I was a sellout. That they would criticize me for thinking that government could be more effective at improving people's lives than organizing and providing direct services. I didn't want either of them to question my loyalty to the farm workers, the labor movement, or my family.

Despite all of my fears, they responded with the three words that have catalyzed and characterized the farm worker movement since the earliest days, *sí se puede*. But they warned me that politics was tough, that it could be ugly and sometimes bitter, and I needed to stick to my values and never lose sight of who or what I was working for: the people.

They were right. My first year in the administration was incredibly difficult. Not because of the job, but because I had the opportunity—at times, it felt like the misfortune—to serve as deputy press secretary for the Department of the Interior during the BP oil spill in 2010.

It was on-the-job training in crisis communications. We worked eighteen-hour days, fielding calls from every investigative reporter in the country, trying to pull together as much data as we could to clearly communicate what we had done and were doing to stop the oil from gushing into the ocean—even though no one really had any idea how to stop it. Fortunately, growing up an organizer prepared me for the intensity of the work, but working at lightning speed with no room for mistakes required a new level of precision under fire. It pushed me to my limits but taught me that I could perform under pressure. It made me realize that I loved organizing and strategic communications. It also made me realize that I did not want to work with reporters.

I loved the work and the people at Interior, but I also wouldn't give up on the dream of working directly for a president who shared the same values I held so deeply, especially after meeting him in 2009 when he signed the first César Chávez Day proclamation in the Oval Office. I was so nervous to meet him: a man who had run a political organizing operation that was, in many ways, a modern version of my grandfather's work with the Community Service Organization in East L.A. during the 1950s. In usual form, he was engaging and attentive. He talked about the significance of my grandfather's work and the importance of community organizing, and he listened intently as my aunts and uncles shared a little of our family's memories and experiences. President Obama in the flesh was the real deal. I knew I wanted to do whatever I could to make his vision for America a reality.

A little over two years later, I walked into the lobby of the West Wing for a job interview with sweaty palms but the confidence of an organizer who doesn't take no for an answer. I told only my father about the interview because I didn't want to let too many people in my family know, just in case I didn't get the job. I also wanted to make sure my candidacy had as little to do with my family relationships as possible. I might have done that a little too well; I later found out that White House chief of staff Denis McDonough didn't even know I was related to César Chávez until I introduced the President at a 2014 screening of the film *Cesar Chavez* three years later.

When I got the offer to come on board as the President's liaison to the Latino community and point person on immigration-related outreach, I could not think of a better fit for my skills and experiences. My grandmother Nana Helen was so proud, but of course gave me my first marching orders—to "tell President Obama that we need immigration reform. We need to help the farm workers and the immigrants in the country."

One of my earliest events with the President was an address celebrating Hispanic Heritage Month. Waiting with him in the Green

Room as he was getting ready to walk onstage to deliver his remarks, I stood there, frozen. Eventually Cecilia Muñoz, who served on his senior staff and was a mentor to many of the Latino staff at the White House, introduced me as the newest member of his team. He didn't remember me from the short Oval Office meeting back in 2009, but the brief minute I had with him now, as a member of his team, solidified my commitment to helping him realize his vision for a progressive America.

A daughter and granddaughter of farm workers was working for the President of the United States. Things were different this time. The vision for government that President Obama and his entire administration brought to bear felt different from past administrations, especially the notion that the best ideas don't come from Washington—and actually operationalizing it, not just saying it. This time, we—the organizers, the advocates, the idealists—were on the inside rather than banging on the doors outside. And we came with an agenda and a responsibility to the millions of people we brought with us and represented at the highest levels of power. I felt the strength of the shoulders I stood on; the people who came before me who organized for change, freedom, and inclusion so people who looked like me and lived my experience could claim their rightful seat at the most powerful table in the world.

That's why I spent every weekend of my first ten months at the White House on the road, organizing twenty-three White House Hispanic Community Action Summits from North Carolina to Denver and everywhere in between where I could find a sizable Latino population (which is basically everywhere in America). We traveled across the country with regional representatives from federal agencies to talk about the issues most pressing in the Latino community, like small business growth and development, education and college affordability, health care and the Affordable Care Act, in addition to immigration. We brought the federal government to the people.

We confronted issues head-on, especially the record number of deportations the Obama administration oversaw. Most of our conversations were not comfortable, but they were critical, because people throughout our community needed to understand how government works, where there were critical pressure points, and how we could work together to provide relief for our communities. I had the benefit of my experiences on both sides of the divide. As a government insider and organizer, I could explain where they should push from the outside to maximize the levers we were pulling on the inside. The most uplifting part about the summits was always the end, when everyone came back together, and despite some of the concerns raised, people felt like their concerns had been heard and they knew what to do next. They were empowered and motivated, and realized government was a vehicle and tool for change, even though it didn't have all of the answers and solutions at its immediate disposal.

Barack Obama has always been proud of his roots as a community organizer, but I wonder if even he was fully prepared for the power of organizing during his presidency. It was seasoned organizers that helped pass the Affordable Care Act and continue to keep it intact today by working in our communities. Organizers helped fight for DACA and built a campaign to provide protection for over eight hundred thousand Dreamers. Organizers ran Supreme Court campaigns to support marriage equality and fight Arizona's anti-immigrant law SB 1070. We created programs like Champions for Change to use the White House's platform to lift up everyday organizers in communities across the country and My Brother's Keeper to provide an opportunity for young men of color to succeed.

We, the organizers, also made sure the President and his team had constant interactions with regular Americans so they would never forget that the work was never about policy, it was always about people.

The inflection point of this connection—between my roots in the farm worker movement and my job at the White House—came in October 2012. We were about a month out from the President's reelection campaign and I was getting ready to head to Colorado to volunteer on the campaign when I received a call from my boss. He told me that the President was going to use the Antiquities Act, which permits the President to authorize a segment of land for specific historic or conservation use, to designate a new monument. President Obama had used this authority before, but this time it was personal. He was coming to the community where I grew up—Nuestra Señora Reina de La Paz (Our Lady of Peace)—to designate the César E. Chávez National Monument in recognition of my grandfather, the farm workers, and the thousands of volunteers who forever changed the trajectory of farm workers' conditions in our country. To etch them into the American story, never to be erased, undone, or unseen.

This is the community where I rode a Big Wheel down the hills and built forts in the nearby creek. I couldn't have imagined this in my wildest dreams: the President of the United States coming to my small, farm worker community at the foothills of the Tehachapi Mountains, the headquarters of the United Farm Workers and the burial place of my grandfather and now my grandmother.

I was on the ground five days out from the event to help with logistics, including where to stage the event and how to get over ten thousand people down a narrow winding road. I was responsible for negotiating the details of the program and the President's meeting with Chávez family members—and thank goodness, because I know how stubborn my family can be (after all, we all bear Tata César's last name) and wouldn't have wanted any of my fellow staff in that position. Nor would I have trusted any other member of the White House staff to ensure that my Nana Helen's wishes were met at every turn, to keep the dedication less about my grandfather and more about the movement he inspired.

I also wouldn't have wanted to be anywhere else when the President met my family, entering the room casual and cool as always, especially when he felt he was among friends. "Hi, everybody," he began. And then he continued, "Now, before I meet all of you I just want you to know how proud we are of Julie and the tremendous job she is doing for me at the White House. You all should be proud, too." I was stunned. It didn't matter that I knew Valerie Jarrett had probably told him before he entered the room that it might be a nice gesture to give me, his employee, a shout-out in front of my entire family. What mattered was he did it, and he said it, and it was heartfelt.

I earned my activist credentials at age nine, when I was arrested while handing out leaflets outside a supermarket. But I often felt like it was hard for my family to see me as anything other than that budding activist, eager to head back to the picket line and get arrested again the next day. But that day, with President Obama's help, I became something more in their eyes. I became respected as a leader among them.

As the official program began, I stood a little off to the side as the President watched backstage. When my father walked out to the podium to introduce him, I heard the President say very adamantly, "Go get 'em, Arturo," as though he were cheerleader in chief for a moment. I couldn't help but smile with pride seeing my two worlds collide in such a deep and meaningful way. To hear the President pay tribute to the "generation of organizers who stood up and spoke out, and urged others to do the same" was one of my proudest moments. I felt this profound sense of acceptance and recognition for the work I had committed myself to doing at the age of five when I told my parents I was ready for my first job in the Farm Workers Credit Union. The President, a former community organizer himself, lifted up the role of organizers in our country by building a campaign that fostered a new generation of organizers like my grandfather had in the 1960s, and by filling the halls of government with people committed to institutional change that wouldn't take no for an answer.

Later, the President took my grandmother by the arm and walked with her to lay a red rose at my grandfather's grave site. She was so moved by how humble the President was and how respectfully he treated her. She told me that when the President entered the room he addressed her first, which she wasn't accustomed to because she preferred to work behind the scenes and hated recognition or the spotlight. She refused public interviews and tried to avoid asserting her leadership in the farm worker movement. But because she was also a supreme organizer, she made sure I knew what she told him. "I want you to do something about immigration as soon as you get re-elected"—and she said he promised her he would. She cherished that day and that moment in particular until her final days.

Not every day was as happy or proud as that one. There were hard, frustrating days when it seemed like the levers of government were impossible to move quickly, or move at all. But I left the experience firm in my belief that the pursuit for justice and equity has to be as strong inside government as it is outside. The generations that fought so hard for our right to vote, to march, to organize, to hold office, and to exercise our power demand that we take our pursuit for justice and freedom to every inch of our country, including and especially in our government.

As I was starting my transition out of the White House in 2016, all

I could think about was sleep, rest, reflection. I wanted time to absorb the lessons I learned working for the first African American, organizer president—until Wednesday, November 9, hit. Like so many Americans, I was in a state of shock after the election that lasted even longer than I anticipated. But in that state of shock, I realized that now was not the time to abandon the halls of government; now was the time to continue to organize from within. Fortunately, there was a new, smart, fierce senator from my home state of California who had just been elected: Kamala D. Harris. I was moved by Senator Harris's Jamaican and Indian immigrant roots coupled with her civil rights upbringing and lifelong work to advance justice. In her, I recognized the next wave of authentic leadership reshaping politics in our country. Leaders like Stacey Abrams, the first African American woman to run for governor in Georgia; Mayor Michael Tubbs in Stockton, California, testing new ways to address income inequality; Congressman Ruben Gallego in Phoenix, Arizona, a Marine Corps veteran who has fought Arizona's anti-immigrant agenda and leaders; Mayor Ras Baraka in Newark, New Jersey, building street teams block by block to provide critical support and services to communities most traumatized by poverty and violence; or Mayor Robert Garcia in Long Beach, California; and so many more who have decided to run for office and organize at every level because, as my grandfather said, "Once social change begins, it cannot be reversed. You cannot uneducate the person who has learned to read. You cannot humiliate the person who feels pride. You cannot oppress the people who are not afraid anymore . . . I've seen the future and the future is ours." My grandfather's work is not yet done, and neither is mine.

Sí se puede.

RIGHT WHERE WE BELONG

Rumana Ahmed

Ms. Ahmed, is your escort on their way?"

I looked up. The voice came from a Secret Service officer stationed between the entrance to the West Wing and the Situation Room. He had biceps the size of my head.

I sank farther into the cushions of an old blue sofa, hoping to disappear. I was in awe of my surroundings. The West Wing was surprisingly small and old-fashioned with its low ceilings, narrow corridors, and worn yellowish carpeting. But being in the presence of all its history and grandeur was both empowering and terrifying.

One of the Situation Room doors swung open, and a stream of hurried staffers poured out into the lobby, some still in conversation. Every time the door opened I straightened up to catch a glimpse of the world inside, but all I could see was a narrow hallway. It was hard to believe I was seated just steps away from the small room where President Obama and his team crammed together to take down Osama bin Laden.

Slowly, I began to notice people glancing at me, looking up from their conversations or catching a glimpse as they walked to the Navy Mess just around the corner to pick up their lunches. I suddenly felt anxious. I felt my throat clenching and mind racing as I tried to interpret their looks. I knew this feeling. I had spent my teenage years being given these looks. All I could think was, *Not again*.

I stood out. A twenty-three-year-old woman with a headscarf in the West Wing of the White House.

I chose to start wearing hijab when I was twelve years old. For me, wearing hijab was a reminder of faith, humility, and identity. I also copied everything my sister did, and she chose to start covering her hair even before my own mother did. For many years, it felt normal. No one looked or treated me any differently.

Until September 11. On top of the shock and horror of that awful day, I now had to cope with being cursed at, spat at, called a "terrorist," and told, "Go back to where you came from!" It was everywhere: customers in a store, a car stopped next to us at a red light, people walking down the street. Almost overnight, memories of a normal American childhood were replaced with feelings of fear and alienation.

Born and raised in a diverse suburb of Maryland, I was unprepared to respond to the sudden unfamiliar new reality of having my patriotism questioned. My parents, who immigrated to America from Bangladesh in 1978 in search of a better life for their kids, taught my siblings and me the importance of faith, compassion, and perseverance. My mother worked as a cashier at a Rite Aid, trying to perfect her English, and later started her own day care business. My father spent late nights working at Bank of America, and, despite complaints by colleagues about "the immigrant" having a leadership role, he was eventually promoted to assistant vice president. He was pursuing his PhD when he was killed in a car accident in 1995.

My parents battled with being undermined by colleagues for their accents and the color of their skin. They worked long hours and endured to prove their worth and dedication. They excelled, and they did it with a level of humility that I wanted to embody. Whenever I debated taking off my headscarf, I tried to remember their struggles and sacrifice.

It wasn't always easy. In 2003, at the start of my freshman year in high school, I was walking down a stairwell to get to my next class when I felt a tug on the back of my hijab and a push on my left shoulder. I looked back, hoping it was just an accident. Instead, I saw a fellow freshman staring down from the step behind me, grinning wide through his braces.

"Terrorist!"

It's okay. Ignore him. That was what everyone—school counselors, friends, most adults in my life—told me to do. After all, no one really wants to address the issue or confront the perpetrator. Instead, we learn to ignore it.

Then came a second, more forceful shove. I lost my balance and stumbled forward, grabbing the railing to prevent a humiliating fall. To my own surprise, I whipped around and pushed him back and said through clenched teeth, "Don't touch me."

It was the first time I had ever responded directly to such hostility. Not because I wanted a fight, but because I was exhausted to my core. I'd had enough of being robbed of my identity. I was just a fourteen-year-old who longed to be able to stand up and say: *I exist. This is me.*

That day, I discovered a new strength. I couldn't give in to others seeking to suppress me with fear and hate. Instead, my hijab became a source of pride, the foundation for my resilience, a reminder and bold statement of who I am.

With my newfound confidence, I started to take on more challenges. I started our school's Muslim Students Association and by senior year was elected the student body president—by a student body with very few Muslims. Between organizing school socials and student visits to soup kitchens, I hosted events like Muslim Awareness Week, to patiently address the array of "burning questions" people had, based upon inaccuracies in the news: *Why do you hate America? Are you forced to cover your hair? Do you sleep with it? Shower with it? Do you have hair?*

I hoped that one day all this scrutiny would end and I could return to a normal life again.

Then came election night in 2008. An African American with the name Barack Hussein Obama became president—a thought previously unimaginable. The prospect of a new era felt within reach. For millions of people like me—who felt like second-class Americans because of their skin color or name or faith, who felt restrained from pursuing their American dream—the impossible suddenly felt possible.

I felt Barack Obama's victory as a debt owed to me and my community for enduring years of harassment and abandonment as Americans. His galvanizing messages of inclusivity and equality, human dignity, and strength in the face of adversity spoke to my own experiences and frustrations. His words were our words. His victory was our victory. "Our time" meant *my* time.

I felt that I had an enormous stake in this potential new future and wanted to be a part of it. Living so close to DC, I decided to apply for a White House internship, and in 2010, I joined the White House Office of Presidential Correspondence as an intern. I was ecstatic. Interning thirty-five hours a week, taking five classes my junior year at George Washington University, and working to pay for school while commuting was strenuous, to say the least. But this was a once-in-a-lifetime opportunity.

On my first day, I was greeted by hallways and desks stacked with thousands of letters. I never even knew you could write a letter to the president! It blew my mind that someone actually read them, and more so, that President Obama even responded to ten of them each day.

Reading about the hopes, needs, and struggles of everyday Americans across the country was humbling, and gave me perspective beyond the political bubble of Washington. I read letters from a father struggling to find a job to support his family, a daughter left to raise her siblings after her mother was deported, a man trying to fight for his home against the colonization of oil investors and pipelines, a child pleading with the President to pardon the minor crimes of her incarcerated father.

Then there were all the joyful letters—baby pictures accompanying requests for presidential greetings, stories of lives that had been changed because of a letter from the President, and kindergarteners of every race and ethnicity wanting to be president one day just like him. These letters, and the voices behind them, meant something to the President, and to us. He shared the letters he read with his staffers and members of Congress. One of those letters, from a cancer-stricken woman, became a centerpiece in the legislative campaign for health care reform.

At the end of the internship, as all 120 of us lined up for our group departure photo below the Truman balcony, I was positioned in the front row. I looked down to see a blue-taped X on the floor. My heart was pounding. For the first time, "random selection" played in my favor: I was going to be right next to the President!

President Obama addressed the group and stood for the photo, placing his arm around my shoulder. I couldn't help but wrap my arm around his waist. He was so lean I thought I could probably reach around him. Being only five-three—and stupidly wearing flats that day—I felt the President tower eleven inches over me. Afterward, when he turned to me to shake my hand and ask for my name, everything I had planned to say got stuck in my throat. All I remember was gawking at him and replying with an awkwardly prolonged "hiiiii."

Working in the Correspondence Office made me realize and appreciate the power and resilience of the American people—and the impact individual voices could have, including my own. I wanted to continue the work, so I occasionally came back to help out as a volunteer. Then, three months before graduation, I was invited to return for a full-time position in the summer of 2011, and ten months later, the director of my office approached me about an opening . . . in the West Wing.

And that's how I ended up sitting on that blue sofa outside the Situation Room on my first day of work in the White House Office of Public Engagement. As I sat there, worrying I might not be welcome, a staff member I did not recognize or expect approached me. He enthusiastically introduced himself, asked me about myself, and offered to walk me to my desk. I later learned he was Chris Lu, a member of the President's senior staff and a longtime advisor.

Despite my initial fears, I quickly found that kind of treatment to be the norm. As I helped OPE in its mission to engage a broad range of communities on issues like health care reform and small business accessibility, I saw firsthand the power and impact of the President. He could make a call for action, unite and empower marginalized communities, and provide strength and calm in times of fear.

I wanted to create a similar opportunity for Muslims in America. After years of being the target of the former administration's xenophobic policies, my community desperately hoped to regain trust in their government. They wanted to be affirmed as full members of American public life. Engaging Muslims had been a priority from early on in the administration—the President had visited mosques during international trips and invited American Muslims to events like the annual White House Iftar—but he had yet to visit an American mosque or hear just from American Muslims on domestic issues. Over the next two years, a few of us in the White House—as well as community leaders—requested that the President host a meeting or visit a mosque in the United States, but to no avail. It was no secret that there were some staff who opposed the idea of the President visiting a mosque, fearing a backlash from right-wing critics who claimed he was secretly a Muslim.

A new window of opportunity opened in 2014. While helping with public engagement efforts around Israeli-Palestinian peace efforts and initiating the first White House Persian Nowruz celebrations, I had the chance to work with colleagues at the National Security Council who were enthusiastic about my efforts and seemed willing to make the case for it, despite others' fears and reservations.

Ben Rhodes, one of President Obama's closest advisors and his deputy national security advisor, took notice—and was willing to support our request to get a roundtable with American Muslims on the President's calendar. As a result of our conversation, he also invited me to join the NSC, where my role would include expanding their outreach efforts to advance U.S. policies with Cuba, Burma, and Laos. I had the opportunity to lead engagements with Cuban Americans leading up to and following the President's historic announcement to open U.S.-Cuba relations and witness negotiations between our countries; hear from Rohingya activists and young leaders in Burma; meet families and children in Laos continuing to suffer from unexploded ordnances dropped by the U.S. during the Vietnam War and help plan the President's announcement to double aid to remove them.

While my new office—just down the hall from the Situation Room—was significantly smaller, my ability to do more and make a greater impact grew a little wider.

A few months later, in February 2015, President Obama finally met with Muslim leaders, youth, and parents. It was a pivotal moment for the community and, as a member of the community, a privilege to prepare the President for it. As I briefed him in the Oval Office prior to the meeting, he mentioned his surprise at how long it had taken for this meeting to happen. It seemed as though the cautions expressed by some of my colleagues did not necessarily reflect the President's perspective.

In the Roosevelt Room, the President listened attentively and promised follow-up on issues like disparities in funds allocated for mental health support between Muslim communities and other faith communities. One of the attendees handed him a valentine from an eleven-year-old girl named Sabrina that said, "I enjoy being an American" and "if some Muslims do bad things, that doesn't mean all of them do." She asked him to "please tell everyone that we are good people and we're just like everyone else."

Just five days after the meeting, three young American Muslims were brutally executed in their home in Chapel Hill, North Carolina. Their devastating death further shook the community, especially young people who suddenly felt more vulnerable than ever.

Further exacerbating the situation and fueling hatred against Muslims, later that year, Republican front-runner Donald Trump called for a "complete shutdown" of Muslims entering the United States. Within weeks of his call for a ban, a car nearly hit me in a parking lot while the driver laughed. On another occasion, I was cursed at and told, "Trump will send you back to where you came from!" at a Metro station. Despite trying to keep a strong face and heart, there were days I found myself acting apprehensive and cautious. On some nights when I worked late, my boss, Ben, concerned for my safety, would email to check if I got home safe.

At the time, I was also volunteering at a Sunday school, teaching fifth graders at my local mosque. They started asking me if their families would get deported, and how to stop being bullied by teachers and peers or harassed in public. Even though I could relate to their anxiety, I could not bear to see such small, terrified faces. I had hoped this new political era would mean they never had to experience a childhood like mine. My sister, a public school teacher, and I organized a school assembly to coach the students on standing up to the various types of discrimination and staying safe. I reminded them, as I often remind myself, that we're not the first to face and overcome such hatred and intolerance. We have figures like Martin Luther King Jr. and Muhammad Ali to give us strength.

Nonetheless, I felt like I owed those children more. I felt like *their president* owed them more. I wanted these kids to have what I never did when I was their age—a president who was willing to go to bat for them, passionately and publicly.

The next day, I saw a colleague who stopped covering, fearful for her and her family's safety after being threatened on social media. I learned from other Muslim White House staffers that they had experienced similar threats themselves or had heard about it from their kids.

I felt like my faith was under attack from all sides. I was disheartened to hear some colleagues talk about hate crimes against Muslims as, first and foremost, a national security issue. They worried, without any real evidence, that a rise in discrimination would lead to greater marginalization of Muslims, making them vulnerable to ISIS recruitment. However, they failed to realize that recruitment by terrorists abroad was the last thing on the minds of American Muslims who were agonizing over how to protect their families here at home. This was, above all, a matter of religious freedom, civil rights, and humanity.

I felt like I needed to do something. I could not sit by and watch a replay of the previous administration's mistakes. I emailed Denis McDonough, the White House chief of staff, who responded immediately and invited me to meet with him the same day. He later hosted a meeting with White House staffers who were experiencing racism and bigotry, after which he approached me to ask if he could hear from and speak to the kids at my mosque himself. We had known each other only in passing, but I was moved by the genuine concern, care, and gesture at his own volition.

As senior White House officials became increasingly aware of the growing severity of the situation—and the need to act—they held another meeting with American Muslim leaders.

Moved by their heartbreaking accounts, the senior staff began discussing a range of options. When one official asked whether we should in fact consider a mosque visit, as had been requested for years, another responded strongly, "Yes, it needs to happen. It should have already happened. We need to get it on the calendar ASAP." Persuaded, the senior staff asked us to identify potential mosques and begin planning the visit.

Finally.

After the meeting, two of my colleagues, Huma and Manar, and I embraced each other, elated, relieved, almost in tears. Here we were, three Muslim women who in addition to our daily jobs had been strategizing and pushing for months for a presidential visit to a mosque. Yes, it was long overdue; but the timing could not have been more urgent. We understood the impact the President's visit would have on millions of people. It was a message America and the world needed to hear.

And we had less than five weeks to plan it.

I knew it would be a challenge to find a mosque that would fit everyone's expectations and hopes. Just like most other religious institutions, not every mosque shares the same perspectives or values, and the background of any single congregant does not represent that of the whole congregation. Picking the right mosque was critically important. Its origin and history, contributions to the local community, diversity of congregants, location, infrastructure, and visuals all mattered. Every detail carried sensitivities and a significance that could allow people to relate or challenge their own assumptions and biases.

Denis had his deputy call me one weekend to ask whether the President should visit my mosque. As much as I personally loved the idea of it, I knew it wasn't the perfect choice. I wanted an option that could accommodate a larger and more diverse crowd, to reflect the momentousness of the visit.

After reviewing multiple options, the Islamic Society of Baltimore (ISB) stood out. Like so many other mosques around the country, it had an all-American story with a community that worked on the front lines of some of the city's most pressing issues: urban development, equal housing, environmental preservation, and social justice. The ISB community started in the 1960s as a small gathering of students and physicians at Johns Hopkins University and has since grown to comprise a nursery, an accredited full-time K–12 school, athletic programs, Girl Scouts, a health clinic that serves patients regardless of their faith, and programs to integrate immigrants. It's a place of worship, education, interfaith dialogue, and civic activism.

Immense care went into planning the event. At a time when images of Muslims and symbols of Islam are perverted by ISIS and demonized by the right-wing media, too many Americans have been conditioned to perceive Muslims fearfully, cautiously, and narrowly. It was important for the broader public to see mosques in a different light. And it was imperative that we use the moment to showcase, through members of the audience, the diversity of American Muslims, including service members, first responders, and various ethnicities, sects, and academic backgrounds. We included family members of the late Muhammad Ali, congressional leaders, and world-renowned American fencer Ibtihaj Muhammad, who, in a few weeks, was to become the first hijab-wearing American Muslim woman to compete for the United States in the Olympics.

Most importantly, we had to get the President's remarks just right. In the lead-up to the visit, the President's speechwriter asked me to work with him from the start to accurately capture the experiences and stories of everyday American Muslims and call on every American to stand against hate. The President's words held the power to help reassure an already anxious public, give hope and fortitude to those being attacked, subdue some offenders, and demand action from complicit bystanders.

I worked with my former colleagues in the Correspondence Office to identify letters from American Muslims that the President could share in his speech to humanize their stories to allow people to grasp the devastating impact of bigotry. One of those letters, from a girl in Texas, asked, "When will the world realize that terrorism has no religion, race, or color?" and was signed, "Sincerely, a confused 14-year-old trying to find her place in the world." Another boy wrote, "We just want to live in peace . . . Please if you could show people that we're not all bad."

Early on the morning of February 3, 2016, the White House sent out an email previewing the President's speech at ISB. I was asked to be the author and express, through my own words and experience, the significance of his visit. It was a message I wanted to share with every American:

> Muslim Americans who teach our future generations in the classroom, who take care of us in the doctors' offices, who inspire us on and off the field, who protect us on the front lines of war . . . have always reminded me proudly, that yes, I am Muslim and American. In this country, I don't have to choose. . . . If you work hard and if you play by the rules, you can make it if you try in America—no matter who you are or how you pray. It's how a young girl—once mocked and called names—can . . . proudly serve her country as a head-covering Muslim American woman in the White House.

As the presidential motorcade made its way into Maryland, I found myself overwhelmed by the influx of supportive emails. Friends, family, and colleagues all grateful this was happening. Elated knowing thousands were eagerly looking forward to his speech and what it meant for them. Hopeful it would have the intended impact. Crushed by the unfortunate circumstances it took for his visit to have to happen. Nervous about anything going wrong. And bracing for the online attacks to come.

Like countless Muslims across America, I had spent most of my life feeling vilified, held back, and in the last few months, attacked by political campaigns. Working toward and achieving a moment like this felt like breaking through years of relentless waves that had tried to drown us out. For the first time, an American president would deliver an entire speech to an audience of Muslims in America, to bring to the forefront the struggles, history, resilience, and contributions of Muslims here at home.

As we pulled into the front of the mosque, the marquee read, "There is no progress without struggle." I smiled. In that moment, I needed the reminder.

A few hours later, President Obama stood at a podium—shoeless, as is customary in prayer spaces. He was backed by window panels, each etched with what Muslims reference as the "99 Names of God," attributions universally recognized among all the major world religions: *The Greatest, The Creator, The Peace, The Most Merciful, The Most Gracious.*

He acknowledged the contributions and fears of Muslims in America; not only the fear of terrorism all Americans share, but the added fear of an entire community facing blame for the acts of a few. He called on every American to speak out against discrimination, reminding us that being silent is being complicit.

Directly addressing the youth in the room and those watching who felt threatened by the prospect of getting kicked out as immigrants or children of immigrants and questioned whether they belonged, he reassured them as president: "You're right where you belong . . . You're not Muslim or American. You're Muslim and American." Throughout his speech, children who watched the speech from the more spacious gymnasium next door could be heard clapping louder and longer than those in the smaller prayer hall where the President spoke.

After the speech, the President walked to the gymnasium, where he was welcomed by a large sign decorated with colorful little handprints and a sudden roar of cheers that could be heard across the mosque complex, produced by almost a hundred kids, reaching out their hands, faces lit up with bright smiles, enthusiastically waving American flags. He addressed them briefly, encouraging them to study, work hard, have fun, and reminding them they could be whatever they wanted to grow up to be. He then walked the line, giving fist bumps and taking selfies before departing.

I came across a group of girls and asked what they thought. Some were giggling in excitement, others in tears. One of them hugged me and said, "Finally someone said something. Thank you! This is the best day ever!" They felt abandoned in the silence, until their president reached out and spoke up. I knew that if I had heard his words as a young girl, I, too, would have felt recognized and empowered to fight the daily struggles and excel, and I would have carried that feeling of his words and presence with me for years to come.

Upon my return to my office, colleagues stopped by to congratulate me and praise the President's remarks. Ben Rhodes, who knew my own personal journey to and through the White House, and the challenges I'd faced and overcome, told me, "Hey, you did it. Those kids will always remember this. So, soak it in and f— the haters." We both knew one visit, even a presidential one, wouldn't end racism and bigotry against Muslims in America, but it gave us tools for the fight ahead: strength, unity, inspiration, and hope.

Thousands of letters and emails from across the country came in thanking the President. My friends in the Correspondence Office occasionally shared a few with me, including some that were addressed to me specifically in response to the email that was sent out by the White House under my name. Some made me choke up, and some I even got to keep, such as the one from a little girl who told me she never liked politics but now hoped to grow up to work in the White House just like me.

For weeks, my students at my mosque talked about President Obama's visit. They felt like someone cared. They felt like they mattered.

I could see them developing the same self-respect and confidence that has helped me navigate life, from the halls of my high school to the halls of power. That encouraged me to be bold, authentic, and unde-featable. That brought me, all those years later, to that blue sofa in the West Wing lobby, right where I belonged.

FIERY LATINAS

Stephanie Valencia

H i, I'm Sonia."

There she was: Sonia Sotomayor, nominee for associate justice of the Supreme Court of the United States, sticking out her hand across a table stacked with towers of binders in the "war room"—the headquarters of the day-to-day coordination around her confirmation.

The historic significance of her nomination to the highest court in the land didn't escape me; I had been an advocate inside the White House for it. But in that moment, as we shook hands, we were just two Latinas from two humble communities—a *boricua* from the Bronx and a Mexican American girl from a small town on the border—getting to know each other. We had both experienced success, struggle, and self-doubt on the path to that unlikely moment at 1600 Pennsylvania Avenue. Standing there, the broader impact of what her nomination meant to the country became very clear, and very personal. I could be her. Girls like us, from communities like ours, could look up to her and imagine being her. Getting her confirmed to the U.S. Supreme Court became much more than a political task; it reminded me why I had gotten involved in politics in the first place.

* * *

The first time I saw the White House, I was a sophomore in high school. My government class was visiting Washington, DC, for the 1997 inauguration of President Bill Clinton. We stood outside the White House gates, watching the Secret Service agents changing guard, news reporters doing live interviews, and staffers and other VIPs shuffling in and out of the West Wing.

Just getting there was an accomplishment, one that involved car washes, bake sales, and more or less begging our family and friends to help us each raise the money we needed for the trip. We were a long way from Las Cruces, New Mexico—a small, middle-class town only a few miles from the U.S.-Mexico border. Surrounded by both desert and mountains, the inherent charm and beauty of Las Cruces was and continues to be overshadowed by its dismal performance in national rankings of education, poverty, and places to raise a child. Mine was a hometown rich in culture, yet scarce in opportunity. There were more programs to stop kids from doing things—dropping out of school, getting pregnant, joining a gang, doing drugs, or drinking and driving—than there were AP classes. Temptation and distraction were everywhere, yet somehow we made it all the way to the White House.

As I stuck my little head through the gates to get a closer look, right then, I saw for the first time that there was a huge world outside of Las Cruces. Somehow, laying my eyes on it made it possible for me. If I could see it, I could be part of it.

Fast-forward ten years, and I stepped foot inside the White House for the first time. This time, I was there to work. It was just a few days after President Obama's inauguration. After many months of campaigning on behalf of the first African American president, I was one of the first to be hired in the Office of Public Engagement. We were all eager to translate the energy from the campaign into passing and implementing the President's agenda. Being a part of those early days was special. Exhausted, but exhilarated, my only ambition was to make real the change we had talked about on the campaign and wanted to see in the world.

As I walked through the security gates and up the grand stairs to the Eisenhower Executive Office Building, across the driveway from the West Wing, I was in awe to be on the other side of the gates. Only about an hour into my first day, I was called over to the West Wing for a meeting with the President to talk about our strategy on immigration. This was a president who wanted to elevate the role of Hispanic Americans, and who wanted to move quickly on immigration. I was the liaison to Latinos for the White House, and immigration was a key part of my portfolio. As I walked into the Roosevelt Room, I saw chief of staff Rahm Emanuel, senior advisor Valerie Jarrett, and Secretary of Homeland Security designee Janet Napolitano. I was definitely the youngest person in the room. And I was the only Latina.

When the President walked in, we all stood, and he took the time to greet everyone individually around the table. It was my first time seeing him since the election. Being there now, in his presence as president, felt more serious, more intense. I suddenly felt out of place there and tried to focus on being ready for a firm handshake. When he got to me I started to raise my hand, but instead he gave me a big hug. A huge wave of relief washed over me, and I was reminded I did belong there, and I had a job to do.

* * *

I quickly got used to being one of the few Latinos and Latinas in the White House, especially in the early days when the staff was still being assembled. On the front lines of outreach to the Latino community, I felt the unique weight of being one of the few people responsible for representing a community of millions who saw their hopes and dreams in President Obama.

I had done a similar job for the campaign, crisscrossing the country building strong relationships with Latino leaders while making the case that President Obama was the best choice for our community. It was a bitter primary season and the majority of Latino leaders across the country had supported Hillary Clinton, who had invested over twenty years in building deep relationships with the community. I had to convince them of what I had come to believe, that a new generation of leadership, embodied by President Obama, would be able to bring much-needed change and opportunity when we needed it. After eight long years under President Bush, expectations were high and action could not come quickly enough. I did not want to squander a single moment to live up to the commitments that we had made.

But despite early determination and optimism fueled by the President's landslide victory, in the months that followed, things didn't go as our White House team planned or expected. In fact, it was quite the opposite. We began in the thick of a financial crisis that would eventually cost the country 8.7 million jobs, which meant the President had to first focus on salvaging the economy, using his important first days in office to pass the stimulus and American Recovery and Reinvestment Act. The President next turned his attention to health care reform, hoping it could be accomplished in a few months, so that he could then shift his focus to other big priorities, like fixing the broken immigration system and climate legislation.

Governing, under any circumstances, is hard work, but we also had to deal with Senate Republicans willing to do everything in their power to stop his agenda. It was difficult to translate the energy we had generated on the campaign trail to passing legislation through Congress.

We were frustrated, and I found myself questioning whether Washington could actually change. I wasn't alone; Latino community leaders started to grow impatient. Long before they began to call him the "deporter in chief," I was his liaison, his primary interface to the community, taking the heat directly. There was not a day that I did not have to make several calls and convene meetings to keep the coalition together. As hopes dimmed for immigration reform, the community was eager for a win.

* * *

A president's one hundredth day in office is a symbolic moment. Unfortunately for us, reaching that milestone didn't help alleviate the anxiety that we weren't doing enough with health care and immigration against a rapidly ticking clock. Weeks felt like months. We easily clocked twelve- to fourteen-hour days during the week, so Fridays were extra sweet because we knew it meant a few extra hours of sleep on Saturday . . . before having to come into the office. During that first year in the White House, we only had desktop computers—no laptops—so believe it or not, there was no such thing as working remotely.

May 1, 2009, was a particularly busy Friday following a long week for me. I had been working on my first big immigration event with the President—a military naturalization ceremony for twenty-five active-duty service members, men and women from eighteen countries who were willing to die for this country, even though they weren't citizens. As I stood in the back of the room, watching him recite the pledge of allegiance in front of such a diverse group of new citizens, I could see the pride in his eyes. It was a powerful reminder for me about why I worked for President Obama—because that moment exemplified for him and for all of us in the room the difference his presence meant.

Still feeling the thrill of pulling off my first big event without a hitch, I headed back to my office in the Eisenhower Executive Office Building. After catching my breath and writing a few emails, I glanced up at our office TV to see President Obama doing an unplanned drop-by at press secretary Robert Gibbs's daily press briefing. I knew he rarely did that unless he had an announcement to make, so I turned up the volume.

CNN was covering the breaking news: Justice Souter had just called President Obama to inform him that he would be retiring, which meant there would be a vacancy on the Supreme Court. The commentators and pundits were already throwing out names of possible contenders, but one of them immediately caught my attention because of her last name: Sotomayor. *Could this actually be possible?*

* * *

I wasn't the only one excited about the prospect of a Latina on the Supreme Court. I spent the entire weekend fielding calls and emails about the open seat from the heads of Latino civil rights organizations, grassroots leaders, and the many Congressional Hispanic Caucus staffers I had worked with on Capitol Hill over the past five years.

At the same time, I was taking care of last-minute details for the White House Cinco de Mayo party, which would take place that following Monday. It was the first time the President and First Lady had opened up the White House for an event focused specifically on the Latino community. The guest list was a who's who of Latino leaders: Hispanic celebrities, members of Congress, heads of national Latino organizations, the President's cabinet, and grassroots organizers we got to know on the campaign who had never set foot in the White House.

Monday came, and the atmosphere was festive, with mariachis playing in the halls of the residence, and margaritas and *pan dulce* being passed around. It was a beautiful thing to see—our culture and community being celebrated by the first African American president. It was a rare moment to enjoy and celebrate the journey and all that we had accomplished.

But with Friday's news of a Supreme Court vacancy, people were buzzing. And as with all Washington parties, it's never just about fun; it's also about work. Congresswoman Nydia Velázquez, chair of the Congressional Hispanic Caucus, and Congressman José Serrano, a prominent Puerto Rican congressman from the Bronx, were there on a mission. In a small meeting with some key Latino leaders before the Cinco de Mayo reception, Velázquez and Serrano made a beeline to President Obama to remind him that nominating Sonia Sotomayor would be historic. Nydia physically grabbed President Obama by the arms with both hands, pulled him close, looked directly in his eyes, and told him in her signature Puerto Rican accent, "You have an opportunity here in your hands, to shape the United States Supreme Court for years to come."

That night, as I walked back from the party to my office through the West Wing colonnade, it became clear to me the kind of opportunity this was, and I knew that Sotomayor was a real contender. Sotomayor was *our* chance.

But I also knew President Obama didn't respond well to the kind of political pressure I saw that night, so it was unclear to me how he would react to their direct lobbying. I had seen him bristle on countless occasions when members of Congress came to him with their pet causes or unloaded their unsolicited advice. Having watched him deliberate over important decisions, I knew that he always kept his own counsel, and while he listened to recommendations, he liked to make decisions in his own way, guided by his own thought process—not political influence.

As I heard the President say countless times on the campaign trail and in debates, interviews, and roundtable discussions, his support for judicial nominees was based on their ability to understand the rule of law, exercise a sharp and independent mind, and respect the judicial process. He made it clear that excellence and diversity were not mutually exclusive and, as someone who knew equally well the streets of the South Side of Chicago and the halls of Harvard, believed that it was important to find individuals with empathy who could identify with the realities and struggles of regular people. This proximity to reality was a critical ingredient in the kind of justice he wanted to appoint to the court. He once said that deciding tough cases is like running a marathon, explaining that the first twenty-five miles are determined by precedent and technical understanding of the law, but "the last mile can only be determined on the basis of one's deepest values, one's core concerns, one's broader perspectives on how the world works, and the depth and breadth of one's empathy."

* * *

In the rare event of a vacancy on the Supreme Court, every community and affinity group begins jockeying to lobby for their preferred candidates. The stakes were especially high for the Latino community, which had never been represented on the nation's highest court, and I found myself under immense pressure to deliver. There was a constant flurry of activity among Latino leaders trying to exert public pressure: calls, letters, press releases. And in private meetings, no matter the topic, the possibility of a Latino nominee came up. Even at social events, national movement leaders who I looked up to would press me for information.

From the beginning, I made it clear to Latino leaders they needed to coalesce behind a single candidate if we were going to have a chance of convincing the President and his advisors. I was hopeful, but I knew that Mexican Americans and Puerto Ricans had never before agreed on a single candidate.

Within the White House, the Latino staff had assembled a strong informal task force across departments to coordinate policy and outreach to the Latino community. Cecilia Muñoz, who had spent two decades in Latino community advocacy, headed the Office of Intergovernmental Affairs; Luis Miranda was a dynamic spokesperson in the Communications Office; and Carlos Odio, a brilliant strategist, sat in the White House Political Affairs Office. As the senior Hispanic in the White House, Cecilia was our convener and we held regular meetings in her West Wing office to coordinate and leverage the resources of all our departments. We had all done our part to elevate the importance of selecting a Hispanic Supreme Court nominee through our respective departments. Now we had to wait.

The uncertainty meant we had to put together plans for both scenarios: one if Sotomayor was selected and one if she wasn't. The strategy for the former was pretty simple—lead with Sotomayor's qualifications because we knew they would be questioned (by the liberal elite and certainly by Republican senators who would accuse President Obama of playing politics with an activist judge); rally Latinos across the country for this historic choice; make certain that senators from states with a large Latino population (and specifically Puerto Rican population) know that a "no" vote would have serious consequences.

Then we had to put together a strategy for a scenario in which Sotomayor was not selected. By this point, I was so hopeful that the President would make this historic pick that I just couldn't convince myself to even envision a scenario where her nomination was not a reality. So we didn't write it. The one thing I did know for certain, however, was that if the President did not choose Sotomayor, I would have a total disaster on my hands. Convincing Latinos to rally around any other nominee would have been nearly impossible in that moment.

* * *

To be clear, not everyone was a Sotomayor fan, and that included some members of the liberal legal chattering class who were weighing in with their unsolicited opinions. One particularly memorable case was Professor Laurence Tribe of Harvard Law School, who strongly discouraged President Obama from nominating her, stating in a private memo that was leaked to the press, "Bluntly put, she's not nearly as smart as she seems to think she is."

When I read that memo, I wasn't sure what to think. I never doubted that Sotomayor was well qualified. And if someone as prominent as Laurence Tribe was taking the time to put out a hit job to take her out of consideration, this must have meant she was a serious contender. But I was still worried. I wasn't sure how much weight the President would give to the opinion of such an important and influential legal scholar.

And then I realized how personally offended *I* was. Professor Tribe was attacking her temperament, not how well she could actually do the job. It was hard for me to see him refer to her "reputation for being something of a bully" and not read it as code for a Latina that would be too much for the Supreme Court. As a Latina with a passionate personality and spirit myself, it made me question whether we had to fit into the boxes that people like Laurence Tribe tried to keep us in. He clearly thought a Latina couldn't do the job, and he advocated for a white woman instead.

His words resurfaced the same self-doubt I felt on my first day at the White House, which had a way of creeping back. When I imagined people were not taking me seriously, or questioned my judgment or intellect. When I calibrated a reaction or my personality for fear of being seen as too emotional or fiery. But I knew that Sonia Sotomayor's confirmation would be a reminder to me—and so many people like me—that despite the challenges posed against us, we must persist in being who we are, even in the face of doubt from ourselves and others.

* * *

On Memorial Day 2009, after much deliberation and personal reflection, the President convened his chief of staff, White House counsel, and senior advisors to notify them he had made a decision. My boss, Valerie Jarrett, emerged from that meeting and sent a cryptic email asking our team to get on the phone that evening. Of all weekends to be away, this was a tough one. I happened to be in New Mexico—a rare weekend off to get married—but that didn't keep me from secretly checking my BlackBerry in between bridal events and last-minute wedding preparations. When the email came in, I knew what it meant and didn't want to miss the call. When I joined, Valerie playfully chided me for being on a work call in the middle of my wedding, but then told me she was glad I was able to be part of history. When she said Sonia's name, my heart jumped.

The next morning, I set my alarm for seven a.m. Mountain time. I sat on the edge of the bed in my hotel room, my wedding dress hanging nearby, and watched the television as Sonia Sotomayor walked into the East Room flanked by President Obama and Vice President Biden. In that moment, everything changed for me. It was the same sense of pride and accomplishment that I felt on election night 2008 in Grant Park as I watched the President and First Family take the stage to declare victory. This was sweet in a different way, though. We, the Latino community, had made it. This was *our* victory. Her nomination gave our community an unmistakable validation. We were no longer invisible. As she stood at the podium, on the world stage, Sotomayor personified the same hopes and dreams that I had seen in the eyes of Latinas and Latinos across the country while working on the campaign. I couldn't help but see all the people that came before her and, more importantly, who would come after her.

As the President recounted Sotomayor's life story in his nominating speech, I found myself thinking of our parallels. While the Bronx is very different from Las Cruces, we had both overcome tough obstacles to get out; we had both experienced not fitting in. She went away to Princeton and I went away to Boston College, both fish out of water in a new world where most everyone didn't look like us, both dealing with the experience of not being Latino enough for the Latinos and too Latino for everyone else. I flashed forward and pictured Sotomayor in the courtrooms and elite law firms during the early days of her career where she was the only Latina and the only woman. I saw myself there, too.

I imagined her having to put up with what may have seemed like insurmountable obstacles—the bullshit of not being taken seriously or feeling like she wasn't enough—because she was a woman or Latina, or both. I knew those feelings all too well.

I was proud of our president for choosing Sotomayor—not just because it sent a signal to our community and the country, but because he was recognizing her deep qualifications and experience, and validating the notion that diverse experiences matter on the bench. It was one of those palpable moments that proved that it really did matter who sat in the Oval Office. Decisions have consequences, and leadership is by example.

I couldn't wait to get back to Washington to help get Sonia confirmed.

* * *

Little did we know what awaited us: the "summer of no." What we were hoping would be an easy confirmation wasn't going to be as straight a shot as we had envisioned. Given all of the other moving pieces of the President's agenda, specifically health care reform and the American Recovery and Reinvestment Act, Senate Republicans wanted to make Sonia's confirmation part of their plan to sabotage President Obama's first year in office. They weren't going to make it easy.

There was the demeaning and laughable way in which several male senators mispronounced her name, from "Soda-may-er" (Senator Jeff Sessions) to "Soto-may-ay-or" (Senator Tom Coburn). But worse was how they mischaracterized her life, pursuing not just the predictable lines of attack—some of her rulings on guns and reproductive rights, which would be lightning rods for any Democratic nominee—but also attacking her health and her lifelong diabetes, her membership in the Belizean Grove organization (an elite all-female organization), and even her time on the board of the Puerto Rican Legal Defense and Education Fund (because apparently, fighting for the civil rights of Puerto Ricans equates to "the worst aspects of liberal judicial activism: identity politics, race baiting, and ethnic favoritism," according to the right-wing group Judicial Watch).

Then there was the infamous "Wise Latina" speech that Republicans dug up to try to pin her as a hot-tempered, emotional, identity-politics-driven Latina. To be honest, there wasn't anything racist or blatantly offensive about the speech, which she had given to university students in 2001. "I would hope that a wise Latina woman with the richness of her experiences would more often than not reach a better conclusion than a white male who hasn't lived that life," she had said.

To me, they were simply the words of someone speaking her truth, describing the world as she saw it, and the factors she felt helped to shape her Latina *identidad*—the food she ate, the things she saw as a child, and the culture that raised her. In the heat of the debate, I remember reading the speech and thinking I had my own Mexican American experiences analogous to hers as a Puerto Rican American: my tacos and tamales were her *arroz con gandules* and *pernil*; our families were both long-standing U.S. citizens in a world where many saw Latinos as immigrants (hers as Puerto Ricans and mine as tenth-generation New Mexicans); our Spanish was okay but not fluent, and we knew that also didn't define our *latinidad*.

In this speech, she talked about the tension of blending into the race-blind melting pot while also owning the experiences that make us who we are. For so long, I had wondered how to own my Latina *identidad* in a world dominated by white culture, in which being "too Latina" risks alienating people. Sonia taught me that this isn't mutually exclusive: you can be 100 percent Latina, the proud product of a unique culture, tradition, and experience, and also be 100 percent American. And the irony of the "Wise Latina" controversy was that targeting her this way actually had a unifying effect on Latinas across all generations that has stuck to this day. "Wise Latina" became a badge of honor.

Provoked by this assault on her character and culture, the Latino community kept the pressure up. It was my job to share what we were hearing on the Hill and in the press with key Latino leaders, so that they could help to build a strong defense for Sonia. The Broadway composer and actor Lin-Manuel Miranda and Sonia Manzano of *Sesame Street* fame cut a PSA for her. There were press conferences in states of target senators and lobbying days on Capitol Hill to add to the pressure to support her. The community made it clear that there would be a price to pay for making her confirmation take longer than it should, for moving the goalposts, for not confirming her before the August recess.

And we were not alone. We had help from a diverse group of communities—women, African Americans, Asian Americans, constitutionalists—who coalesced behind her because of the depth of her experience, her character, and her personal story. They knew this was a historic moment. Sonia gave them all something to fight for.

* * *

Finally on Thursday, August 6, 2009, after a long, hot summer, the Senate confirmed Sonia Sotomayor as the first Latina Supreme Court justice by a vote of 68–31. Just nine Republicans came to their senses and voted for her. It was one of the last votes the Senate took before breaking for the August state work period. I was jubilant. And while we still had some big challenges ahead of us—especially health care reform—I was able to relish that moment, knowing that I had contributed to one of the President's first big legacy accomplishments, a lifetime appointment to the Supreme Court.

Sonia Sotomayor changed what was possible on so many levels.

Her story is about being unapologetically *boricua* and Latina, about being someone who cherishes our food and traditions (and never says no to dancing salsa) and knows how these factors have shaped who she has become. Her story is also one about a distinguished career working at nearly every level of the judicial system, and winning praise from colleagues and critics for her fairness and character. She has that critically important ingredient of proximity to the reality of most Americans that President Obama was looking for—a quality that no one else on the court had in the same way. As I have progressed through my own career, I have come to realize how important it is to have this ingredient of proximity in any situation—whether I am bringing it to the table or someone else is—and that my experience *and* my heritage are of value.

When a friend of mine, Damaris Hernández, became the first Latina partner at a very large, and notoriously not-diverse, New York City white-shoe law firm, Justice Sotomayor, who had never met her but read a profile of her in the *New York Times*, casually dropped her a note congratulating her for reaching such an important milestone. When Damaris shared this with me, I was not surprised. It was a total Sonia thing to do. I knew that she had dozens of mentees, former clerks and adopted nieces and nephews that were all part of her extended family, for whom she will always be "Titi Sonia."

Every year, one of Sonia's closest friends organizes an annual birthday barbecue and I always try to attend. It's a gathering of several dozen people making change in their own ways, including lawyers, scholars, and thought leaders. I often feel out of place there, just as I felt in college and later in the White House—but Sonia, the justice, always makes a point to have a conversation with me, not about the past but about what is happening in my life now. She asks about my work and family and what else is important to me. I think at some level she knows and understands what I am feeling and wants me to know that she sees me and wants me to know that, as a Latina from a small town in New Mexico, with a similarly unlikely path to success, yes, I absolutely do belong.

I do not have any aspirations to be on the Supreme Court. But I do want to be like Sonia Sotomayor, someone who cracked glass ceilings for Latinas and told us it was okay for us to be who we are. I want to be someone who, like her, opens new doors of opportunity and excellence for other Latinas. And I want to be someone who can turn to a young Latina who isn't sure she belongs and, just like Sonia has for me, remind her that yes, she does.

BEFORE WE WERE US

Aneesh Raman

Sometimes life-changing moments start with a grand gesture, making it impossible to ignore the start of something transformative. Other times they begin so subtly there are a thousand different reasons why you could miss them.

That's how this one started—with a routine question on an unremarkable day.

It was January 2013. I had been a speechwriter for Barack Obama for a little over a year and, as I walked back to the White House after grabbing coffee with a friend, I did what I had done countless times before—I unlocked my BlackBerry, scanned the in-box, skipped past the news clips and calendar invites, and searched for jump balls.

Jump balls were unassigned speeches or statements that went to the first taker. They were usually tossed up in the air with a "Who wants this?" from the chief speechwriter and could come at any time on any topic. A major conference just asked the White House for an opening video; the President needs a draft script. A notable American just passed away; the President needs a draft statement. Or, as I saw that day, a speech in Las Vegas had just been added to the schedule;

the President needs a writer. The more interesting the jump ball, the faster it went, so if you wanted one, you had to grab it quickly.

By that point, I had written all types of speeches. Big policy and staffing announcements. Statements the President read word for word. Statements the President totally ignored in favor of ad-libbing. The Weekly Address, and its "Hi, everybody" opening line, more times than I can count. Watching words that first came together in my mind make their way into remarks by the President is exactly what you'd imagine—a singular experience. Whether it is singularly good or bad depends on how well the lines land. Did that opening joke make people laugh, or confirm that you're just not that funny? Did the explanation of a new piece of legislation feel clear, or contorted? You quickly realize as a speechwriter that what you imagine in your head can play out far differently in reality. While writing one of my first speeches, a World AIDS Day speech, I imagined the entire audience rising to their feet amidst deafening applause as the President proclaimed the possibility of an AIDS-free generation. Instead, the entire audience, including Bono and Alicia Keys in the front row, sat completely silent until the President reached the Very. Last. Word. Unfortunately, presidential speeches don't come with an Applause sign.

In those moments, I would wallow in self-doubt for a bit but then eventually settle on ways to make the next speech better. Even if a speech went well, I thought about how it could have gone better. All of us speechwriters did, because we never took for granted that when you write for the President, you write for history.

Over time, as my list of lessons grew, one kept coming back. It wasn't about creating an immortal line that could get etched in stone. It was whether the President of the United States—a figure larger than life for most of us—could connect with those listening in a way that only someone who understood their reality, their struggles, and their aspirations could. In short, to make a presidential speech soar you have to make it personal. Not surprisingly, that's why the best speeches are those that, for the writer, are deeply personal. And that's why, on that unremarkable January day in 2013, when that routine question of "Who wants this?" came my way about a topic more personal to me than any other—immigration—I immediately I wrote back, "I got it."

Growing up in the Boston suburbs, almost all my friends could show you where their parents grew up and went to school. They had a path to replicate or reject when it came to navigating things like dating and college. Their grandparents lived in the same town or maybe a few over. Their cousins, too. Their family story was always right there for them to see.

For me, it was different. I may have been born and raised here, but everything that shaped my parents' coming of age was a world away in India, which meant that my family story was harder to find. Instead, what I did have—what I turned to anytime I felt out of sorts— was a black-and-white photo kept safely in an old family album. In it, three teenagers sit on the front steps of a home in southern India. One of them is smiling so wide you can't help but smile back. On the front wall of the home behind them are two charcoal portraits, one of Abraham Lincoln and the other of John F. Kennedy. The nineteen-year-old who took that photo of his younger brother and two cousins is the same guy who drew those portraits. My father.

My dad first learned about Lincoln in high school history in a small town in Kerala, a largely rural region of southwest India. He first learned about Kennedy from newspapers and by sneaking into my grandparents' room at night to listen to world news off my grandfather's radio. Hearing about Kennedy's campaign and presidency, he became fascinated with America's open democracy at work as it ushered in a young, idealistic president and an era of remarkable progress. That fascination deepened as India turned the page from the birth of democracy to a more authoritarian chapter under Indira Gandhi. In America, he saw a place unshackled by the caste system and family dynasties, where all were equal and where anyone could do anything. Including him.

On February 4, 1971, my dad acted on that belief and stepped onto an Air India flight heading from Mumbai to Frankfurt on his way to Boston. I've heard the story so many times that at this point I tell it as if it's my own—except my version always ends with this question: could I have done what he did? Because on that February day, my dad did not just board a flight. He left behind his home country: his mom and aging dad, who he would never see again; his seven siblings, his nieces and nephews, his cousins and friends; the places that shaped his life and the paths that were forged for him to follow. All he had was some luggage and eight U.S. dollars, the maximum foreign currency allowed by the Indian government at the time. Yet, for him, those possessions and his belief in America were enough to make the biggest decision of his life.

My dad wasn't naive. He may have seen the best in America, but he only had to look to the struggles fueling the civil rights movement to see that America didn't always live up to her best. He knew that, as a new immigrant with a funny accent and brown skin, he was likely to encounter racism and ridicule. But looking back at all that was achieved in the 1960s, he also knew that in America, citizens could build a better future not just for themselves and their family but also for their community and their country. To my dad, even if America wasn't yet the land of opportunity for all, it was the land of *possibility* for all. That's what he's believed ever since he drew those portraits of Lincoln and Kennedy, and that's what he raised me to do as well.

Whenever I was asked as a kid, "No, where are you *really* from?" or whenever I felt defensive about the fact that our home sometimes felt more Indian than American—like when Dad would greet my high school friends the morning after a sleepover, shirtless in a *lungi*—I thought about that photo. It was a reminder of something more profound and inspiring than anything I could have gotten with my cousins and grandparents all living around the corner. My parents made one of the greatest sacrifices anyone could make so that they could build a better life for themselves and a brighter future for their children. That's why I couldn't wait to write this immigration speech. And then, just as I put my BlackBerry back in my pocket, my stomach clenched, and my heart rate rose. In an instant, I was terrified.

Having grabbed the jump ball, the realities of the task hit all at once. With President Obama, immigration speeches had a history of being tough speeches. The policy was expansive and the emotions were raw. The President often had specific views on what he wanted to say, as did his senior staff, members of his cabinet, and every advocacy organization that had a stake in the outcome.

Then there was the timing. With reelection secured, a new chief of staff in place, and a number of senior staffers promoted, everyone was focused on getting the second term off to a strong start. In particular, everyone wanted to move quickly on big campaign promises like immigration reform. At the other end of Pennsylvania Avenue, the dynamic was different. The election was over, but opposition to the President in Congress had deepened, making the process of crafting a bipartisan bill all the more delicate.

When you're starting a speech, if you think about everything that is at stake—every constituent you need to please, every policy you need to highlight, every headline you need to produce, and every way the words you write could be twisted by the opposition—it can be paralyzing. You end up staring at a blank screen with no idea where to begin. Eventually, though, you stop trying to solve everything at once and instead build a process that works for you. This was mine:

STEP ONE: Read everything the President has ever said on the topic you're writing about and look for common themes and structures. If the same argument is in every past speech, it should probably be in the next one.

STEP TWO: Get guidance. If it isn't possible to get that guidance from the President himself, either because the speech isn't big enough to necessitate his time or it's coming up so quickly that he doesn't have the time, get it from the chief speechwriter. As I was preparing this speech, the chief speechwriter, Jon Favreau, was working on the second inaugural address. Building off of the themes he was using there, he suggested focusing on the economic impact of immigration reform and the broad bipartisan support behind it.

STEP THREE: Research. This was usually determined by the amount of time you had and how well you knew the topic. You could set up coffees with policy experts inside and outside the White House. You could speak with key activists who would be attending the speech to see what they wanted to hear from the President. You could read influential books on the topic. With this speech, that's what I did first, heading to the White House Library, to grab a book I had last read as a college freshman.

On the top floor of the library, tucked between two less iconic titles, sat John F. Kennedy's *A Nation of Immigrants*. Opening that book was immediately comforting. Kennedy has been a constant in my life, from the portrait my dad drew in his childhood home to the

monuments and markers that surrounded me as a child in Massachusetts to my college years at the Kennedy School of Government's Institute of Politics, where I walked past a portrait of JFK almost daily. I
wanted to reread *A Nation of Immigrants* because I remembered its
powerful summary of how immigrants contributed to the making of
America. What I had forgotten was the equally powerful accounting
of the waves of immigrants who came to America in her first century.
Seeing that again, I knew I wanted to work it into the speech.

STEP FOUR: Get ahead of rewrites from senior staff. Before you
dove into the writing, it was always good to think about who cared
most about a topic so that you could get their thoughts before you sent
a draft. If you rushed to write, the editing process could prove tortur-
ous because the edits would be less about language and more about
the overall structure or, even worse, the core argument. When those
are the edits, you're in for a near-total rewrite, often close to the day of
delivery, sometimes late the evening before, when you've already
called it a day and need to suddenly pour out your beer and replace it
with two rounds of coffee and loud music until you're awake enough
to cram a week's worth of effort into one unforgiving, unending,
sleepless night.

For this speech, I thankfully received the last bits of necessary
guidance late on a Friday afternoon, four days before the trip to Las
Vegas, when members of the President's senior staff gathered on the
top floor of the West Wing to discuss details. *Will we introduce our
own bill or support the Senate process?* Support the Senate process but
say we'll offer up our own bill if Congress doesn't move quick enough.
*What will we call the policy recommendations in the speech—a legisla-
tive structure, a legislative proposal, principles?* Principles, because we
don't want to seem too prescriptive given the dynamic in the Senate.
What are the most important things to convey? Leadership and urgency.

STEP FIVE: Write.

Reaching step five meant it was time to shut the door, say good-bye to the world, and write. As I sat in my office that Friday night, I looked at the clock and then at my screen and typed my first attempt at a perfect opening line. It was okay. I deleted it. I wrote something else. It was worse. The third attempt went the same way. I looked back at the clock. Twenty-five minutes had passed. How had twenty-five minutes passed? I stared at the blank screen, the blinking cursor taunting me to start. I didn't know how. I did, however, know how I wanted to end so eventually I decided to start there. I looked over at *A Nation of Immigrants* and flipped through the chapters that described the first waves of immigrants who followed the English and early European settlers. I took out a piece of paper and wrote them down one by one. The Irish. The Germans. The Scandinavians. The Italians. The Russians. The Poles. On it went.

When I was done, I looked at that list, and I thought about those early groups, all those Irish and German and Scandinavian and Italian and Russian and Polish women and men and what it was like for them to board those ships to America, leaving behind everything they had ever known and family they would never see again. I thought about the waves that followed, all the way up to the present day. And then I thought about my dad and what it was like for him to board that flight to Boston.

Until that moment I had never appreciated that the story of my dad is, in important ways, the story of virtually every immigrant who has come to this country. And if that's true, then it is the story of virtually every American in this country because, unless you are Native American, your ancestors came here from somewhere else. And while not everyone—especially the generations of slaves who arrived in

chains—came by choice, those who did often came for the same reasons, often experienced the same struggles, and often persisted with
the same resolve.

That insight—that the power of my family's story comes from being, at once, unique and universal—struck hard given the moment
playing out. The President, over his entire first term, had been labeled
by some opponents as less American because of who his father was
and where he grew up. The renewed focus on immigration reform
had caused natural-born citizens to push back against newcomers.
The debate had taken on an "us" versus "them" dynamic, which was
personal for me because I spent most of my childhood trying, in my
own mind, to affirm my place in the "us" camp.

Normally when I wrote a speech for the President, I would hear
his voice in my head and think about whether the words I was typing
would resonate with the crowd in front of him and in the country at
large. This time, though, I was hearing the voice of a president who
had his patriotism routinely questioned, and as I typed the words, I
was fully aware that I was doing so as a first-generation American
who grew up feeling he always had something extra to prove when it
came to his patriotism. For the first time, I was writing something for
Barack Obama to say *to me*.

When I was hired at the White House, I researched every past
presidential speechwriter I could find. I even spoke to one I knew
from college, trying to get as much advice as I could gather. None
were Indian American. None seemed to have the upbringing I had.
So, for most of my time, I did what I had done before when there was
no set model for how to operate as a person of color. I tried to fit in, to
become my best version of the norm, mimicking the mind-set of the
people I worked with. That night felt different. For the first time as a

speechwriter, I felt as though I had put my family's story out there. And what made it so affirming was that it wasn't just out there as my family's story; it was America's story.

The next day, after triaging edits that came in from senior staff and after a final check by the chief speechwriter, the draft went into the President's briefing book. Sending a speech to the President is a bit like turning in an exam. Once submitted, all you can do is wait. Sometimes you get feedback right away, like the time the President called me at my desk to say I should make a National Prayer Breakfast speech more vivid when talking about how Martin Luther King Jr. and Abraham Lincoln turned to their faith in moments of uncertainty. But most of the time, early the next morning, an email would arrive from the President's personal secretary notifying you that his edits were ready outside the Oval Office. That walk would always be a mix of awe and anxiety. Awe because, as a regular requirement of your job, you got to walk to the Oval Office. Anxiety because you never knew how many edits were coming your way.

President Obama edits by hand, crossing out words here, adding phrases or paragraphs there. His handwriting is impressively legible, a skill valued by speechwriters. As I walked back to my desk, I skimmed the edits, reflexively grading myself on the effort and doing some rough math on how long they would take to incorporate. That time estimate mattered, especially if the speech was happening outside of Washington, DC, because, if at all possible, you wanted to send the final version before you got on Air Force One. Flying on Air Force One is an incredible experience but the internet connection leaves a lot to be desired.

With this speech, there were a few open questions that required agreement between the policy team and the research team, which could sometimes take a while because the questions were nuanced.

That meant, as I loaded into the staff van headed for Andrews Air Force Base, as I headed up onto the plane and into my seat, as I opened my laptop and saw the slow drip of incoming emails, I was still waiting for the speech to go final.

By the time we were halfway to Las Vegas there was one last part unresolved and, in the back-and-forth on email, it was unclear how we were going to get to a decision. Right on cue, the President walked by, looked over to me, and said, "The speech looks good." I signaled to my computer and said, "There is this part that we're waiting on to get a final answer." He strolled over, took a look, heard me summarize the back-and-forth, and said, "Leave it." That moment produced my favorite email I ever sent to the research team—"I think we have a decision. The President says leave it."

With that, the speech was locked. But speeches are only partly about the words. They're also about the delivery, which is why the first thing you clue into as the speechwriter is how much energy the President brings to the opening lines. On average, President Obama spoke publicly every day, sometimes just a few hours after he returned from an overseas trip or at the end of an intense stretch of negotiations with Congress. It was unfair to assume he would bring his best to every speech, but as he started this one, he was clearly energized, flashing his trademark smile and moving his shoulders and arms to punctuate lines. I could tell this was a moment when he was going to bring the full weight of his talent as a speaker.

For most of the speech, I sat where the speechwriters normally sit, in the back. But as the President reached the ending, I went out from behind the stage to watch in person. "Immigration's always been an issue that inflames passions," he said. "That's not surprising. You know, there are few things that are more important to us as a society than who gets to come here and call our country home, who gets the privilege of becoming a citizen of the United States of America. That's a big deal. When we talk about that in the abstract, it's easy sometimes for the discussion to take on a feeling of us versus them. And when that happens, a lot of folks forget that most of us used to be them." The crowd started applauding. Some started smiling. Some started laughing, perhaps amused that the President was reminding all the natural-born citizens who were disparaging new immigrants that they, in fact, shared the same past. He continued, "The Irish, who left behind a land of famine; the Germans, who fled persecution; the Scandinavians, who arrived eager to pioneer out west; the Polish; the Russians; the Italians; the Chinese; the Japanese; the West Indians; the huddled masses who came through Ellis Island on one coast and Angel Island on the other—you know, all those folks, before they were us, they were them." Again, applause. Again, smiles. Standing on the side, I was applauding and smiling, too. Lost in that moment was my role as a speechwriter. Instead, it was about the President of the United States so fully and forcefully embracing our immigrant past.

After the speech was done, as the President was heading back to the limo, he looked over at me, gave a thumbs-up, and said, "Great job." I almost never got feedback from him after a speech—everyone moved on to the next event—so those two words carried lasting weight. Barack Obama was not just my president, but a role model who changed my life in meaningful ways. He was the motivation behind the biggest decision I ever made—leaving my job as a CNN correspondent in 2008 to become an unpaid intern at his Chicago campaign headquarters. He proved it possible for America to elect an African American president and to embark on a new era of equality, one that is proving to be potentially as contentious and consequential as those in our past. He set a standard as a feminist husband and father that I strive every day to meet. And, as a president, he inspired in me an unending reserve of optimism and an unshakable focus on service. That's why President Obama saying two words—"Great job"—with a thumbs-up will always be one of the great memories of my life.

On our way back to Washington, DC, on Air Force One, I did something I hadn't done on any previous trip: I ordered a beer. I wasn't alone on that front. All of us on the flight were excited. The momentum behind immigration reform felt unstoppable. We knew the issue had the broadest possible coalition of support. We knew the Senate was moving forward in rare bipartisan fashion. As we watched the cable networks cover the speech, on the bottom of the screen in big letters was one of the President's biggest applause lines: "Now is the time." Every poll showed that the vast majority of Americans agreed.

Immigration reform would get done. How could it not?

In the weeks that followed, our optimism quickly turned to disappointment. The Senate passed a bill, but the House never took it up. Comprehensive immigration reform never became law. In fact, almost no meaningful piece of legislation became law in the second term. Opposition to President Obama had grown impenetrable, fueled by a mix of Republicans who felt he had done too much too quickly in his first term and Republicans who, for a variety of reasons, never wanted him to succeed on anything.

That November, I left the White House for the world of start-ups, eager to try to make real the potential for technology to expand opportunity. By that point, Congress had become incapable of doing the people's work. As if to belabor the point, my last day fell during a government shutdown, which meant I never had the chance to properly say good-bye to the majority of people I worked with at the White House.

While the 2008 election was the most inspiring experience I will likely ever have as an American, 2013 was different in almost every imaginable way. It certainly gut-checked my optimism, but it also re-minded me that progress is not something that happens on its own or that, once secured, remains. Progress requires constant vigilance and ongoing activism. As the President often reminded us, hard things are hard. Moving this country forward, given how big and diverse our democracy is, will always be hard.

That easily could have been the end to my White House story: optimism giving way to cynicism, hope giving way to resignation. Thankfully, it wasn't.

As a member of the White House staff, when you leave, you get a departure photo with the President and members of your family. When the day came and I introduced my family to the President, I told him about what brought my parents to America, the careers they forged and the impact they made in their community, including join-ing a few other families to build one of the earliest Hindu temples in America. I told him about my in-laws, doctors on the South Side of Chicago who served people with limited access to health care. I told him about my wife, Haley, who was doing clinical research at the National Institutes of Health to find new therapies for devastating diseases. Each of them had an area of impact that they were passion-ate about and the President connected with each in a way that made them feel like that conversation was the most important of his day.

An experience like that takes a while to digest. At first, you think back to it constantly, trying to isolate every part that made it memo-rable. In the days and weeks that followed, Haley and I spent a lot of time talking about our parents' journey to that day. We also, for the first time in depth, talked about our own journey. Growing up the children of immigrants, we had come of age with all types of insecuri-ties as we tried to reconcile the culture of our parents' homeland with our own. But something else came with being a child of immigrants.

We grew up with a relentless drive to seize every opportunity this country had to offer so that we could be worthy of our parents' sacrifice and so that our contribution could be worthy of all that America has given our family. My parents and in-laws came to America because they believed this was the land of possibility for all. Haley and I spent our lives proving them right.

If we raise our kids right, they will, too, as they inherit our American story and pass it on to their kids and all the generations of our family yet to come. Over those years, our American experience will certainly change, as will this country. Beneath it all will remain a foundation built, and rebuilt, by immigrants and their descendants. That is a truth—held up by President Obama on that January day in 2013—that we must never forget. No matter how long your family has been here, we are each living just the latest chapter of an immigrant story. It is a story that is filled with patriotism, idealism, sacrifice, resolve, persistence, and impact. It is why we stay optimistic, even in our darkest days, and it can be what unites us, even in our most divided days. But only if we remember—and embrace—our history as a nation of immigrants.

Contributors

RUMANA AHMED interned in the White House Office of Presidential Correspondence before becoming a full-time staffer. She then was a liaison to Muslim American and other communities in the Office of Public Engagement, where she also worked on highlighting community-based efforts to address issues such as gun violence. Later, as senior advisor in the Office for Global Engagement and Strategic Communications in the National Security Council, she worked on advancing relations with Cuba and Laos.

DEESHA DYER first came to the White House in 2009 as an intern in the Office of Scheduling and Advance. In 2010, she returned as associate director of scheduling correspondence and was later promoted to deputy director and hotel program director, traveling with the President and First Lady working on press, lodging, and site logistics. In 2013 she was promoted again to deputy social secretary, and in 2015 she took on the role of special assistant to the President and social secretary of the White House.

HEATHER FOSTER served as both director of African American outreach and advisor in the White House Office of Public Engagement. Before joining the White House, she served as the policy and outreach advisor at the Center for Faith-based and Neighborhood Partnerships at the Department of Education.

HOPE HALL worked as a cinematographer on the documentary *By the People*, which followed then senator Obama's trajectory into candidacy, before joining the 2008 campaign's new media team as a staff filmmaker, and then serving on the presidential transition team. In May 2011, she became President Obama's principal videographer at the White House in the Office of Digital Strategy. Her personal work has taken her to artist residencies all around the world, has been shown in more than fifty film festivals and exhibitions worldwide, and has won numerous awards, including at Sundance.

BRAD JENKINS worked as an investment professional for six years before joining the Obama campaign in 2008. On the campaign, Brad worked on youth media, helping Obama turn out one of the largest youth vote numbers in history. Brad joined the White House in 2011, serving as a liaison to the creative community, working to inspire millions of Americans to take action.

LEAH KATZ-HERNANDEZ first joined the Obama family as campaign volunteer, and then interned in the White House after graduating from Gallaudet University. Later, she worked as a research associate and press assistant in the First Lady's Office before becoming the West Wing receptionist, known informally as the Receptionist of the United States, or "ROTUS."

CECILIA MUÑOZ served all eight years on President Obama's senior White House staff, first as director of intergovernmental affairs, and then as assistant to the President and director of the Domestic Policy Council, which coordinates the domestic policy-making process in the White House. Prior to joining the Obama administration, she spent twenty years at UnidosUS (formerly known as the National Council of La Raza), the nation's largest Latino civil rights organization.

DARIENNE PAGE, a former U.S. Army noncommissioned officer and an Operation Iraqi Freedom veteran, joined the 2008 Obama campaign as a volunteer, working her way up from the campaign mailroom to become the first West Wing receptionist in the Obama White House. Later she served as director of veterans, wounded warriors, and military families outreach in the Office of Public Engagement, acting as a liaison between the White House and the veterans community.

NED PRICE began his career in the CIA as an intelligence analyst in 2006, later becoming a spokesperson for the agency. In 2014, he joined the Obama administration on the National Security Council, advising the President on matters of foreign policy and national security, first as director of strategic communications and later as NSC spokesperson.

GAUTAM RAGHAVAN served as President Barack Obama's liaison to the LGBTQ community as well as the Asian American and Pacific Islander community from 2011 to 2014. Earlier in the Obama administration, he worked for the U.S. Department of Defense and served on the Pentagon's "Don't Ask, Don't Tell" working group. Earlier in his political career, Raghavan worked for Progressive Majority, the Democratic National Committee, and the 2008 Obama campaign.

ANEESH RAMAN was a speechwriter for President Obama from 2011 to 2013, following a year at the Pentagon and two years as speechwriter to Treasury secretary Tim Geithner amidst a historic financial crisis. From 2004 to 2008 he was a foreign correspondent for CNN, first based out of Southeast Asia and later the Middle East, where he spent a year as the network's Baghdad correspondent during the Iraq War.

MICHAEL J. ROBERTSON started working for Barack Obama on his 2004 U.S. Senate race and later served on his U.S. Senate staff as legislative coordinator and deputy to the chief counsel. After working for the 2008 campaign and transition team, Robertson then worked as the United States General Services Administration's chief of staff before joining the White House as deputy cabinet secretary, leading the team that liaised with cabinet departments and agencies on President Obama's behalf.

JULIE CHÁVEZ RODRIGUEZ served for five and a half years in the White House Office of Public Engagement, initially as the point person on immigration and Latino issues and later as special assistant to the President, managing a team responsible for engaging leaders in the LGBTQ, AAPI, Latino, veterans, youth, education, labor, and progressive communities.

LYNN ROSENTHAL was the first-ever White House advisor on violence against women. At the White House, she also represented the Vice President on the White House Council on Women and Girls and co-chaired the President's Working Group on the Intersection of HIV/AIDS, Violence Against Women and Girls, and Gender-Related Health Disparities. She has over twenty-five years of experience advocating on behalf of women, including serving as executive director of the National Network to End Domestic Violence from 2000 to 2006.

MICHAEL STRAUTMANIS has known the Obamas for more than twenty-five years, starting when he joined Sidley & Austin where Mrs. Obama was working as a young lawyer. Later, he served as chief counsel on Barack Obama's Senate staff. Strautmanis continued to be a close aide to the President throughout his first term, serving as counselor for strategic engagement, deputy assistant to the President, and chief of staff to senior advisor Valerie Jarrett.

RAINA THIELE worked in the White House Office of Intergovernmental Affairs, where she focused on tribal governments and advised on climate change, Arctic, and energy issues. She was also a lead organizer of President Obama's trip to Alaska in the fall of 2015. Earlier, Raina served for nearly five years in the White House Office of Management and Budget, where she worked on a wide variety of issues, including tribal legislation, international affairs, and energy. She is Dena'ina Athabascan and Yup'ik and is a proud Alaskan.

STEPHANIE VALENCIA worked for Barack Obama for nearly a decade, starting as deputy Latino vote director on the 2008 campaign, and then serving on the Obama-Biden transition team before joining the White House at the start of the first term. Valencia ended her time at the White House as special assistant to the President and principal deputy director in the Office of Public Engagement.

BILL YOSSES was the White House executive pastry chef from 2007 to 2014, where he was closely involved with First Lady Michelle Obama's Let's Move! initiative. Prior to his time at the White House, Yosses was the executive pastry chef at the Dressing Room, Tavern on the Green, and Bouley Restaurant. He is the coauthor of three books on baking, including *The Sweet Spot: Dialing Back Sugar and Amping Up Flavor.*

Acknowledgments

In retrospect, the only thing more improbable than working at the White House is writing a book about it.

There's no way this could have happened without our fabulous book agent, Cindy Uh at Thompson Literary Agency. What began as a passing conversation over New Year's Eve drinks turned into a wholly unexpected and incredibly rewarding experience, and it was only possible because of Cindy's passion, tenacity, and patience.

Lightning struck twice when we landed Sam Raim as our editor at Penguin Books. From the very beginning, it was clear he shared our vision for what this book could be—and then held all of us to the highest possible standards to ensure we delivered the best writing and storytelling possible.

Stephanie Valencia, Heather Foster, and Monique Dorsainvil were invaluable in getting this project off to a strong start by helping identify fellow Obama White House alumni with unique perspectives and important stories to tell. In addition, a number of our former White House colleagues were especially thoughtful and generous with their guidance, most notably Valerie Jarrett, Yohannes Abraham, Paulette Aniskoff, Brian Bond, Jon Carson, Jamie Citron, Bess

Evans, Aditi Hardikar, Sarah Hurwitz, David Litt, Chris Lu, Tarak Shah, Tina Tchen, and Louisa Terrell. We are also grateful to Sheryl Sandberg, Adam Grant, and Kalpen Modi for their early and ongoing support for this project, and to Alex Horwitz and Jack Greenbaum for their feedback, partnership, and—most important!—our book title; and Congressman John Lewis, who honors us with his support and inspires us every day.

All of us have relied on love, support, and advice from family, friends, colleagues, and mentors over the years—including, but also extending past, our time at the White House. I am grateful to my parents, Kamini and Raga (especially Dad for the crazy idea!), my husband, Andy, and our daughter, Maya, whose 2052 presidential campaign is off to a strong start.

My fellow West Wingers contributors would also like to express their profound personal thanks to Rokan and Saleha Ahmed, siblings Rehana and Shafiq, and Terry Szuplat (Rumana Ahmed); Justice Dyer, Jasmyne Dyer, and Isaac Dyer IV (Deesha Dyer); Earl and Joy Foster, Dr. Holly Foster Haynes, E. J. Foster, and Dr. Sharon Malone (Heather Foster); Carin Besser, Beck Dorey-Stein, Hal Greenfader, and Sadia Shepard (Hope Hall); Marina, Sadie, and Oscar Jenkins, Mike Farah, and Zach Galifianakis (Brad Jenkins); Lizabeth Katz and Dr. Ricardo Hernandez, Daniel Katz-Hernandez, Howard Rosenblum, and Rachel Arfa (Leah Katz-Hernandez); Amit Pandya, Cristina and Meera Muñoz Pandya (Cecilia Muñoz); Donna Page, Gustin Page, and daughters Dylan and Dawson (Darienne Page); Samantha Noel, Elizabeth Price, and nephews Nic and Harry Noel (Ned Price); Haley Naik, Trichur and Latha Venkataraman, daughters Isha and Maha, Ricki Seidman, and Avinash Raman (Aneesh Raman); Sahar Wali-Robertson and our son, Wali Michael Robertson, John and Karyn Robertson, and Hashmat and Samar Wali

(Michael J. Robertson); Linda Chávez, Arturo S. Rodriguez, Olivia Irlando, and Christine Chávez (Julie Chávez Rodriguez); Tina Tchen, Cynthia Hogan, Demetra Lambros, and Jennifer Hinchey (Lynn Rosenthal); Valerie Jarrett, Pete Rouse, Damona, and our kids, Michael, Jori, and Nia (Michael Strautmanis); Sarah Thiele and Carl Thiele, June and Carl Thiele Sr., and Mary and Gus Jensen (Raina Thiele); Oscar Ramirez, the Valencia and Rivera families, Ricki Seidman, and Team Latino (Stephanie Valencia); Peter Kaminsky, Wendy Ripley, Joan Nathan, and Susie Morrison (Bill Yosses).

Finally, we would like to thank President and Mrs. Obama, Vice President and Dr. Biden, and all of the dream chasers, change makers, and hope creators for and with whom we worked. The strength and depth of our team was such that their stories could replace ours and this book would be no less passionate, thoughtful, or inspiring.